PENGUIN PLAYS

NEW ENGLISH DRAMATISTS 14

STEWART CONN was born in 1936. His volume of poems *Stoats in the Sunlight* was published in 1968. His other plays include *Breakdown* (1961), *Birds in a Wilderness* (1964), *Broche* (1965), and *I Didn't Always Live Here* (1967).

IAN HAMILTON FINLAY was born in 1925. He has published short stories (*The Sea-Bed*, 1958), and many volumes of poetry, both traditional and 'concrete', including *The Dancers Inherit the Party* (1960), *Glasgow Beasts* (1961), *Rapel* (1963), and *Telegrams from My Windmill* (1964). Four of his one-act plays were published in German translation in Vienna in 1966 under the title ... *und alles blieb wie es war*. His play *Walking Through Seaweed* was performed at the Falcon Theatre, Glasgow, in June 1962.

DAVID STOREY was born in 1933 and is best known as a novelist: *This Sporting Life* (1960), *Flight into Camden* (1960), *Radcliffe* (1963). His second play, *In Celebration*, was produced at the Royal Court Theatre in 1969.

PETER TERSON was born in 1932. He worked for a period as resident playwright at the Victoria Theatre, Stoke on Trent, where some of his plays were first produced. His plays include *A Night to Make the Angels Weep* (1964), *Zigger Zagger* (1967), *The Ballad of the Artificial Mash* (1968), *Mooney and his Caravans* (1968), *The Apprentices* (1968), and *Fuzz* (1969).

B. S. JOHNSON was born in 1933 and has published several novels: *Travelling People* (1963), *Albert Angelo* (1964), *Trawl* (1966), and *The Unfortunates* (1969) His films include *Up Yours Too, Guillaume Apollinaire* (1968), and several T.V. documentaries.

GEORGE MACBETH was born in 1932. He has published several volumes of poetry, including *The Broken Places* (1963), *A Doomsday Book* (1965), *The Colour of Blood* (1967), and *The Night of Stones* (1968), and has edited the Penguin Books of *Sick Verse*, *Animal Verse*, and *Victorian Verse*.

NEW
ENGLISH DRAMATISTS
14

Introduced by Edwin Morgan

THE RESTORATION OF ARNOLD MIDDLETON
David Storey

THE MIGHTY RESERVOY
Peter Terson

THE KING
Stewart Conn

WALKING THROUGH SEAWEED
and
THE ESTATE HUNTERS
Ian Hamilton Finlay

YOU'RE HUMAN LIKE THE REST OF THEM
B. S. Johnson

THE DOOMSDAY SHOW
George MacBeth and J. S. Bingham

PENGUIN BOOKS

Penguin Books Ltd, Harmondsworth, Middlesex, England
Penguin Books Australia Ltd, Ringwood, Victoria, Australia

—

—

Made and printed in Great Britain by
Cox & Wyman Ltd, London, Reading and Fakenham
Set in Monotype Bembo

CONTENTS

INTRODUCTION

THE two full-length and five one-act plays in this volume have no common denominator of either style or theme, and in this they reflect the extremely unsettled state of contemporary theatre in general, but one linking factor is that most of the authors are non-metropolitan in their origins or in their concerns. Three of them – Stewart Conn, Ian Hamilton Finlay, and George MacBeth – are Scottish, though only the first two of these live and work in Scotland. David Storey and Peter Terson have strong associations with York-shire and the Vale of Evesham respectively. And B. S. Johnson's originality and independent-mindedness make him, in his own way, one of their non-conforming company.

This is not to suggest that the plays themselves come springing fully-fledged from some physical or spiritual North with no marks on them of the influences that have been agitating the London or international theatre. But certainly in the case of Storey and Terson, where a degree of London success has been achieved, more than a drop of regional independence is injected into whatever they may contribute to the West End. Storey may know his R. D. Laing (himself, of course, a northerner), but he has also read the Brontës and something of their hard frustrated longing for love and com-munion seems embedded in his work. Terson brings together the Potteries and the Malvern Hills, D. H. Lawrence and Dylan Thomas, mines and loam and home-made wine and local accents, a rough earth-poetry that is concerned about man's links with nature as well as with the daily problems of living. And a playwright almost un-known to London, such as Ian Hamilton Finlay (though he is known in his quite different capacity of concrete poet), has a flavour that virtually requires to be related to Scottish environment and tradi-tions, whatever simplicity his plays have as statements.

It would be wrong to make too much of this local thrust, a fighting one in Terson, a gentle one in Finlay, and yet one has a decided sense at the moment of non-metropolitan forces and growing centres of independent activity, whether regional or national. On a larger per-spective, there is no doubt some relation between these developments and the continuing influence and *réclame*, in London especially, of

American theatre, whether avant-garde (McClure, Van Itallie, Foster) or more conventional (Albee). The relation is something of a back-lash. The more idiosyncratically vigorous American theatre is seen to be, the more it may be felt as a splendid but alien body in the bloodstream of these islands. Hence Terson and Stoke-on-Trent; hence Storey and Robin Hood; hence Arden and Johnny Armstrong; hence English Osborne, throwing an unexpected hand to English Coward. Hence also Cecil Taylor and Stewart Conn reviewing the last thirty years through the smoke of Glasgow (in *Bread and Butter* and *I Didn't Always Live Here*).

In the present volume, however, as in the tangled situation the theatre presents, local flavours and widespread influences inevitably mingle. The hero of *The Restoration of Arnold Middleton* is a history teacher who is engaged in the school production of a Robin Hood play, and the historical idea of a northern revolt against a bad central government is used simultaneously to present a modern anti-hero whose mental crack-up, though never fully explained, is related to an alienation from family and society that has become almost a com-monplace. There is a distinction, and even a power, in this play, which comes from facing honestly the perplexities that accompany the encroachment of a fantasy life upon everyday experience, and its eventual retreat. It is the first play of a man who is better known as the novelist of *This Sporting Life*, *Flight into Camden*, and *Radcliffe*. These are strong novels which made their mark by a tenacious, often physical intensity and a relentless probing of frustrated feelings and purposes. That he is conscious of such frustrated feelings as being very much his concern was shown by an interview published in *Books and Bookmen*, in which he said: 'Everything in our heritage, our laws, our culture, prevents a person giving himself to another . . . . Every-thing in life today is put in compartments. No, I don't know if this has always been so or not – I always imagine a Walter Raleigh kind of man who might have been nearer achieving a wholeness and completeness in his life.'

These remarks would seem relevant to the play. We have a hero who is unable to give himself to his wife and whose lack of wholeness and completeness is shown both in the perverse attraction he feels towards his mother-in-law and in his using the house as a museum of fetish-like collected objects that stand between him and human relationships – the stuffed eagle and model boat, the rifle and panga, the stones on the mantelshelf and the full suit of armour are a futilely self-protective gesture towards history and action. As he cannot be a Walter Raleigh or a Robin Hood, let alone a king, he will nurse his isolation, enjoy disconcerting his friends, toy with the idea of going mad, go mad, and at the end fight his way back to an ambiguous restoration. He is partly a clown, partly Jimmy Porter, partly Hamlet. (The Hamlet echoes are pretty central: the antic disposition, the mother, the fencing, the play within a play, the soured idealism.) Good theatrical use is made of the physical larking about, whether in the strange Strindbergian incident when wife and mother-in-law get Arnold down on the floor and cut off a lock of his hair, or at the extremely funny moment when the hero does a handstand with his feet impatiently drumming on the wall, while a woman guest pretends nothing has happened, and Arnold's wife asks, 'Would you like some tea, Maureen?' There is also a fine range of verbal comedy, from the orotund–facetious schoolmasterly style which is hit off with horrid accuracy in Arnold's friend Hanson, to the hero's doggerel rhymes and inconsequential but memorable stories:

This is quite extraordinary. [*He touches some imaginary person's arm.*] About two days ago the Director of Education came up to me and said, 'Bancroft,' he said – I mean my name isn't even Bancroft – 'Bancroft, I don't know quite how to tell you this, and I should hate it to get around. But the fact is, Bancroft, my wife has recently begun to manufacture money. Periodically she lowers her knickers and from inside takes a miscellaneous collection of coins. The process, as far as I am aware, Bancroft, has completely taken over her excretory organs. And it's mostly silver. The coins, I mean.' You know – would you believe it – the only comment he made after telling me all this was 'Pity it isn't gold, Bancroft. Just like that rotten bitch to produce second best.'

Whether the serious ideas in the play are worked out with sufficient clarity is another matter. There are a number of murky thoughts lurking in the last act which are never quite brought into focus. The hero, particularly in his madness, talks much about kingship and dignity and sees himself as a kind of king (to put it no higher; for God is in the background too). Perhaps, had he been put on, he would have proved most royally. But what does that mean in terms of modern suburban society? In his gripping verse soliloquy facing the wall (Act 3 Scene 1), Arnold would seem to be the victim of an impossible perfectionism instilled in him by his dominant mother:

> So remember, even if the means are insufficient, rather
> Than die in pieces subside by preference as a whole
> For disintegration is inimical to the soul
> Which seeks the opportunity or the chances
> To die in the circumstances
> Of a prince, a saviour, or a messiah –
> Or something, perhaps, even a little higher . . .

In other words, it is better to break than to bend, and the 'sense of secret dignities and rights' which he is inheriting from his mother can only lead him to disaster in ordinary life unless he can find the twentieth-century equation for dignity. We are not shown in the play that he has found this, but his 'restoration' at the end, to his wife and presumably to sanity (though this is not crystal-clear) may be taken as a hopeful indication.

Less tantalizing in its meaning, but equally forceful in its language and dramatic quality, is Peter Terson's *The Mighty Reservoy*. It is interesting to see this play, like many of the other plays in the volume, trying to recover somehow some kind of poetry which will be valid in terms of today's theatre. The verse passages in *The Restoration of Arnold Middleton*, both serious and comic, have already been referred to. The heightened lyrical prose of the central seduction scene in Stewart Conn's *The King*, and the winding, repetitive word-patterns in Ian Hamilton Finlay's *Walking Through Seaweed*, are also working very much as poetry works. B. S. Johnson's play is written in verse, and George MacBeth's employs singing and chanting effects. All these plays, therefore, usefully illustrate from different directions the huge problem of rediscovering dramatic poetry, though none solves it. With Peter Terson's play, the 'poetry' mounts like a pungent tang or smoky bloom from the racy downright dialogue of Dron, the keeper of the reservoir:

I could make it pay. I could make it pay. I used to have lettuce, and sprouts, and parsnips, and radish; nothing posh you understand? But I made a living. No glass mind you, but then, the Vale didn't have glass in those days. Not like now. It's a field of glass now. But in them days it was honest toil. I used to sweat. Sure, I liked a cider, sure, I liked a cider. It gets hot down there in the Vale. 'You're drinking too much cider,' she would start to say. No I am not drinking too much cider, I can drink a glass of cider with the next man and we would sing 'Farmer's Boy', in the Plough and Harrow; and she'd say, 'Well, I hope you ent that's all,' and I says, 'I work hard, I eat hard, I drink hard.' And then, you see. Things got bad like. I mean, there were hard years. There were hard years. Drought, bad market, frost nipping the blossom, things like that. I said, 'I've had enough, I can't make the land pay in this year. We'll sell out and I'll get a job outside and just keep the land on the hill, for our own veg.' But she said, 'You've allus been a land man, you can't let this land beat you.' But I said, 'I'm not beaten, not beaten, but I'll defy any man to make money out of this land.'

The setting of the play has in itself an imaginative appeal. The enormous water-tower with its 500,000 gallons broods as a new technological marvel over the gardens and orchards and scattered villages of the Vale of Evesham. It is like 'a pig's belly upside down', and onto this pig's belly the two characters clamber in all their human insignificance to drink damson and plum wine and discuss nature, work, marriage, and the dark forces of the elements. The two men are in dramatic contrast. Dron drinks, is virtually estranged from his wife, has given up his village smallholding and retreated to the job with the waterworks which he tries to present as scientific, useful, and responsible but which in fact attracts him because of the images of dangerous and destructive power the mighty 'reservoy' evokes in him – the cracks it might develop, the flooded valley, the babies swept out of their beds to death. He loves to think of the reservoir as alive, as 'she', as a moving, moaning thing that will never settle till it is calmed by a human sacrifice. 'I think she needs her man. She needs her man, that would settle her.'

His companion, Church, with his suburban garden and plastic gnomes, his office in Cheltenham, his working wife, his little car, and his quiet desperation, finds the pseudo-Promethean Dron irresistible, and Dron draws out his dissatisfactions and longings one by one as the home-made wine begins to work. Church's father had been a miner, and Church is just as much haunted by the earth-powers as Dron is by the water-gods. 'I've lost the earth,' he cries. 'And I've lost my independent soul.' The eerie crisis grows out of all this as naturally as a fruit. Church, in attempting to swim in the black depths of the reservoir as his father had once swum in the pit-pools, becomes the ritual sacrifice Dron needs.

The mixture of grotesque comedy and mounting excitement in these first three acts is admirable, but when Dron in the fourth act soliloquizes in sodden delirium, talks to Church's ghost, and dies to the imaginary cracking of the reservoir walls, the riproaring melodrama asks for a good deal of suspension of disbelief. Yet we are today more than a little interested in melodrama, and this Terson evidently senses. Whatever melodrama may have lacked in intellectual sophistication, it clearly fed a need for communal entertainment and audience involvement that twentieth-century theatre has treated cavalierly and is only now endeavouring to return to, by a number of devious and uncoordinated routes. Terson's other plays – I am thinking especially of *Zigger Zagger* and *The Ballad of the Artificial Mash* – acknowledge the importance of popular elements that include the communal and the earthy and can still find in them a real poetry and irony.

Terson's chthonic appeasement, and the king-obsession of Storey's play, come together (as it happens) in Stewart Conn's *The King*. This might be classified as an anthropological fairy-tale, though Pinter's comedy of menace has also contributed something to the basic situation. Yet the actual origin of the play, as Conn himself has related, was an incident in his own experience: seeing an old fisherman called Attie King try on a mock crown, and being unable to shake off this strange image which struck him as having a mingled absurdity and horror. Shades of the Fisher King and *The Golden Bough* gather fast around such an incident, though the resemblance of the name Attie to Attis (or Adonis) is apparently coincidental. At least we are reminded, by knowing this *donnée*, that it is a poet's play, and Conn has referred to the development of his dramas as 'an overflow from poems'. But *The King*, whatever its origins, is good theatre, and reaches two moments of real intensity.

It is a fable which has to modulate between realism and magic, and this it does with considerable success, no doubt building on previous workers in this vineyard such as Pinter, Ionesco, and de Ghelderode. The Attie of the play is a gardener, and when he is engaged by Mr Farrol to tend his wife Lena's rose-garden we are neatly pushed into that area where the lines of Frazer's Adonis and Freud's Eros cross. Attie, plied with naturalistic beer and cigarettes and given a sofa for the night, is soon made aware that he is an actual prisoner, unable to leave the house, but then he becomes a prisoner in a deeper sense, visited by Lena and seduced in a poetic flurry of vegetational images. The erotic frenzy of this scene is all the more remarkable in being so dominatingly and boldly verbal:

The petals thrust back, giving off their perfume, soft as silk, the silken petals, the honey dropping and flowing and running, the whole garden dripping and flowing with honey, and you deep at the centre, the centre of it all . . . . The roses, Attie . . . . The roses, the rose-garden all yours, to take for your very own, the petals opening, your fingers flexing and slipping inside, sliding between the opening petals, the stamens erect, then drooping, the scent of pollen perfuming the air, the blue midnight air heavy and dripping with the scent of honey, of pollen drifting, the scent of honey, of spices, blue in the night air, blue and green, and shot with gold . . . with velvet . . . and gold . . .

Although the play returns again to realism, Attie is now a sacred person, and doomed. He is no longer allowed to smoke and drink. He is in the hands of a queen who now owns him, who proceeds to crown and robe him, who gives him an iron rod and a brass bell and asks him to try out his powers as king by stopping the thunderstorm which has sprung up and threatened the flower-garden. The increasing desperation of the would-be king, ringing his bell frantically and uselessly against the thunder, makes a strong climax, and the ritual murder and ritual weeping over the body, do almost but not quite succeed on the level of the thriller which the plot has now become. The fable is imperfect, and does not convince to the hilt. But the power of suggestion, and notably the power of words, make themselves felt in this concentrated little piece.

Wistful charm is not the first quality anyone would associate with the 1960s, yet Ian Hamilton Finlay's *Walking Through Seaweed* innocently sets out to cold-shoulder the bow-wow battalions, whether of Artaud, Hochhuth, or psychedelia. The author's favourite pop-singer is, not surprisingly, Donovan. Sir James Barrie would not feel alienated in the world of Finlay's plays. These three Scots can all be related, in fact, to the (unjustly) despised kailyard tradition which at its best simply reminds us of small things that would otherwise be hammered into the ground. When the present play was first produced in Glasgow, the two girls spoke with a marked Glasgow accent, the local flavour depending not on vocabulary but on the distinctive intonational sing-song of that city. The text, as now printed, may be taken to be fairly universal, but would certainly gain from a local rendering wherever it happened to be produced. The point of this is that the universally disseminated pop-and-telly culture the play uses as its background is being shown as insufficient in that it is powerless to reach into the nooks and crannies of every individual mind, even when a mind is semi-articulate and only half-aware of its own mythology. Little pockets of individual feeling and experience, everywhere, become significant not because they oppose pop (they probably don't) but because they allow the non-central, the non-metropolitan, to make a small sound of its own.

Here, only one of the two girls has heard this sound, and she is nicely contrasted with her friend. The friend is conventional and a would-be realist. She won't eat toffee-apples in the street because girls don't do that sort of thing at the age of sixteen; she dreams about having 'a great big telly' and 'a beautiful radiogram' and being married to a disc-jockey; she takes the common-sense view that sea and seaweed are alien and scary and wants to have no more to do with them than with the childish toffee-apples. But the other romantic and imaginative girl is more scared of 'every day' than of walking through slippery crab-sheltering seaweed with her shoes off; she not only likes toffee-apples, but when she sees liquorice-straps in the window her mind leaps poetwise to the brown straps of seaweed. Her magazine-culled imaginary boyfriend Paul is properly deflated by the realist, but the feelings she has about the sea are endorsed by the author in a pointedly heightened part of her dialogue near the end:

You and I – we could hold hands – we could go walking – like dancers – like on a tight-rope – all down through all that seaweed – and we'd tell each other things – all our secret things. – Yep, you and me – we could walk through the seaweed – all the way – right to the sea! [*Pause.*] You got to walk through seaweed or – or you don't get anywhere. And seaweed – it's full of crabs and things . . . . But you got to walk through it – hand in hand – with some other person – be-

cause it's lovely too – you got to walk like a dancer – like two dancers –
all through the seaweed – right to the sea . . . !

Like Blakean forests of experience, the tangles of seaweed have to
be gone through, resiliently, hopefully, the slippery dangers trans-
formed into a dance, if life is not to remain humdrum, mapped-out,
an unawakened thing. Some will find this a shade fey, and admittedly
the sea (which the girl describes as her goal, as her 'home') is a very
ambiguous image hovering between life more abundant and certain
death. The feyness, however, is arguably a part of the dramatic
effect.

The Estate Hunters substitutes a father and son for the two teenage
girls, but its theme is similar: an intense longing for something that is
simple and physical, and within normal experience, but rare and in
fact not found within the play. The girl has walked by herself through
the seaweed, but not hand-in-hand with 'some other person' as she
will have to do for the magic to work. The boy in *The Estate Hunters*
has not found the 'little burn that has never been fished', and his
father is no nearer buying that country cottage with 'no shop to go
hurrying down to'. Typical of Finlay's work is the narrow range of
recurrent imagery. The tea, the fishing, the poor old horse, the
cottage, the burn all make their appearance in his poetry, and are
used here for the same basic purpose: to stretch out, between the
compass-points of familiar things, a net of comment on human
aspirations. There is nothing fey this time; only a sadness. The play,
with its old Russian motto to emphasize a Chekhovian or pre-
Chekhovian paralysis of action, presents an essentially static, almost
fairy-tale situation where the dramatic movement, though forward
in time and involving expectation and climax, coils back on itself
and completes a circle: the characters will not escape from the dream
they are in, from the tenement kitchen, from the hopes they have
watched thinning to an elaborate game which is played with newspaper advertisements and delayed outings to the country. Pathos
closes the circle. The ending, which in one sense is outrageously
kailyardy with its golden light falling on the smiles and tears of the
two raised faces, works, in the way that so much of Barrie still
works, or some precarious moments in Tennessee Williams. The
poetry of melodrama can be re-invented, perhaps, if a patterned

simplicity of feeling is allowed its theatrical head. Here, the aesthetic patterning produced by the boy's near-repetition of his father's speech at the end of the first scene (the reiterated rising of the trout used like the Moscow of *The Three Sisters*) may be too obvious a device, but the appeal through an obvious device, like the appeal through feyness, does not preclude impact.

B. S. Johnson's work, in the novel, drama, poetry, and film, clearly shows a fascination with technique and for what he calls 'pushing my limits back'. Ian Hamilton Finlay has said that he detests the word 'experimental' because the serious artist should have a clear idea of what he wants to do, and B. S. Johnson too has complained of reviewers who discuss his innovations (e.g. all-black pages, pages with holes) in terms of surprise rather than of function. There seems no harm, however, in calling *You're Human Like the Rest of Them* experimental, since it is a play which has had a double life as a film, being presented in a bill of experimental films at the National Film Theatre in 1967 and being revised as a stage play for the present collection. Its experiment was an attempt to find out how words, syllables, lines, and pauses in verse dialogue could be married to the shots of a camera in a more minutely corresponding way than had been tried before, even having ten cuts in a ten-syllable line. In its theatre form, the play still has a strict ten-syllable line-structure with a pause at the end of each line, and although inevitably the conversational movement of the spoken lines will impose its own stresses and blur the syllabic count, it is clear that the syllabic structure is important and should be retained even at the doing of some violence to naturalism. Johnson's dislike of *cinéma-vérité* can be carried over into the theatrical line-mechanism which deliberately snaps and grinds its gear-teeth through the theme of bodily malfunction and death.

Autobiographically emerging from the shock of a close friend's early death from cancer, this play also bears a strong resemblance to *The Restoration of Arnold Middleton* in its presentation of the disturbed, joke-cracking, isolated teacher hero who is going mad because the world seems at utter variance with human dignity. Blame for the imperfections of the human spine, which slips a disc simply because it can't do what we need it to do, may not readily be assignable in an unbelieving society. To become suddenly aware of these flaws, and by that suddenness to feel a whiff of the grave on your face, is to become sceptical of heroics. The best you can do is emulate the wretched locusts in Haakon's parable:

> There were these lizards, at the zoo, lizards/
> In a sort of glass-fronted cage, prison/
> And they fed these lizards with big locusts/
> The lizards were about twelve inches long/
> And the locusts were about two inches/
> The locusts couldn't get away, of course/
> They had no defence against being killed/
> The only thing a locust could do was/
> To make itself an awkward thing to eat/
> By sticking out its arms and legs and wings/
> To make itself an awkward thing to kill/

And even his attempt at self-assertion may have the ground cut from under its feet. In Haakon's 'comic apotheosis' the world rewards him for his noble suffering – a drop of frying oil on the struggling locust.

In form, the play is reminiscent of film, with its careful use of spots, blackouts, fading, and slides. Its claustrophobic effects could have a menacing power in a small theatre.

George MacBeth's *The Doomsday Show* offers a more complex orchestration of non-conventional theatre effects. A pop electronic nightmare cabaret which makes full use of microphone and tape-recorder, metronome and searchlight torch, stylized dress and split-second timing, it scatters macabre entertainment on the theme of post-atomic survival. The interesting idea that the survivors will develop ritual games in order to keep the horror of their situation at bay is projected into the whole frame of the play, which is itself a kind of game, so that the audience (necessarily an intimate one) is played upon, with, and to, all at the same time. Satire on atomic civil defence melts into the straight fascist Götterdämmerung of Hitler's bunker, and that into a future fantasy of giant ants. Pervading consciousness of disaster is channelled through the tantalizing sex-and-violence card-games of 'The Ski Murders' and 'Fin du Globe' until the final Doomsday Chant re-enacts the catastrophe and sets the whole cycle ready for operation again.

The very strict cues and tightly disciplined acting and speaking on the one hand, and on the other hand the permutated poem and the permutational card-games which give a sense of missing-jigsaw-piece uneasiness to the audience even if they are therapeutic to the Metrognomes in the play, combine to make this a piece that is extraordinarily detached from its subject, yet capable of generating a variety of responses and excitements. The printed text in this case is virtually a score for performance, and it is one aspect of contemporary theatre that this should be regarded as important. The lengthy and precise stage-directions *are* a large part of the play:

[*The leader stops the metronome. At this point there is the dry rasping of a single pair of scissors, opening and shutting in the darkness. It should sound like the joyless copulation of a metal insect. The leader cocks his head at this noise, as if listening. His next words are spoken as a mocking question, almost an interrogation, as if speaking to an unseen presence.*]

The sometimes elaborate technical effects called for in a play like this have themselves an added element of the game about them, and it might be a fair criticism of *The Doomsday Show* to say that technique can obtrude too much. But the nervous flicker of cabaret has few laws, and perhaps none that are not for breaking.

EDWIN MORGAN

DAVID STOREY

The Restoration of Arnold Middleton

The Restoration of Arnold Middleton was first produced at the Traverse Theatre, Edinburgh, on 22
November 1966, with the following cast:

(in order of their appearance)

MRS EDIE ELLIS	June Watson
JOAN MIDDLETON	Marian Diamond
ARNOLD MIDDLETON	David Collings
JEFFREY HANSON	Paul Williamson
SHEILA O'CONNOR	Ann Holloway
MAUREEN WILKINSON	Rosemary McHale

The play directed by Gordon McDougall
Setting by Denzil Walker
Lighting by Paul Miller

Subsequently produced at the Royal Court Theatre,
London, on 4 July 1967, with the following cast:

MRS EDIE ELLIS	Noel Dyson
JOAN MIDDLETON	Eileen Atkins
ARNOLD MIDDLETON	John Shepherd
JEFFREY HANSON	Tenniel Evans
SHEILA O'CONNOR	Gillian Hills
MAUREEN WILKINSON	Andree Evans

The play directed by Robert Kidd
Setting by Bernard Culshaw
Lighting by Andy Phillips and Bill Dufton

ACT ONE

SCENE ONE

A cosy, well-furnished, scrupulously clean living-room, equipped with dining table and chairs as well as a three-piece suite and sideboard.

Arranged round the room, on the walls and furniture, are various objects, mounted and in excellent state of preservation: a stuffed eagle, a sword, a ship, a model aeroplane, a model engine, etc., which may suggest the rudiments of a museum, but bereft of any specific human connotation. Over the mantelpiece hangs a Lee-Enfield rifle.

The centre of the room is dominated by a full-size suit of armour, standing in a pile of brown paper and string from which it has just emerged. A two-handed sword runs down from its hands.

Regarding this object with a mixture of amazement and distaste are two women: JOAN, *an attractive, good-humoured if tenacious-looking woman in her early thirties, and* MRS ELLIS, *her mother, a rather unconsciously-sensual woman in her late fifties. Like her daughter, she is neatly and prettily dressed. They are also both wearing pinafores:* JOAN's *full,* MRS ELLIS's *petite and frilly and fastened around her waist.*

JOAN *has a label in her hand.*

MRS ELLIS: Well...
  They must have sent it here by mistake.
JOAN [*glancing at the label*]: It's the right address.
MRS ELLIS: But it should have gone to the school, surely? That's where he has all the others.
JOAN: The man said that he'd asked for it to be delivered here.
MRS ELLIS: Here? But why here? We've nowhere to keep it here. Whoever would want a thing like that in their house?
JOAN: Perhaps it's his idea of a joke. [*She looks round the room.*] At this rate we shan't be here at all soon.
MRS ELLIS: He must *mean* it to go to the school, Joan. Eventually. That's where all the others are. And he's had it sent here so we can see it.
JOAN: Well, it's strange if he has, because it's the only one I've seen. Queen Elizabeth, George V and all the rest. I'm the only person

who hasn't been allowed in. 'Some other time. Some other time.'
While any school child can go in and out as he pleases.

MRS ELLIS: I'm sure that's where this will end up. The history
museum. Just you see.

JOAN: Clean the paper up, mother, will you? I'll put his tea on.
[*Goes through into the kitchen; she treats her mother strictly, as she would
a servant.*]

MRS ELLIS [*clearing up*]: Well, it's a surprise, and no mistake.

JOAN [*calling through*]: Have you got all the string? I don't want bits
left lying about.

MRS ELLIS [*looking up at the armour as she stoops*]: Of course . . .
it's as you say. His idea of a joke. [*She laughs uneasily.*]

JOAN [*reappearing with the teatray to set the table*]: Or an insult.

MRS ELLIS: Insult? It needs time to sink in. I can see now . . .

JOAN: Could you put it all in the kitchen. There's a piece of string.
[MRS ELLIS, *her arms full of brown paper, stoops down, retrieves the
last morsel of string, and carries her load into the kitchen.*
JOAN *is setting the table: as she goes to the sideboard during this
conversation to get the tablecloth she passes the armour one way, then
changes her mind and goes the other, as though it were a person to be
avoided.*]

MRS ELLIS [*calling through*]: Of course, if you were really stuck for
somewhere to put it, you could keep it in the bedroom.

JOAN: In the bedroom!

MRS ELLIS [*calling through*]: No one would see it, would they?

JOAN: No one?

MRS ELLIS: Not in the bedroom.

JOAN: What about me?

MRS ELLIS [*reappearing*]: Well. I'm sure I don't want to quarrel about
it.

JOAN [*lightly*]: Well, then, at least I'm glad of that.

MRS ELLIS: I do live here as well, Joan.

JOAN [*disregarding*]: Could you do the bread? [*Checks her watch with
the clock.*] He'll have forgotten altogether that we're going out
tonight.

MRS ELLIS: You're so inconsiderate, Joan.

JOAN: It would be different, wouldn't it, if he ever showed any
interest in them. But he spreads them all over the place then never

looks at them again. Accidentally move one and he comes down on you as though it were the house you'd shifted.

MRS ELLIS: Why can't you let it rest? He doesn't give you anything else to grumble about. You can't complain about him. Not really.

JOAN: He's never out of the damned house. [*She picks up one or two of the pieces.*] He puts on his coat, goes out to school, and leaves them like this. They're like spies. He never lets you rest. Everywhere you look there's some part of him watching and waiting. Even in the bathroom . . .

MRS ELLIS: It's just you, Joan, that.

JOAN: Two slices. That's enough. Well, it's not staying there.

MRS ELLIS: Where are you going to put it?

JOAN: Don't just stand there. [*She's taken hold of it, leaning it back, and with* MRS ELLIS *she drags it over to a built-in cupboard near the kitchen door.*] In the cupboard.

MRS ELLIS: In the cupboard! Do you think we should?

JOAN: It's obscene. Something like this in the house. It makes you feel terrible just to touch it. . . . These houses weren't built for things like this. Mother: will you open the door?

[*They put it in the cupboard and* JOAN *hands out a few brushes, mops and an umbrella which she gives to* MRS ELLIS *before shutting the cupboard doors on the armour.*]

Put those in the kitchen, will you?

MRS ELLIS: Are you going to hide it from him?

JOAN: It'll do for now.

Why did he have to have it here? Aren't there enough people here already?

[MRS ELLIS *has gone to the kitchen.*

JOAN *goes to the door to talk in at her, instructionally.*]

No, in the cupboard, mother. There's his mother and father coming in two days' time. Can you imagine what *they* are going to think?

MRS ELLIS [*re-emerging*]: They'll hardly complain, Joan.

JOAN: Coming to somebody's house only to find out as you step through the door it's a museum. It's not a home it's an institution.

MRS ELLIS: They've never seen *either* of you all these years. They're hardly in a position to judge anybody.

JOAN: But that's just what they will do. They're just about total strangers, aren't they? Come to that, it's just as well they are.

MRS ELLIS: I don't know . . .

[JOAN *turns restlessly about the room,* MRS ELLIS *watching her concernedly.*]

If only you had something.

JOAN [*beginning to re-arrange the tea-table already scrupulously prepared by both of them*]: Had something what?

MRS ELLIS: An interest.

JOAN: Interest! I have an interest.

MRS ELLIS: You could go out to work, get a job. You're qualified to do any number of things.

JOAN: This is my house.

MRS ELLIS: I know it's your house, Joan.

JOAN: And it takes some looking after.

[MRS ELLIS *doesn't answer.*]

I run this as I want it.

MRS ELLIS: All I'm saying is I could run the house while you do something else.

[JOAN *sits down:* MRS ELLIS *begins to re-arrange the table now.*]

And there would be so much more coming in.

JOAN: And your widow's pension.

MRS ELLIS: I don't just mean money. But all those opportunities for other interests as well.

JOAN: You think, then, we'd all be better off if we each had an interest?

MRS ELLIS: What's life for if you can't have an interest?

JOAN [*examines her mother shrewdly*]: You know, mother, you're too much like me.

MRS ELLIS: People can laugh at interests, but it's like religion. He who laughs . . .

JOAN [*shouting*]: We've got an interest here already! *His!* It's scattered in every cranny of this building. You can't sit down without finding a stone 'with an interesting mark' on it, or a bit of wood that fell off Noah's ark, or a rotten old nail that dropped out of somebody's rotten old chariot. And just look at that thing. Standing behind that cupboard door listening to every word I say. It's not fair. It's not fair.

MRS ELLIS: Joan, I do my work here.

[*They are silent a moment. Then, contemplative:*]

24

JOAN: Do you remember once when you bought him a little statue – a man's head and shoulders? God only knows where his body had got to. And he accidentally knocked it off the sideboard and broke it?

MRS ELLIS: He was more concerned with my feelings than with the thing.

JOAN: He wanted to get rid of it.

MRS ELLIS: He did not.

JOAN: He wanted to get rid of it. It was the only thing that resembled a human being in the entire house.

MRS ELLIS: You've never understood him, Joan. You never have.

JOAN: And now he brings this thing. There's something strange about it. It's the first life-like thing he's ever had here. He usually keeps them all at school. [*She gets up.*]

MRS ELLIS: Joan. You don't understand my position here.

[JOAN *begins preparations to go out.*]

Where are you going?

JOAN: Out. [*She goes to the door leading to the hall.*]

MRS ELLIS [*alone*]: If you're hoping to go to the cinema you'll have to leave almost as soon as he comes in. . . . He'll be back any time now.

JOAN [*calling through*]: I won't be long. [*She enters with a coat she puts on over her pinafore.*] He's not going to find me waiting here, that's all.

MRS ELLIS: Waiting here?

JOAN: Stuck here amongst his trophies.

[MRS ELLIS *watches* JOAN *make up her face in the mirror.*]

I'll go down to the corner, or something.

MRS ELLIS: It's ridiculous.

JOAN [*turning to her*]: I'll go out the back way, then there's no chance of meeting.

MRS ELLIS: Joan. This is silly. [*Suddenly, looking at the cupboard*] You won't be long, will you, Joan?

JOAN: Don't mention *that* until I come in. [*She indicates the cupboard.*] Do you understand?

MRS ELLIS: Yes. But . . .

JOAN: And for God's sake don't say I've just gone out. Say I've been gone an hour. All right? [*She leaves by the kitchen door.*]

MRS ELLIS: You won't be long, love, will you?

[MRS ELLIS *glances at the cupboard again, then goes to the table, fingers and re-arranges the various tea-things, then moves uncertainly about the room, avoiding the cupboard area completely. Finally she comes face to face with the mirror, glances at it, then becomes increasingly interested in her reflection. She begins to examine her face, its various expressions of hope and dismay, glee and uncertainty, unconsciously producing animal noises, purring and cooing. She becomes lost in herself; her body heaves for a sigh, then suddenly relaxes in a huge, vaguely grotesque smile.*

ARNIE, *a well-built man in his thirties, has appeared in the hall doorway. He watches awhile, expressionless, then comes quietly into the room until he is almost behind* MRS ELLIS. *Then he suddenly barks like a dog.*

MRS ELLIS *gives a scream of fright. Then:*]

MRS ELLIS: Oh, Arnie! Arnie!

ARNIE: Loved one!

MRS ELLIS [*recovering*]: It's just what you'd expect from a school-master.

ARNIE [*Takes off his old raincoat.*]

Master, Edie. Master. Watch this, Edie. [*Using his coat as a whip he begins to beat the floor.*]

MRS ELLIS *watches this with interest and pleasure, yet as though she's seen it all before. She sits down at the table to watch.*]

Take that. And that. And that – you sniffling snot-gobbling little crat. And *that.* I'll teach you to take my stick of chalk. [*He growls and roars as he drives the imaginary child into the floor. He steps on the spot and spreads the remnants thoroughly over the carpet.*] Got it! Got it! Now. How do you like that, Edie? I know how to take care of these little crats.

MRS ELLIS: I don't know. It's a wonder any of them stay alive.

ARNIE: Know? Edie! You know. You know everything.

MRS ELLIS [*pleased*]: What! Me!

ARNIE: You.

MRS ELLIS: More than a schoolteacher?

ARNIE: Yes.

MRS ELLIS: Well ... I don't know ... [*She holds her cheek with pleasure.*

ARNIE *watches her, suddenly intent. Then:*]

ARNIE: Look. . . . [*His mood relaxes again.*] Did you see his face? The way he looked when I hit him the first time. He thought I didn't mean it. He thought I'd *let him off* for taking my stick of chalk. Mind you – he'd every reason to think I wouldn't beat his lousy head in. These *dwarfs* think you're frightened of being reprimanded, of being handed over to the . . .

MRS ELLIS: And will you get the sack?

ARNIE: No such fortune for me. [*He sits down and begins to tug off his shoes. His mood changes again. Reflective.*] If I rape two, or perhaps it may have to be three, I might be asked if I'd mind being moved to another school. But chances of promotion like that are increasingly rare. [*He gets his last shoe off with a struggle.*] Rape apart, it's all a question of dead men's shoes, Edie.

MRS ELLIS [*concernedly*]: I wish you wouldn't use language like that, Arnie.

ARNIE [*holding up his shoes*]: Ill-will; that's the cargo these shoes carry. Along, that is, with my own personal misfortunes. [*He searches round, sees* MRS ELLIS's *feet and, on hands and knees, crawls across to them as though they were shoes he was hunting.*] Why . . . Why, these are full of hopes.

MRS ELLIS: Oh, now . . .

ARNIE: Can't you feel them: growing beneath your feet? Why, Edie, your shoes are full of hope. It's sprouting through your toes . . .

MRS ELLIS: All I feel is how glad I am I didn't know what teachers were like when our Joan went to school.

ARNIE: Where is SHE, by the way? Not gone off on my bike, her dress tucked into her bloomers.

MRS ELLIS: Really, Arnie. . . . She's just gone out. I mean, *merely* gone out.

ARNIE: Merely gone out?

MRS ELLIS: She's only gone out. That's what I mean.

ARNIE: Only gone out. Not merely gone out.

MRS ELLIS: She's . . . out.

ARNIE: I see.

MRS ELLIS: Your tea's on the table.

ARNIE: We're supposed to be going to the cinema. Let me see. [*Consults his wrist watch.*] Half an hour ago.

MRS ELLIS: She'll only be a few minutes. . . . [*Hurries into the kitchen.*]

ARNIE [*knowingly and quickly searching the room*]: It all seems carefully timed. What's going on?

MRS ELLIS [*calling through*]: She's so restless. She can't sit down two minutes these days without getting up again because there's something not satisfactory. I don't know . . . it's just everything.

[ARNIE *turns at this and goes to the table. He sits down and begins to put some jam on the bread.*]

MRS ELLIS [*calling through*]: How's your play going at school?

[ARNIE *plays with the bread abstractedly.*

MRS ELLIS *re-appears in the kitchen door with a teapot.*]

You. Can't you hear me when I talk to you?

ARNIE: What's that, chump-chops?

MRS ELLIS: None of your cheek. Haven't you been rehearsing this afternoon?

[ARNIE *breaks his mood to give a dramatic recitation.*]

ARNIE: Said Robin Hood to Friar Tuck,
'How are you my fat fellow?'
'I'm very well,' said the cheerful monk,
'But I'm sorry you're looking yellow.'

'Is that a jest or would you dare
To challenge your captain staunch?'
'Nay,' said the Friar, 'don't threaten me,
Or I'll kill you with my paunch.'

MRS ELLIS [*giggles*]: Is that it?

ARNIE: A generous portion of it, Edie. On the whole, I think it will appear neither conspicuous nor insignificant on the contemporary theatrical scene.

MRS ELLIS [*pouring his tea*]: Is it going very well?

ARNIE: A minor alarm this morning when the Lionheart tripped over his scabbard. He'll appear on stage with a bandage round his leg – a wound sustained, while fighting the Turks outside Damascus.

MRS ELLIS: They're only boys. What are you calling the play?

ARNIE: I don't know. [*Thoughtfully*] 'Hands up, Sheriff, your Money or your Wife.'

MRS ELLIS: Oh, now.

ARNIE: 'The Good King Richard and the Bad King John!' Probably, 'Robin Hood and His Merry Men', Edie.

MRS ELLIS: Oh, that's nice. [MRS ELLIS *sits down opposite* ARNIE *and watches him eat his tea.*] And is it adapted from William Shakespeare, then?

ARNIE: No. Jeffrey Hanson. He's the head of the English Department. He's coming round tomorrow evening to discuss the less serious aspects of the play. So that'll be tea for two, Edie.

MRS ELLIS: Oh, I'll be out late tomorrow, getting things in. [*Silence.*] Are you looking forward to them coming? Are you listening?

ARNIE: Yes.

MRS ELLIS: What are they like?

ARNIE: Who?

MRS ELLIS: You know. Silly.

ARNIE: Oh. [*Dismisses it.*]

MRS ELLIS: Of course, I only met them that once at the wedding. Ten years. [*She broods.*] It's not often you meet decent people nowadays. [*Suddenly*] You complain that they never come to see you. Yet you've never been to see them.

ARNIE: No.

MRS ELLIS: Did you have a happy childhood, Arnie?

ARNIE: Did you?

MRS ELLIS [*laughs*]: No: I'm asking you. I bet you were a model child.

ARNIE [*pleasantly*]: I was. Facsimiles of me could be seen all over the place at one time, Edie.

[MRS ELLIS *becomes preoccupied with her thoughts, getting up and wandering round the room distractedly.*]

MRS ELLIS: You know, Arnie . . .

[ARNIE *is getting out a pipe and looking round.*]

Joan. She's been in such a funny mood today.

ARNIE: Yes.

MRS ELLIS: You've stopped listening, haven't you?

ARNIE: I have not.

MRS ELLIS: She's been suggesting, you know . . . that I wasn't much use to anyone.

ARNIE: You know, Edie, I've told you before. I'm not stepping in between your women's fights.

MRS ELLIS [*coming to the table*]: Do you want another cup?

ARNIE: Thanks.

[MRS ELLIS *pours a cup.* ARNIE *fusses with his pipe.*]

ARNIE: It would be nice to have a proper job and a decent home, wouldn't it?

MRS ELLIS: Arnie! You have a decent home. And it could be even better if you'd let me.

ARNIE: Better?

MRS ELLIS: Cleaner and neater.

ARNIE: Cleaner than this?

[*He stirs up his tea with milk and sugar.* MRS ELLIS *watches him acutely, the teapot still in her hand.*]

MRS ELLIS: In a way.

ARNIE: In a way! Why can't we ever hold a decent conversation in this house? I teach in a madhouse all day, then come home to another at night.

MRS ELLIS [*outraged*]: Arnie!

ARNIE: It's not right. You and Joan. . . . If you would only say what you meant. Just once.

MRS ELLIS: You don't begrudge me staying here, do you?

ARNIE: No.

MRS ELLIS: I could go away. I'm not so old . . .

ARNIE: Edie. What are you talking about? [*He gets up from the table and moves about the room, apparently looking for matches.*]

MRS ELLIS: Fancy . . . . Do you remember that little statue I bought you once as a present? That was accidentally broken?

ARNIE: What? [*Taps out his pipe abstracted.*]

MRS ELLIS: Joan said this afternoon – that you broke it deliberately. Because you didn't like it. And you hadn't the heart to tell me.

ARNIE: Now, look. I don't have to stand here and listen to all this, Edie. You're a woman in your own right: you must stick up for yourself.

MRS ELLIS: I don't want to cause any bother. I don't. But Joan's always making me feel I haven't got anything at all . . . nothing.

[*She's clearly upset.* ARNIE *watches her. Then crosses to her, and takes her shoulders.*]

ARNIE: I didn't break it on purpose, Edie. And it wasn't a statue. It was a piece of pottery made to look like stone. I appreciated you giving it to me. All right?

[*She looks into his eyes, then nods.*]

So there's no need to start an argument, is there?

MRS ELLIS: No.

[*The front door bangs, and* ARNIE *releases her.*]

ARNIE: Quick. Hide under the table and tickle her knees.

MRS ELLIS: Get on with you, you devil!

[*She's laughing as* JOAN *comes in: then goes to clear the table.*
ARNIE *has taken a comic from his pocket and propped it on the mantelpiece to read aloud.*

JOAN *looks at them both, then goes to the mirror and takes off her coat.*]

ARNIE [*reading like a child*]: G . . g . . g . . gooood . . . ness g . . g . . g . . gra . . gra . . gracious! Ssss . . ssss . . ssssaid th . . th . . th . . the F . . Ffff . . Ffff . . . Fairy Qu . . Qu . . Qu . . Queen . . .

JOAN: That girl's followed you home from school again. I suppose you realize.

[ARNIE *goes casually to the window.*]

ARNIE: What?

JOAN: O'Connor. Isn't that her name?

ARNIE [*looking out*]: I don't know what I'd do without her. Always that faithful twenty-five yards behind. . . . Like a progressive following the revolution.

[MRS ELLIS *joins him to look out too.*]

JOAN: She moved smartly across the road when I came in. And no wonder.

MRS ELLIS: What does she hope to get out of it?

ARNIE: Some people do things, Edie, not for what they can get but for what they can give . . .

JOAN: Oh, very nice. For two damn pins I'd go out there and give *her* something she *wouldn't* be grateful for!

[*As* ARNIE *turns from the window*]

And I thought we were going out tonight?

ARNIE: I'm ready when you are. I'll just finish this instalment then I'll be right with you.

JOAN: Is that a child's magazine?

ARNIE: It's all right. I didn't buy it. I stole it from a desk. [*He takes the comic and goes to the stairs: the sound of his feet ascending, then a door closing.*

JOAN *goes to the window.*]

JOAN: Has he seen that?

MRS ELLIS: No.

JOAN: Are you sure?

MRS ELLIS: I'm positive.

JOAN: What have you been crying about?

MRS ELLIS: I haven't been crying. [*She finishes clearing the table.*]

JOAN: It doesn't look like that.

MRS ELLIS: We were talking about his parents, if you must know.

JOAN: What about his parents?

MRS ELLIS: Nothing you would understand.

   [JOAN *watches her intently. Then:*]

JOAN: I don't like this. I don't.

MRS ELLIS: What?

JOAN: This! *This*! [*She grabs and tugs at her mother's pinafore.*]

MRS ELLIS: What?

   [JOAN *doesn't answer.*]

  What's the matter with . . .

JOAN: It's all wrong! [*She swings on the room. Neither can speak.*]

MRS ELLIS: I'll take mine off, then.

JOAN: Take *yours* off?

   [MRS ELLIS *takes her apron off slowly: she lays the petite-looking
   thing absent-mindedly on Arnie's raincoat on the chair.*]

  Not there! Not there! [*She snatches it up and throws it on the floor.*]

MRS ELLIS: Joanie . . .

JOAN: I don't like this. I don't.

MRS ELLIS: What is it, pet?

JOAN: Don't *pet* me.

MRS ELLIS: Joan . . .

JOAN: You weren't talking about his parents. You were talking about
  me.

MRS ELLIS: Do you think we've nothing better . . .

JOAN: Don't say *we*! You were talking about me. You were talking
  to him about me. Did you tell him . . . did you say anything about
  that? [*She gestures at the cupboard.*]

MRS ELLIS: No.

   [ARNIE's *feet are stamping down the stairs:* JOAN *goes to stand by the
   cupboard doors.*

   ARNIE *comes in smoking a pipe. He begins to put on his shoes.*]

ARNIE: Well, ready?

JOAN: I have a surprise for you first.

ARNIE [*genially*]: Yes.

JOAN: Are you ready?

ARNIE: Yes. . . . Just a minute. Right.

JOAN: All right?

ARNIE: Yes.

[JOAN *swings open the cupboard doors.*]

JOAN: There.

ARNIE [*smokes on*]: Oh, that's where it is.

JOAN: How do you mean, that's where it is?

ARNIE: I couldn't imagine where you'd hidden it. It wasn't upstairs; I've just looked.

JOAN [*crying out at* MRS ELLIS]: You told him! You liar!

ARNIE: As a matter of fact, I asked the man to ring up the school and let me know when he delivered it.

JOAN: You *sneak*!

ARNIE: I'm not sneaking. I've been waiting for it to come.

JOAN: You rotten, bloody sneak. I've been walking around out there . . .

ARNIE: Walking round?

JOAN: What's it doing here?

ARNIE: Walking round?

JOAN: What's it doing *here*?

ARNIE: Walking *round*?

JOAN: *What's it doing here?*

ARNIE: It looks to me as though it's standing in a cupboard. [*To armour*] Aren't you coming in, old man?

JOAN: I mean *here*! Here! At this house. You usually have all this junk thrown into your mausoleum at school.

ARNIE: But I didn't buy this with school funds.

JOAN: What?

[ARNIE *is smoking still.*]

ARNIE: It's mine. I bought it myself.

JOAN: Yours? [*Pause.*] What sort of tale is this, Arnold?

ARNIE: I've always wanted one. [*He puts his pipe in his mouth, and eases the armour out of the cupboard: he sets it upright in the room.*]

JOAN: When did you buy it?

ARNIE: What?

JOAN: When did you buy it?

ARNIE: A few days ago.

JOAN: Why? What for? Don't you think we've enough with this already?

ARNIE: You're very aggressive, Joan. Has it assaulted you or something behind my back?

JOAN: It's going back where it came from.

ARNIE: It even smokes a pipe. I told you it was respectable. I don't know. It might easily entertain political ambitions.

JOAN: I've tolerated everything else, Arnie. But not this.

[ARNIE *takes no notice: he's detaching the sword.*]

Can't you see? The place isn't built for a thing like this.

[ARNIE *leaps with a shout and swings the sword at* MRS ELLIS, *who escapes with a scream.*]

MRS ELLIS: Arnie!

[ARNIE *snorts at her.*]

JOAN: Where do you think you're going to keep it for one thing? In the garden?

MRS ELLIS [*standing behind a chair*]: Oh. We can't keep it there. [*Jumps.*] Joan! Everybody would see it.

JOAN: And I'm not having it in the kitchen, peering over my shoulder. And not in the bathroom, the bedroom, the living room or the hall.

[ARNIE *stalks* MRS ELLIS: 'No, Arnie! No!']

ARNIE [*holding the blade to her*]: D'you think it's blood?

JOAN: It's not staying here, Arnie. It's ugly. That's enough!

ARNIE: Well. Are we ready? [*He fits the sword back into place.*]

JOAN: Ready?

ARNIE: To go out.

JOAN: Are we going out now? And leave this?

ARNIE: What do you want me to do? Hug it and give it a kiss? It won't run away. Well, Edie . . . how about you then?

MRS ELLIS: Going out? I don't mind going out. Why, it's ages . . .

JOAN: It's all right. [*She goes to her coat.*] Tomorrow, first thing: that's going.

ARNIE: Aren't you going to take your apron off?

JOAN: What?

ARNIE: Your how d'you do.

[*She sees she's still got on her pinafore.*]

ARNIE: Don't you want to come, Edie?

MRS ELLIS: Well . . .

[JOAN *has almost wrenched off her pinafore and, watching her mother, pulls on her coat.*]

JOAN: She'll be quite all right at home.

MRS ELLIS: I wouldn't have minded going out. I don't really fancy being left alone with this, Arnie.

ARNIE: Get your coat, Granny, and away we go!

MRS ELLIS: Ay, now . . .

[ARNIE *puts his arm round* JOAN *as* MRS ELLIS *gets her coat.*]

ARNIE: It's not half as bad as it seems.

JOAN: It's too much, Arnie, that's all. [*But she is appeased by his coaxing gestures.*] Stop playing around . . .

ARNIE: O sing us a song, you hearty woman,
　　　Of all your dark crimes and your fears;
　　　And we'll swallow our pride and lie down by your side,
　　　And digest all your grief in our tears.

JOAN: Do you hear . . .

[MRS ELLIS *has returned with her coat.*]

ARNIE: Ah, now, a gorgeous old lady of twenty-one . . .

MRS ELLIS: Inches round the neck. I know.

ARNIE: Oh, now Edie. You enlargen yourself. . . . [*He goes to help her with her coat.*]

MRS ELLIS: Oh, I know. Don't worry. I wasn't born yesterday.

ARNIE: If you insist.

MRS ELLIS: There you are, you see. . . . And I ought to have done my face.

ARNIE: Only a disservice, my dear.

MRS ELLIS: Goodness. What's got into him?

[ARNIE *takes her hand.*]

ARNIE: Pray take advantage of my goodwill:
　　　Let us share it between the two;
　　　Take all you can and in return
　　　I'll do the same for you.

JOAN: Come on, we better be going out before he breaks into song.

ARNIE: A moment. [*He sidles with exaggerated caution to the window, carefully lifts the curtain, and looks out.*] The coast's clear. [*To* JOAN] Your glance spoke as eloquently as your thoughts, my dear. Her loyalty knew no bounds – and now you've presented it with several.

JOAN: At least we can go out now, without being molested.

ARNIE: You always could. It's me who is the loser. [*He puts his arm about the two women. As they go out:*]

Gay Robin Hood to town did ride
With maidens fair on either side:
The evil Sheriff and the bad King John
Ne'er recognized the gentlemon.

[JOAN *waits patiently.*]

ARNIE [*hesitates*]: . . . Yes. [*He sweeps them out of the room. A moment later, however, he dashes back in, knocks his pipe out on the armour, boxes it briefly, pats it, then hurries out.*

His voice is heard crying with pleasure, then a door crashes to, and it's silent.]

[*The room slowly darkens.*]

SCENE TWO

The door bursts open, there's giggling and laughter: then MRS ELLIS *and* ARNIE *enter, followed a moment later by* JOAN.

ARNIE. We should . . . we should . . . we should . . .

MRS ELLIS: But we didn't. [*She breaks into outrageous laughter.*]

ARNIE: But we should have!

JOAN: We'd have been home a damn sight sooner if we had. Weee!

[*She throws her shoes into the air and runs across the furniture.*]

ARNIE [*instructionally*]: If we had we wouldn't have had to stand all the way back. [*He belches.*]

JOAN: I'll be sick if I drink any more.

MRS ELLIS: It was your idea.

ARNIE: She doesn't have ideas, mother. Only prejudices.

[JOAN *barks angrily like a dog at* ARNIE, *snarling then growling.*]

MRS ELLIS: Whatever anybody says, I enjoyed myself. I enjoyed myself. [*Telling herself*] How about you, Joan?

JOAN: All the time. . . . All the time . . . asking each other if we've had a good time? All the way back [*mimicking*] 'Have you had a good time, *Arnie*? Have you had a good time, Edie?'

ARNIE: Well, have you had a good time, Edie?

JOAN: What did you call me?

[ARNIE *has turned from her and taken* MRS ELLIS *by the shoulders, looking into her face.*]

You called me Edie!

[ARNIE *turns from* MRS ELLIS, *one hand still holding her shoulder, and he begins to recite with a boy's mechanical, tutored gestures to an imaginary audience.*]

ARNIE: I have lived a long time, mother,
    And seen strange sights beyond the seas,
    But never a one have I seen, mother,
    To match the dimples in your knees.

[MRS ELLIS *has burst out laughing.*]

JOAN [*calling out*]: You called me Edie, you swab.

ARNIE: There are women who shout and women who moan,
    And women who titter down the phone,
    But the only women that I ever see
    Are the ones that need hanging from the nearest tree.

JOAN [*calling*]: You're disgusting!

ARNIE: My wife Joan has a heart of stone,
    And eyes as black as charcoal,
    She wouldn't have looked bad
    If she hadn't have had
    A mouth the shape of her arsehole.

JOAN: I'll kill you!

[MRS ELLIS *attempts to drag her back:* ARNIE *has leapt with great alacrity behind the Knight who, until now, has gone unnoticed.*]

ARNIE: If you touch me I'll set him onto you.

JOAN: And tomorrow that thing's going first thing.

ARNIE: He'll tear you to pieces!

[*For a moment they stand poised, silent. Then:*]

MRS ELLIS: I think you both better get to bed.

ARNIE: Did you hear. . . . [*He steps cautiously from behind the Knight, reassures himself from* JOAN's *look that he's safe.*] Did you hear, as we passed them in the street, what those . . . *children* called me?

Children – I might add – whom I teach and instruct in my own classroom.

MRS ELLIS: It's nothing I'd care to repeat.

ARNIE: And it's nothing, I can assure you, mother, that I've taught them. Those words are not in the curriculum. I even thought once that they liked me.

JOAN: You shouldn't go round getting plastered where they can see you.

[ARNIE *takes* MRS ELLIS'*s hand suddenly.*]

ARNIE: Here . . . here darling. [*He leads her to the arm of a chair, sitting beside her to recite:*]

> There are things in your life
> Not even your wife
> Would think could pass through your brain.
> But give me a light
> And I'll show you a sight
> That would turn even Satan insane.

[MRS ELLIS *laughs, shocked, and breaks away.*]

MRS ELLIS: I think I'll be getting to bed . . .

JOAN: Oh, no, mother.

MRS ELLIS: What?

JOAN: You're not going to bed till you've helped me shift this.

ARNIE: Where to?

JOAN: I'm not going to bed, I'm not. I'd never rest. Not with this wandering loose in the house.

ARNIE: What's it going to get up and do?

JOAN: It's going back in its kennel. And tomorrow . . .

ARNIE: . . . morning it's going out first thing. [*They finish the phrase together.*

JOAN *has begun to struggle with it back to the cupboard,* MRS ELLIS *going to help her.*

ARNIE *watches them ironically, arms folded, though he's still bleary with drink.*]

ARNIE: Rub-adub-dub, three nuts in a tub,
> Who do you think they can be?

JOAN [*struggling*]: I've told you. Tomorrow morning . . .

ARNIE [*together*]: . . . it's going out first thing. [*He has switched on the wireless.*]

JOAN: You don't seem to believe me. But it is. The minute you've gone to school.

[*Dance music has started as the women haul the armour slowly to the cupboard.*

ARNIE *has begun to dance, taking a bottle to drink.*]

JOAN: And I don't want to see it again. Do you hear? [*She hiccups.*]

[ARNIE *dances on, oblivious to them. As* JOAN *fastens the cupboard doors* MRS ELLIS *turns to watch* ARNIE *dance, amused.*]

MRS ELLIS: That's a sight for sore eyes. He can hardly put two feet together. [*Laughs. Then claps.*

ARNIE *looks up at her with sultry affection, eyes half-closed.*]

ARNIE: Oh, I don't know ... all that there and so forth. Hup-dee. Hup-dee.

JOAN [*hiccups*]: Do you hear?

[ARNIE *takes* MRS ELLIS's *hand and they dance loosely together,* MRS ELLIS *laughing still.*]

ARNIE[*swaying his hips*]: That's it, Edie, That's it. Swill it all around.... Give it a good shake.

[JOAN *has picked up a bottle: she seems about to use it both on the wireless and* ARNIE, *then some instinctive coquettishness overcomes her and, bottle dangling, she puts her arm round* ARNIE, *who's spouting his own bottle to his lips.*]

JOAN: Move over, babe. [*She bumps her mother.*] Let's have a dance, honey.

[*The three of them, holding together, dance slowly and lugubriously.*]

ARNIE: Sing us a song, Joannie.

JOAN: I can't sing. ... [*Hiccups.*] I can't sing. [*She makes several near-noises approximating to the music.*]

ARNIE: Oh, lovely, beautiful. [*He belches.*]

[MRS ELLIS *dances away on her own; a slow waltz, not ungraceful. She holds her skirt and dances with a slow nostalgia.*]

Oh, lovely, Edie. Lovely.

[MRS ELLIS *dances on.* JOAN *and* ARNIE *stop to watch her, intrigued.*]

JOAN: Go on, mother. Let 'em have it. [*Hiccup.*]

MRS ELLIS [*dancing*]: Do you like it?

ARNIE: Go on, Edie. Don't stop. She's good. She's good. Oh, she's good. Just look at her little old legs going!

MRS ELLIS: What's the matter with my legs?

JOAN: You should see yourself, darling.

ARNIE: Take no notice of her, Edie. They're all right. You can take my word for it.

MRS ELLIS [*stopping, looking down at her legs*]: I've got good legs. . . . I always have had, since I was a young woman.

JOAN: Mother!

MRS ELLIS: What's the matter? [*She lowers her skirt.*]

JOAN [*with sudden bravado*]: Those [*hiccup*] are legs, if you want them! [*Lifts her skirt discreetly and poses her legs.*]
There's no comparison. . . . Lift your skirt up. Lift. Come on. [*She pulls at her mother's skirt.*]
You just look. Arnie. What do you say? [*Hiccup.*
ARNIE *has already turned away.*]
Hold it up, mother. [*She turns round, for the first time aware of* ARNIE's *lack of attention.*]
Go on. What do you think? [*Pause.*] Arnie, for God's sake!
[ARNIE *blearily turns round.*]

ARNIE: What . . .

JOAN: What do you say?
[MRS ELLIS *turns to him, holding her skirt like a child paddling, her mood a vague stupor between elation and tiredness.*]

ARNIE: What . . .

JOAN: Look, damn you! [ARNIE *is overcome with weariness.*] Tell her, for God's sake. [*She has still one hand guardedly holding her mother's skirt, the other her own.*]

ARNIE: Tell her . . . ?

JOAN: What you think.

ARNIE: You want me to, Edie?

MRS ELLIS: I don't mind, love. [*Giggles.*] It's getting draughty here.

JOAN: Look, look. We're walking. How's it look?
[ARNIE *sits down, drunkenly and tired. He watches, frowning, and belches.*]

ARNIE: Like a camel. [*He finishes off the bottle, toasting the cupboard doors.*]

JOAN: Just look at her, then. Mother, you walk up and down. And keep your skirts up. [*Suddenly aware of* ARNIE's *diversion.*] You're not watching! [*Hiccup.*] For God's sake. We're walking! Here!

Give me that! [*She snatches the bottle from him.*] All gone. Pig.
[*She throws the bottle down, and suddenly snatches his hair.*] NOW –
choose!

[ARNIE *sinks down in the chair calling out.*]

Who's got the best legs! [*Hiccup.*]

ARNIE: Help! Let go! You're hurting .... Yarooo!

JOAN: I'm going to hurt you. Open your great mouth and tell her.

ARNIE: Edie! Tell her to let go. She's drunk. She doesn't know. OW!

MRS ELLIS: Why don't you do as she says, Arnie?

ARNIE: OW!

[*The chair slips:* JOAN'S *grip tightens:* ARNIE *falls to his knees,
calling out, more helpless than he'd realized, his humour, however, still
apparent.*]

For God's sake let go, Joan. I'm an historian.

JOAN: Choose. [*Hiccup.*]

ARNIE: If you don't let go I'll maim you.

JOAN: You try, then.

[MRS ELLIS *has picked up some sewing scissors from the sideboard.
She's laughing, holding her skirt still with one hand as though she were
paddling.*]

MRS ELLIS: If you hold him still I can cut his hair!

JOAN: Go on, then, Mam ...

MRS ELLIS: I'll cut it all off, Arnie!

ARNIE: Get off!

JOAN: Go on, Mam. Give him a cut. [*Hiccup. She pulls at his hair and*
ARNIE *gives a real cry of pain, and can only bend more ineffectually to
the floor.* JOAN *holds up the hair while, one-handed – her other holding up
her skirt –* MRS ELLIS *cuts it off.*]

MRS ELLIS: There! ... There! He looks younger already!

JOAN: And another. Go on, Mam!

ARNIE: Let go. Or I'll kill you. Both of you.

JOAN: Go on, then. You stupid devil.

MRS ELLIS: Choose, Arnie. Then she'll let you go.

JOAN: Choose!

ARNIE: Edie! She's got the best legs. All the way.

JOAN: What? [*Hiccup.*]

ARNIE: Edie's! Edie's, all the way.

[JOAN *has released him.*]

JOAN: You prefer *her* to me!

ARNIE: Completely. [*He's still kneeling, clutching his head, still humoured, considering how best to take his revenge.*]

JOAN [*hiccup*]: You don't love *me*!

ARNIE: No!

JOAN: You've never loved me.

ARNIE: Never!

JOAN: You just wanted *that* [*hiccup*] and then it was all over.

ARNIE: Absolutely.

JOAN: You don't love me.

MRS ELLIS [*chastened*]: Let's get to bed. For goodness sake. We're not in our senses. Come on. Let's get up.

JOAN: Yes. Yes! I know. . . . I know . . . [*implying.*]

MRS ELLIS: Joan . . .

    [JOAN *hiccups.*]

ARNIE: Make way! Make way! Move back!

JOAN: You've never loved me.

ARNIE: Oh! Oh! Oh!

JOAN: I know what's going on. Don't worry.

ARNIE: Why. Why. Why. All the time. Nothing but this, baby!

MRS ELLIS: Take no notice. None of you. It doesn't mean anything. It's nothing.

JOAN [*to* MRS ELLIS]: Well, what are you doing here, then? [*Hiccup.*] Come on. Come on. You be honest just this once.

MRS ELLIS: Joannie! Joannie!

JOAN: History or no bloody history. Don't think I haven't noticed. [*Hiccup.*] And that *thing*! All the time. Stuck in there listening to every word. [*She gestures at the cupboard.*]

ARNIE: I'm going up . . .

JOAN: Arnie. Tell her. Tell her to go.

    [ARNIE *pauses on his way to the stairs.*]

    Tell her to go. [*Hiccup.*]

ARNIE [*pauses, then*]: If your Bob doesn't pay our Bob that bob that your Bob owes our Bob our Bob will give your Bob a bob on the nose.

JOAN: Arnie! Tell her! Tell her!

ARNIE: Tiger, tiger, burning bright,
    In the forests of the night,

    If you see a five pound note
    Then take my tip and cut your throat.

JOAN: Tell her to go!

MRS ELLIS: No, Arnie!

ARNIE: The man in the moon has a chocolate spoon,
    And eyeballs made of custard;
    His big fat head is a loaf of bread,
    And his whiskers are peppered with mustard.

JOAN: Arnie!

    [ARNIE *pauses again, bows to them with a flourish. Then:*]

ARNIE: Ladies. Ladies. Ladies. [*He goes.*]

JOAN: Arnie!

MRS ELLIS: Arnie!

    [*Lights fade.*]

ACT TWO

SCENE ONE

Late afternoon.

JEFF HANSON *slumps in an easy chair. He's dressed in sports coat and flannels, a very long college scarf with tassels, bowler hat and yellow gloves: the eternal student. The gloves he eventually peels off, but the bowler hat remains on his head. He also retains a stout walking stick which he uses to amplify and reinforce his conversation. He is about forty, a middle-aged man with certain, perhaps obsessive desires to retain his youth.*

Standing behind him is the suit of armour.

ARNIE *himself sits at the table smoking a pipe.*

JOAN *is out of sight, cleaning the stairs with a hand-brush and pan.*

HANSON [*raised voice*]: My dear Joan, I wouldn't believe a word of it.
JOAN [*heard*]: It was absolutely nothing at all.
HANSON: Absolutely.
JOAN: We were drunk.
HANSON: Of course.
JOAN [*heard*]: We'd all had too much.
HANSON: Naturally.
   [JOAN *appears in the door.*]
JOAN: So whatever he's told you . . .
HANSON: My dear china, he's told me nothing. All we've heard are hints from you.
JOAN: You never know. . . . [*Watching* ARNIE *suspiciously.*]
HANSON: And if he had it would be of no account. Our long friendship [*indicating* ARNIE] is based on the simple precaution that I never believe a single word he says. I hate to indulge in scepticism of any sort but events have always justified my foresight.
ARNIE: He's lying as dextrously himself . . .
HANSON: Arnold, I'm the last person to step between a man and his mother-in-law, as well you know. Despite all your accounts of domestic felicities I have always refrained from intruding. The only reason I don't agitate my hands about my ears is the faint hope that I may hear an explanation. . . . [*He is looking steadfastly at* ARNIE.]

44

JOAN: Of what?

HANSON: A remarkable occurrence that took place at school this morning, my dear. [*Suddenly looking up at* JOAN.] I'm astonished you're not already acquainted with it.

JOAN [*watching* ARNIE]: Well, I'm not.

ARNIE: It was nothing.

HANSON: Nothing!

ARNIE: A slight miscalculation.

HANSON: My dear Joan – hardly were we assembled in the hall – eight hundred *youthful* spirits about to make the most *hearty* obeisances to the one and only – when what should we glimpse through the door backing on to the stage but the most incredible apparition you can imagine! Beyond the Headmaster's stout and noble figure – its eyes raised, somewhat prematurely it now appears, towards the Heavens – could be discerned a man accompanied by a suit of armour, stealthily creeping by under the obvious delusion that our devotions concealed him from our view. At first our benevolent autocrat mistook the huge and hideous roar that greeted this astonishing sight for one of religious fervour, his eyes travelling quickly downwards in a mixture of horror and surprise. [*Pause.*] Standing there in all his furtive glory was Arnold, smiling shyly in the arms of his new-found friend, and making unmistakable gestures with his one free hand that we should ignore his presence as best we may. God in Heaven, I said to myself, is this a manifestation – the not-unforeseen consequence of our rigorous vocation – or has Arnold, my dearest and closest friend, taken complete and utter leave of his senses?

ARNIE: She wanted to get rid of it. I had to protect it the only way I could. If I hadn't taken it to school, she'd have thrown it away.

JOAN: They must have laughed themselves sick!

HANSON: Except for the Head, my dear. Assuming it to be a comment upon his own austere régime – perhaps even on the strenuous nature of his religious practices – he ordered its immediate seizure and removal from the premises. It spent the remainder of its day, I believe, in the coal cellar, until its owner could take it home. [*He looks expectantly at* ARNIE.] Well?

[ARNIE *puffs contentedly at his pipe.*]

Aren't you going to tell us? [*Pause.*] Is it some cheap means,

Arnold, of publicizing your subject at the expense of others on the curriculum? [*Pause.*] Perhaps an indication to us of the kind of company you actually prefer.

ARNIE: I've told you why I took it to school.

JOAN: You won't get anything out of him.

HANSON: What is this, Arnold? Are we no longer sufficient for you? Your dear wife, your friends, your devoted pupils. . . . Or is it that you feel a sword is necessary to prompt us to a proper admiration of your extraordinary talents? Ungrateful may be the world, but, Arnold, surely not those who know you.

ARNIE: It won't be here much longer. You better take advantage of it while you can.

JOAN: Not here? [*Pause.*] Where's it going?

HANSON: Not – back to school?

ARNIE: No.

JOAN: Where, then?

ARNIE: As a matter of fact it's a present.

JOAN: A present!

HANSON: A present. Not for . . . [*Gestures at himself.*]

ARNIE: No.

HANSON: Nor . . . [*He gestures at* JOAN.]
     [ARNIE *moves away.*]

ARNIE: For my parents.

JOAN: Your parents!

ARNIE: That's the last I want to hear of it.

HANSON: But . . . of course, I'm not acquainted with the couple . . . and far be it from me to judge from preconceptions. But are they . . . I mean, is it something they've always wanted? Do they have a fondness for metallic men?

JOAN: You've never said it was a present. You never said it was.

ARNIE: I take it I'm entitled to a little privacy of intention.

JOAN: Privacy of *what*?

HANSON: You mean they collect suits of armour?

JOAN: You let me shout down the house. [*Catching hold of him.*] Look . . . have you just invented this?

ARNIE: That's all I want to hear of it. I've told you. Now you know. It's a present.

JOAN: He's always inventing things when he thinks it suits him. Why . . .

ARNIE: It's over.

JOAN: My God!

HANSON: All these alarums, then, were merely to conceal the natural benevolence of your heart. What stratagems men will go to to disguise their proper virtues!

[JOAN, *however, is watching* ARNIE *with a mixture of disbelief and condemnation.*]

JOAN: Do you expect me to believe that? What's the point of buying them that? Of all things.

[ARNIE *doesn't answer.*]

Aren't you going to *talk?* [*Pause.*] All right. Just do as you damn well please.

JOAN [*to* ARNIE]: And tell him to take his hat off in the house.

[*She goes to the kitchen: sound of cups.*]

HANSON: Have at you, man! [*He thrusts at him with his stick.*]

ARNIE: Have at you!

[*They fight with much groaning and exertion,* ARNIE *with his invisible sword,* HANSON *with his stick.*]

Back! Back! Th . . . th . . . th . . . i . . . i . . . i . . . ssss . . . sssss THIS! i . . . i . . . i . . : ssss . . IS! g . . g . . g . . gay! r . . r . . r . . r . . ROBIN h . . h . . h . . h . . HOOD!

[HANSON *gives a great and ugly scream and dies writhingly in a chair.*]

HANSON: Actually, could you lend me five pounds?

ARNIE: I haven't a cent. It all went on this.

[HANSON *has got up. He eyes the armour suspiciously.*]

HANSON: Oh. [*Pause.*] Actually. Why did you buy it?

ARNIE: As a present.

HANSON: For your parents?

[ARNIE *nods.*]

HANSON: Mmmmm! [*Watches him a moment. Then:*] The purpose of the loan was to entertain a lady. Temporarily, I'm without the wherewithal without.

ARNIE: A lady?

HANSON: A Miss Wilkinson, to be precise.

ARNIE: Not our Miss Wilkinson? From school?

HANSON: 'Fraid so. [*He talks a little in* JOAN's *direction.*] Naturally the school premises – where normally I make assignations of this nature – are the most propitious place for the dalliances I have in mind. But of late Old Thompson, despite rheumatism, a protopsic condition of the right eye, and an audibly leaking bucket, has acquired in stealth what he has so patently forfeited in spontaneity. The Park, though ample in resources, and open to all classes and creeds of men, is constant victim to the inclemency of the weather; the lady herself lives with elderly parents in a charming country cottage several miles from town; and my landlord resents frivolities of every nature.

ARNIE [*watching him cautiously*]: She's a damn fit woman, I'm told, Jeffrey.

HANSON: You were correctly informed. While we clamber daily through the portals of our plight, she is nimbly leaping over bucks, vaulting-horses and horizontal bars as lightly as . . . a frog, say.

ARNIE: I had always assumed her to be the soul of integrity, Jeffrey.

HANSON: I have a curriculum to straighten out with her.

ARNIE: That would be nice.

HANSON: And her permission to examine the subject on an evening suitable to both.

ARNIE: I see.

[HANSON *finally turns from the armour just as* JOAN *re-enters carrying a tea-tray.*]

HANSON: So what's to do?

ARNIE [*perceiving* JOAN]: Entertain her here.

HANSON: In public?

ARNIE: A party. Or whatever festivities you feel she might approve.

HANSON: Tonight?

JOAN [*setting down the tray*]: Is someone coming here tonight?

ARNIE: It is a debt of honour I am endeavouring to pay with a frenzied bout of hospitality. Nothing more.

JOAN: What do you think all this is for?

ARNIE: All what?

JOAN: This! All this tidying up!

ARNIE: Any evidence of the pleasures we may have sustained will have long been removed by then.

[JOAN *stares at him in silence. Then:*]

JOAN: What *is* all this about, Arnie?

ARNIE [*to* HANSON]: You might bring a few bottles with you, Jeffrey. No reason why your pleasures should not entertain our own particular miseries.

HANSON: Oh, but of course.

JOAN: There's your tea. If you want anything else help yourselves. [*She returns to the kitchen.*]

ARNIE [*loudly*]: Talking of religious fervours, Miss O'Connor followed me home again today. The distance of twenty-five yards has increased slightly to thirty, perhaps even thirty-five. Idolatry, I fear, has given way to something verging on detachment.

HANSON: Sheila O'Connor ...

ARNIE: The one.

HANSON [*leaning on kitchen door*]: Is a girl ...

JOAN [*heard*]: I've seen enough of that.

HANSON: ... Upon whom a mischievous deity has bestowed two attributes, the largeness of which – in all humble deference – must be an embarrassment even to Himself. [*He salaams to the ceiling.*]

JOAN [*reappearing with cleaning utensils*]: Is that how you talk about the children?

HANSON: A child in the eyes of the State, my dear, but a woman in the eyes of God.

ARNIE: She actually approached me at four o'clock, just as I was entering the staff-room prior to retrieving my armour, and asked me to take her out. Tonight. [*Pause.*] Those are the first words that have passed between us.

HANSON: Oh, she's never asked me that. She never has.

JOAN: What arrangements did you come to?

ARNIE: I suggested we rendezvous at the picture palace at nine o'clock. 'Nine o'clock sharp, mind!' I said sternly, if not officiously – reminding her as casually as I could that I had a position to maintain. As it so happened, she would have followed me into the staff-room there and then if it hadn't been for the fact that old Manners was marking her arithmetic book along with several thousand others. 'Oh, Sheila,' he said, looking up obliquely from his tattered ledgers, 'I've just got to yours, my dear. Would you like to stand by me while I glance through your problems?' Wherein she vanished in the twinkle of an eye.

HANSON: There are incentives to the profession the Minister never dreamed of.

JOAN: Yes. [*She goes to the stairs but* ARNIE *takes her shoulders.*]

ARNIE: You're very contained, my little sparrow.

JOAN: I've to fly up there and finish the stairs if you don't mind, then fly back down and tidy here.

HANSON: A woman's work is never done!

JOAN: *What!*

HANSON: I. . . . Merely a tribute, my dear, to your . . . profession.
   [JOAN *releases herself from* ARNIE.]

JOAN: God, I love you, honey. [*She blows a kiss and goes.*]
   [ARNIE *goes to the table, gets his pot, and sits down. He doesn't drink.* HANSON *watches him. Then:*]

HANSON: Say, old man. Isn't your hair somewhat oddly arranged for an historian? Or, indeed, for a man?

ARNIE: What?

HANSON: You're not short of food, I take it? It appears someone has consumed two mouthfuls of your tonsure.

ARNIE: It was a slight accident on the way to the kitchen.
   [HANSON *holds up his walking stick guardedly.*]

HANSON: Ah.

ARNIE: Mind your own business, loppy-lugs.

HANSON: Snot-nose.

ARNIE: Carpet-breath.

HANSON: That's revolting.
   [ARNIE *turns away to his tea.*]
   By such inadvertent gestures cancer is induced. Secrets go bad and affect the very flesh.

ARNIE: Cabbage knuckles.

HANSON [*with his stick*]: Have at you, Gay Robin!

ARNIE [*without gesture*]: Have at you, Big John.
   [*Pause.* HANSON *taps the armour reflectively. Then he glances at* ARNIE.]

HANSON: You think, then, it's conceivable I'm mistaken about Miss Wilkinson. One grave disadvantage is that she's physically so very *fit*. It would be imprudent continually to have recourse to this stout staff while she merely relies upon the dexterity of her limbs. But my daily exercises are entirely cerebral, whereas hers, day in, day out, are designed exclusively to extend the already phenomenal resilience of her physique.

ARNIE: It could be an advantage, no doubt, in one way. And then again, in another ...

HANSON: But you do not think it strange. ... [*He glances round*] ... that women are gradually acquiring a physical superiority to men? Do you think. ... [*Goes to the stairs, listens, then returns to say slowly, putting his arm round the armour:*]

Do you think there's some sort of organization behind it?

ARNIE: A conspiracy ...

HANSON: Which we are very foolish to ignore. [*He glances quickly behind him.*] I mean, one hears so much of judo and professional equality these days.

ARNIE: Does the King know?

HANSON: The King? My dear Arnold, the very sources are corrupt. [*Moves away thoughtfully flexing his stick.*] I mean, it can't have failed to have reached your attention that we – that is men *and* women alike – emerge at some point of our lives from the body of a woman. But has it also occurred to you that whereas we are always under this obligation to them, they are never under a reciprocal obligation to us? They, as it were, *divulge* us: whereas we – we are simply *exposed*. This is an extraordinary advantage bestowed on one sex at the expense of the other.

[*As he talks he re-approaches* ARNIE *who takes* HANSON's *stick and, as he listens, flexes it over his shoulders.* HANSON *leans over him with the confidence of a spy.*]

Have you noticed that women live longer than men? [*Pause.*] They do not fight wars, only occasionally do they murder their fellows, and they seldom, unfortunately, commit rape. Relate this to our original observation that it is *they* who breed *us*, then things like politics and finance, even philosophy and art, become like playthings bestowed on us by women merely to amuse and divert our un-breeding functions!

ARNIE: What time are you meeting her?

HANSON: What? [*Glances at his watch.*] Yes, I shall have to go.

[JOAN *has re-entered from the stairs.*]

HANSON: It is one thing to sit there and smile at present danger. It's quite another to rest there until you are *gobbled up*.

ARNIE [*quickly*]: You have caught Jeffrey in the very act of leaving.

HANSON: Ah, I did not hear you dismount, madam. [*He takes his stick from* ARNIE, *and pulls on his gloves.*] I must be about my business before it is about me. [*He suddenly turns round on* ARNIE *with his stick.*] On guard!

ARNIE: To be sure.

[HANSON *salutes with his stick.* ARNIE *has stood up and now he stands by* JOAN, *putting an arm about her shoulders.*

HANSON *glances at them a moment.*]

HANSON: I shall take my leave quickly. Imagine I am killed in the street the moment I have stepped beyond the door, and allow that poignancy to inform your farewells. [*He takes* JOAN's *hand and kisses it, salaams to* ARNIE, *then crosses to the armour. He taps it lightly with his stick.*]

That, Arnold. That. I'm not altogether sure of. Well. . . . [*He regards it thoughtfully for a moment. Then, turning briskly:*] Remember, no fisticuffs when I introduce Miss Wilkinson to this abode. And may all our cavortings be as discreet and as anonymous as alcohol allows.

[*He ceremoniously bows and exits backwards, closing the door. A moment later there's the sound of the outer door shutting.*

ARNIE *releases her. She watches him a moment. Then:*]

JOAN [*lenient*]: You needn't be afraid.

ARNIE: Afraid?

JOAN: Of showing in private the affection you display in public. [*Pause.*] I could have told him.

ARNIE: You could?

JOAN: I heard your 'discussion' from the stairs. I could have told him how you came to lose your hair.

ARNIE: An embarrassment to both of us I would have thought.

JOAN: Doesn't *he* ever grow sick of it?

ARNIE: Of what?

JOAN [*pause*]: You despise him really.

ARNIE: I do not.

[*She watches him a moment then goes to the kitchen.*

ARNIE *sits down at the table. A moment later* JOAN *re-appears.*]

JOAN: Has something sunk through all those layers at last?

ARNIE [*pause*]: Has what sunk through which layers?

JOAN: Disgust.

ARNIE: You're being boring.

JOAN: Isn't it that underneath . . .

ARNIE [*calling out*]. You're being boring! I've never known anyone make such commonplace observations in so revelationary a tone!

[*They're both silent.*]

JOAN [*quietly*]: Do you have any feeling left for me at all?

ARNIE: Are you trying to be frivolous?

JOAN [*pause*]: You make me feel I don't exist. You hide away. You don't look. You show nothing but a parody of yourself. You deride even your own weakness. Isn't that self-contempt?

ARNIE: You're sickening.

JOAN: Am I . . .

ARNIE: You're sickening. Your allegories are sickening, woman.

JOAN [*crying out and gesturing at the room*]: And what's this, then, but sickening! What's this!

[ARNIE *makes no response.* JOAN *watches him. Then, more quietly:*] If you'd just break up this – pretence!

ARNIE: What? What? What? What?

JOAN: Anything so long as you don't have to step up here. [*Gestures at herself.*]

ARNIE: You think that's an eminence worthy of ascent?

JOAN: You did once. [*Silence.*] Why do you stay with me, Arnie?

[ARNIE *watches her intently.*]

Go on.

ARNIE: Go knot your nose.

JOAN: Tell me. Why do you stay here?

ARNIE: Run up a flag.

JOAN: Try and answer me.

ARNIE: Leave me alone.

JOAN [*slowly*]: Why do you stay with me, Arnie?

[ARNIE *glances round at the doors.*]

Well, off you go then.

ARNIE: I can detect a piece of dust. Wait a minute, yes. It's under the near left-hand leg of the dressing-table in your mother's bedroom: a quick outflanking manoeuvre and it will be within your grasp.

[*Silence. Then:*]

JOAN: You must make yourself so *sick*.

ARNIE: Ladybird, Ladybird, fly away home:
    Your house is on fire and your children have gone.
    [*Silence.* JOAN *waits patiently.*
    ARNIE *suddenly shouts with burlesque affectation, slamming the table.*]
  Will sombody get me out of here!
  Help! Help! . . . HELP!
    [JOAN *watches a while. Then:*]
JOAN: It's not a game is it?
ARNIE: Leave me alone.
JOAN: No. You run away instead.
ARNIE: All right. [*He doesn't move. After a while:*] Assume I've run away.
JOAN: You insulting little *snot*!
    [ARNIE *closes his eyes.*]
  Come on. Get down on your knees and cry. Do something to attract some *pity*! Come on. Get down! Cry!
  Come on. Cry, *baby*, cry!
    [ARNIE *turns his head away.*]
  Nobody's going to love you unless you show us *something*.
ARNIE: Go away.
JOAN: Let's have some rage. Isn't there anything in this world, Arnold, that you'd like to put right?
ARNIE: Go away.
JOAN: Come on, baby. Isn't there anything that offends you? Isn't there some tiny little wrong that can rouse your indignation?
ARNIE: Get out.
JOAN: Come on. Make me sickening.
ARNIE: Hop it!
    [*She comes and studies his face more closely.*]
JOAN: Just look. For God's sake, Arnie.
    [*They're silent. Then:*]
  What are you frightened of?
    [*He makes no response. Then quietly:*]
  All right. All right. [*She watches him, waiting, for a response. Quietly, she goes.*
    ARNIE *sits remotely at the table.*
    After a while JOAN *re-enters.*

She watches him a moment, sitting exactly as she left him.]

JOAN: As a start, Arnie . . . I suggest we get rid of all these. [*Indicating the objects.*]

ARNIE: Yes.

JOAN: You agree, then?

[*Pause.* ARNIE *looks up.*]

ARNIE: Certainly.

JOAN: We get rid of all this.

ARNIE: Yes.

[*She seems about to start.*]

Not yet.

JOAN: Isn't this the best time?

ARNIE [*Pause*]: No.

JOAN: All right. When?

ARNIE: Tomorrow.

JOAN: After *they've* been?

ARNIE: Er. . . . Yes.

JOAN: You promise that?

ARNIE: Yes.

JOAN: And this? [*Indicating armour.*]

[ARNIE *regards it in silence. Then:*]

ARNIE: That's going in any case.

JOAN: As a present.

[ARNIE *makes no response.*]

And if they won't have it?

ARNIE: What?

JOAN: I can't imagine they will. [*Pause.*] If that's what you really intend to do with it.

[*Pause.*]

ARNIE: They'll have it because I'm giving it to them.

JOAN: Oh.

ARNIE: I like it.

JOAN: Yes.

ARNIE: And I'd like them to have it.

JOAN: Suppose they don't.

[*Pause.*]

ARNIE: This is not a battle.

JOAN: No.

ARNIE: They'll be pleased with it because I am. And the other way round.

[*She watches him.*]

Some people are actually like that.

JOAN: Yes.

ARNIE: All right?

JOAN: I'll believe it when I see it.

ARNIE: I doubt it.

JOAN: Well, then, while we're clearing everything away, there's one other thing. It's time my mother left and went and lived on her own.

ARNIE: What?

JOAN: In this case you'll just have to accept *my* word if you don't believe it.

ARNIE: She's harmless.

JOAN: It's time she went for all our sakes. You'll be better off for it. I will. And so will she.

ARNIE: I don't want her to go. It'd break her bloody heart.

JOAN: I'm sorry. But she'll have to.

[*The outside door bangs.*]

That's her now.

ARNIE: Well, don't say anything to her. Not yet.

JOAN: It's my decision.

ARNIE: I've told you. Don't. [*He waits, almost threatening.*] You understand?

[JOAN *makes no response. There are sounds outside the door, and* ARNIE's *mood changes abruptly as* MRS ELLIS *appears. She's smartly dressed, a fur round her shoulders, and she carries a full shopping basket which she puts on the table.* ARNIE *greets her with a dashing gesture.*]

Here comes a spy to parry at our scheme:
I shall retire, and make it – all a dream.

MRS ELLIS [*pleased*]: Oh . . .

[ARNIE *goes with a flourish.*]

MRS ELLIS: What's got into him?

[JOAN *doesn't answer.*]

It's a lovely evening out. A beautiful sunset.

[*Pause. The two women confront each other;* MRS ELLIS *with some perplexity.*]

What's the matter?

JOAN [*goes to her*]: Let me help you off with your coat, mother.

MRS ELLIS: What?

JOAN: Your coat.

[*Surprised, she submits.*
The light fades.]

SCENE TWO

The same evening.

ARNIE, *in shirtsleeves, tieless, lies on a couch. The suit of armour has gone.*

JOAN [*heard*]: Aren't you going to get changed?

[*There are sounds of her working in the kitchen.* ARNIE *makes no response: his eyes are closed, apparently in sleep.*]

JOAN [*entering*]: Aren't you going to get shaved?

ARNIE [*eyes still closed*]: I thought you wanted no one here. The place kept tidy and clean.

[JOAN *has dressed herself attractively, and her hair is tied in a ribbon.*]

JOAN [*briefly and briskly tidying the room*]: I've changed my mind. . . . Aren't you going to get ready at all?

ARNIE: Oh? [*He opens his eyes, watches her a moment.*] They might never get here.

JOAN: My mother's gone out for nothing, then.

ARNIE: She didn't have to go out.

JOAN: She didn't feel like meeting people this evening. That's all.

[*Pause.*]

ARNIE: The sacrifice of one old woman . . .

JOAN: She can look after herself.

[ARNIE *rouses himself, sitting up.*]

ARNIE: You can't turn people out like that, that's all. Not when they rely on you. You either do it at the beginning or not at all.

JOAN: I'm not arguing about it.

ARNIE: That's settled then. [*Sitting on the couch, slaps his thighs and looks around contentedly. Then he puts his hands together and blows between them, hooting like an owl.*

After a while:]

JOAN: You know . . .

[ARNIE *hoots.*]

JOAN [*pause*]: With my mother it's my decision whether she goes or not. She's *my* mother.

ARNIE: I've told you.

JOAN: But it's my decision, Arnie. I make it!

[*The door is crashed back on its hinges and* HANSON *puts his head round.*]

HANSON: *Pray!* Hold thy hand good Robin Hood,
   And your merry men each one,
   For you'll swear this is the finest maid
   That ever your eyes fell on.

JOAN: Don't you usually knock when you come in?

HANSON [*taking her hand*]: If thou wilt forsake, housewife, thy craft,
   And wend to the greenwood with me [*kisses her hand*]
   Thou shalt have loving all the year long,
   And forty gold crowns for thy fee.

ARNIE: All right. All right.

HANSON [*to* ARNIE]: And Robin leapt up full thirty good foot,
   'Twas thirty good foot and one,
   And he cleft the rude fellow with a blow of his fist –
   And his light went out like the sun. [HANSON *disappears immediately through the door. His voice is heard.*] Go on, dear. Straight ahead.

[SHEILA O'CONNOR, *a precociously developed girl, though by no means loutish, enters. She's dressed in slacks and a bright sweater. Her shyness tends to disappear first when she sees* ARNIE, *then the interior.*]

SHEILA: Hello, sir.

[ARNIE *is up quickly from the couch where he's been lounging.*]

ARNIE: Oh, hello, Sheila.

Didn't expect to see you here.

HANSON: Odd thing. Passing the gate just as we came in. Thought: what a coincidence! Then: why one be damned when rest sanctified by celebration!

ARNIE: Yes. [*To* JOAN] This is Sheila O'Connor, Joan.
This is my wife, Sheila.

SHEILA: Hello, Miss.

JOAN: Hello, Sheila.

[MAUREEN WILKINSON *and* HANSON *have followed* SHEILA *in.
The schoolmistress is dressed tastefully: a respectable and fairly
attractive woman in her late twenties.*]

ARNIE: Evening, Maureen. I don't think you know my wife. Joan –
this is Maureen.

MAUREEN: It's very nice meeting you, Joan.

[*They shake hands.*]

JOAN: Let me take your coat.

ARNIE [*to* HANSON]: Well, let's sit down, and so forth.

HANSON: Look here, Arnold, would you mind awfully if Sheila and
I betook ourselves to the hostelry to purchase an armful of drinks?
Things came up. Distracted the intention . . .

ARNIE [*to* SHEILA]: So soon arrived, so soon departed.

HANSON: You don't mind, do you, Sheila? I swear I heard you had
been appointed milk monitor this term for the Lower Fifth.

SHEILA: It's not far, is it?

HANSON: Good girl! We shan't be long. Adios, caballeros.

ARNIE: Shall I . . .

HANSON: Oh, we'll manage, old man.

[*They go.*
ARNIE *has got up to go with them but, rejected, returns.*]

JOAN: Does that irritate you?

MAUREEN: Oh, you get used to it.

JOAN: What is it, do you think?

MAUREEN: The school play this year is 'Robin Hood and His Merry
Men'.

JOAN: No, I meant . . .

ARNIE: You're being unnecessarily adventurous, aren't you, coming
out with Jeffrey?

MAUREEN: He's asked me out so often it's less tedious to agree.

ARNIE: Is that all?

MAUREEN: I'm sorry.

[JOAN *watches* ARNIE'*s almost vindictive manner with* MAUREEN,
curious and intrigued.]

There was nothing I could do about him bringing Sheila in. It's very foolish.

ARNIE: It'll give her a break from her usual sentry-go. I never know whether she's keeping me in, or keeping the others out.

JOAN: It's inviting trouble: walking through the streets with her like that, and going into pubs.

MAUREEN [*pleasantly*]: Oh, he'll take a pleasure in it.

JOAN: After all, we're partly responsible for it.

ARNIE: Of those two, the only one who can be violated is Jeffrey.

MAUREEN: You're not responsible. That's absurd.

JOAN [*indicating* ARNIE]: Oh, he has ways of encouraging her. Don't worry.

ARNIE: She asked *me* out.

JOAN [*to* MAUREEN]: Some days they say it's because they teach in a school; then on other days they say it's the world.

MAUREEN: I never knew you had a philosophy, Arnold. As well as a suit of armour. [*Stretching round*] Where is it, by the way?

ARNIE: Yes. [*He gets up and wanders uneasily about the room.*]

JOAN [*to* MAUREEN]: Are all your men staff alike?

MAUREEN: Oh, very nearly!

JOAN: Doesn't it wear you down?

MAUREEN [*laughing*]: I shouldn't worry about it, Joan!

ARNIE: Watch this. [*Does a handstand against the wall, balancing precariously.*

The women pause to watch.]

JOAN: Would you like some tea, Maureen?

MAUREEN: Love some.

JOAN: I'll just put the kettle on. I was hoping to make some sandwiches as well. Won't be a minute. [*Goes into the kitchen.*]

[MAUREEN *looks round at the objects in the room for the first time.*]

MAUREEN: Are all these yours?

ARNIE: Yes.

MAUREEN: Don't you want me here?

ARNIE: You?

MAUREEN: Us?

ARNIE: It was *my* party. Joan has appropriated it.

MAUREEN [*laughs*]: Yes.

[ARNIE *lowers himself from his handstand.*]

ARNIE: Do you know what happened to the Early Christian martyrs the moment they stopped throwing them to the lions, and loved them instead?

MAUREEN: They went off into the desert to live in caves, haunted by demons.

ARNIE: What?

[MAUREEN *waits.*]

ARNIE: I've told you before. [*Pause.*] Are you sure?

MAUREEN: Yes.

ARNIE: I see. [*Pause.*] Don't you think it's extraordinary?

MAUREEN: In what way?

ARNIE: In what way? [*Pause.*] I don't know really. It seemed extraordinary at the time. . . [*Pause.*]

MAUREEN: Where is . . .

JOAN [*returning*]: I'm making some sandwiches then perhaps one or two people won't get so drunk. Where are you going?

[ARNIE *has gone to the door, picking up his jacket.*]

ARNIE: Out. See if Hanson needs any help.

JOAN: I should think he'd be able to manage well enough on his own.

[ARNIE *still goes.*]

You won't be long?

ARNIE: No.

JOAN: Give us a kiss, Arnie.

ARNIE [*to* MAUREEN]: You'll notice. Always the diminutive.

[JOAN *waits.* ARNIE, *after a moment, comes back, takes her shoulder and kisses her on the cheek.*]

JOAN: You won't be long, Arnold?

ARNIE: No.

[*He goes. A pause.* JOAN *tentatively re-tidies the room.*]

JOAN: His parents are coming tomorrow. We haven't seen them for years.

MAUREEN: The best thing is to ride with it, isn't it? I still live with my parents: I know what a trouble they can be.

JOAN: When *we* got married and his mother came up to kiss me as we were leaving the church, she said, 'Well, you'll look after my only son, won't you, Joan?' And he said, quick as a flash, 'Your only sin, mother.' And she smiled as sweetly as anything; he laughed out loud; and God did I feel a fool! You can see just what a state I'm in. Would you like to see round the house?

MAUREEN: Yes, I'd love to.

[*They move to the stairs.*]

JOAN: I'll show you upstairs. You've seen nearly all there is to see down here. Considering how small they look from the outside it's surprising how large they are.

[*They go. Heard is* MAUREEN: '*Do you intend staying on here, then?*' *Then* JOAN: '*Oh, I suppose so. We've lived here since we got married. There's no point in moving into something smaller. . . . This is the main bedroom . . .*

Their voices grow fainter, then disappear. After a short interval there's the sound of the back door opening in the kitchen and, a moment later, the kitchen door is cautiously opened. MRS ELLIS *enters. She's drunk. She puts a bottle on the table and stands aimlessly looking round, stifling her sobs with a handkerchief. Then she moves to the mirror and stares distractedly at herself, moaning.*

From above come the voices of the women as they move about: '*the bathroom there, and this is the spare room . . .*' '*Well, that's convenient. . . . Goodness. Is that all Arnold's too?*' '*And this is my mother's room . . .*'

MRS ELLIS *swings round, hurries to the kitchen door, then across to the door leading to the hall. Then, as the women begin to descend the stairs, she remembers the bottle, hurriedly retrieves it and goes out by the hall door, leaving it open.*]

MAUREEN [*re-entering*]: His classroom's extraordinary. More like the court of King Arthur than a schoolroom. Have you seen his museum?

JOAN [*re-entering*]: No.

MAUREEN: The children love it. What it has to do with history I've no idea. They seem to spend all their time building model castles, singing ballads and doing great big pictures of William the Conqueror. . . . It's strange we've never met at school, isn't it? You've never been to any of the plays Arnold's produced, have you? They're very good.

JOAN: He prefers me to stay away.

MAUREEN: Whatever for?

JOAN [*shrugs*]: He prefers it, that's all. He's full of prejudices, you know, Maureen.

MAUREEN: Prejudices?

JOAN: We better do the sandwiches, by the way, before they get back. The kettle should be boiling. You promise . . .

[*They go into the kitchen.*

After a moment MRS ELLIS *re-appears and stands hesitantly in the room, uncertain whether to go into the kitchen herself. She stifles a sob, staring at the door. Then, at the sound of a door opening and whispers from the hall, she glances wildly round and, with her bottle, departs unsteadily to the stairs.*

The sound of the women's laughter comes from the kitchen, and MAUREEN's *shout of 'Joan!'* HANSON *appears in the hall door, looks left and right, then signals behind him. Giggling,* SHEILA *follows him in, a carrier bag with bottles in her arms.* HANSON *puts his finger to his lips and gestures at the kitchen.*]

HANSON [*whispers*]: Excellent. Very good, O'Connor. Next week, as a very special reward, you can be in charge of the ink *and* the chalk – and if you're extra good I'll let you clean the blackboard.

SHEILA: Oh, thank you, sir! [*Taking off her coat.*]

HANSON [*aware*]: I think for that you deserve a red star. Or is it a green one? [*He pins an imaginary medal on her chest, then kisses her on either cheek.*

SHEILA *takes him round the neck and kisses him more directly.*

ARNIE *has entered quietly.* HANSON *looks up in mid-kiss to see him.*]

There you are, dear fellow.

ARNIE: Saw you down the street. Thought: bound to resent my intrusion. Kept my distance.

Circumspect. All that.

HANSON: Absolutely, old boy.

ARNIE: Not at all.

JOAN [*heard*]: Arnie? [*She enters from kitchen, followed by* MAUREEN, *carrying a tray of tea and sandwiches.*] There you are.

MAUREEN: Arrived back altogether.

HANSON: Are we supposed to drink out of our hands?

JOAN: You can help yourself in the kitchen.

SHEILA: Can I find the glasses?

HANSON: You find them, love. Anything that will hold liquid. You know what liquid is, don't you?

SHEILA: Course I do, silly.

[HANSON and SHEILA giggle.]

JOAN [to ARNIE]: What are you doing?

[ARNIE stands at the back of the room rubbing his hands energetically, nodding his head at everybody, his face set in a pleased grin.]

ARNIE: Just getting it all organized. Ship-shape. Everyone on the best of terms. Pleasantries, cordialities, sparks within a fire.

JOAN: What's got into you?

MAUREEN [to HANSON]: I hope you know what you're doing with that girl.

HANSON: Oh, definitely.

JOAN: Better leave him alone, Maureen.

MAUREEN: He needs reminding.

HANSON: On whose authority, Miss Wilkinson?

MAUREEN: Those people who hire you to educate the . . .

HANSON: That's their fault for serving up dishes like her. We're not sticks of chalk.

MAUREEN: I never said you were.

HANSON: So put that over your shoulder and start marching.

[There's a cry from the kitchen and the sound of breaking glass. JOAN rushes out.]

Relax, Maureen. Relax.

ARNIE [cheerfully]: Relax.

MAUREEN: I am relaxed. There's a question of behaviour, isn't there?

HANSON: My behaviour's strictly human . . .

ARNIE: It's strictly human.

HANSON: Or are you against that too?

ARNIE: Are you against that too?

HANSON [to ARNIE]: What's the matter with you?

JOAN [re-entering]: One broken glass, that's all.

SHEILA [following with tray of glasses]: I broke a glass!

HANSON: Right, then. . . . [He starts pouring out the drinks.]

ARNIE [to MAUREEN]: What's got into you?

MAUREEN: What?

HANSON: Joan? Maureen? A little for you, Sheila?

JOAN: I'll have a glassful . . .

HANSON: But certainly.

MAUREEN: I'll make do with tea.

HANSON: Naturally. [*To* JOAN] We have a little whisky here for the menfolk. If you like . . .

JOAN: Oh, beer will do.

HANSON: And Arnold?

JOAN: Don't give him whisky. One glass knocks him off his feet.

HANSON: Aha!

[*He hands a glass of whisky to* ARNIE *who downs it in one swallow.*]

JOAN: I've warned you.

[HANSON *tots it up again, and* ARNIE *drinks it off.*

ARNIE *screws his face, holds his stomach, then his head, gesticulates with violent, staccatic motions, lurches erratically one way then another, goes boss-eyed, knock-kneed . . .*]

JOAN: All right. All right.

[. . . ARNIE *stands motionless in the centre of the room.*]

HANSON [*expressionless*]: Oh dear. Oh dear, I haven't laughed so much for ages. . . . Are you sure you're old enough, Sheila?

SHEILA: Course I am.

HANSON: I meant for alcohol, my dear. [*He slaps his thigh.*] Oh, my!

ARNIE: My *friends*!

HANSON: *What?*

ARNIE: I would like to address you, if I may.

HANSON: Oh.

ARNIE [*swallows his next whisky. Hesitates. Then*]: This . . . *celebration* . . . is not an ordinary celebration. Oh, you may say, it *looks* an ordinary celebration. And I admit. It has all the signs, the characteristics, all the *moeurs*, as they say in German. Of a celebration. But the fact is. . . . What? . . . What? [*He looks round questioningly.*]

JOAN: Is that the end?

ARNIE: I have always in my life attempted to deal . . . fairly, with my fellow men.

HANSON: And women.

ARNIE: Ah. [*Holds up an admonitory finger.*] And it would, indeed, be mealy-mouthed . . .

HANSON: It would.

ARNIE: Of me. Ungracious. Prevaricating. To let you assume that this is merely a celebration. This is in fact. . . . What is this? [*He holds up his glass.*]

[HANSON *holds up the whisky bottle to him.*]

HANSON: One of the very worst brands, old friend.

ARNIE [*wipes his hand, surprised, across his forehead*]: I'm *sweating*.

JOAN: I told you he'd fall down.

MAUREEN: Perhaps we better put on the music and calm down.

ARNIE: An event of such gigantic proportions as to be virtually invisible to the naked human eye! It is. . . . Do they wash up in this?

HANSON: Only one of the minor rituals of distillation. Why, I could tell you . . .

JOAN: We'll have that another time.

ARNIE: I want . . . *all* of you. I want all of you to be content. This evening I want you to remember . . . I want you to remember. I want you.

HANSON: What?

ARNIE: What?

HANSON: Well, if not 'what' then 'why'?

ARNIE: I don't want to know why. Any damn fool can give you reasons *why*. All I'm interested in is *how. Why* is a kind of sentimentality I heartily eschew. I *eschew* it. Why is of no more interest to me than *when*. You can put why and when into . . . wherever you'd like to put them, and blow them to smithereens, for me.

HANSON: God! A religious maniac!

ARNIE: I want an evening of . . . ease, of peace, of relaxation. The . . . *flow* of gentle laughter, conversation . . . the natural intimacy between friends.

JOAN: I'd like to recite a poem.

ARNIE: What?

HANSON: Oh, steady, Joan.

JOAN: I think I shall.

ARNIE [*pained*]: You're being revolting. . . . I said the *natural* flow of conversation not a poem.

JOAN: You said the flow.

MAUREEN: Yes. You did say the flow.

[JOAN *begins to recite.*]

HANSON: Have another drink, Sheila.

SHEILA: Oh, ta.

HANSON: You are enjoying yourself?

SHEILA: Oh, super!

[JOAN *has begun to recite, at first her fingers holding her cheeks, then, as she goes on, growing more confident.*]

JOAN: I saw love passing by my window
   Early one morning on a lightsome day ...

ARNIE: Oh, no.

HANSON: Joan ...

JOAN: Its face was warm and its look so hopeful
   And pleasure and happiness in its features lay.

[ARNIE *has covered his face with embarrassment.*]

ARNIE: Oh, no. [*Groaning*] This can't go on.

HANSON: Joan: my dear, dear girl ...

SHEILA: No. Sir, it's super!

MAUREEN: No, let her go on.

[*For a moment they argue over this,* SHEILA *and* MAUREEN *attempting to quieten the other two. Meanwhile* JOAN *carries on reciting.*]

JOAN: I saw love hurrying in the meadow
   Its steps so light over the leaden clay,
   Its breath was quick and its voice beseeching,
   And I heard its cries as I fled away.

   I saw love sitting in a cottage
   About its feet did children play,
   Their sounds were loud, their voices lusty,
   And I saw love smile to see them gay.

[ARNIE *has continued to groan, gradually quietening, finally subsiding on a chair, holding his stomach and leaning forward as if in pain. The others too have quietened, turning to listen to* JOAN.]

JOAN: I saw love bending with the sickle
   Though all the thorns were clustered in its way,
   Its body aged and its head now shaking,
   And with the wind it seemed to sway.

   I saw love trudging by my window
   Late one evening on a darksome day,
   Its face was worn and its look despairing
   And grief and sorrow on its features lay.

[ARNIE *has now looked up to watch* JOAN.]

I saw love carried to the graveside
The day was sunny and the month was May.
Across its brow was a wreath of laurel
And in its hands a clean white spray.

[*They're silent. No one moves for a moment. Then:*]

HANSON: Oh, I say. That's very good.

MAUREEN: Lovely.

SHEILA: It was super, Miss.

HANSON: No, I really do think that was very good.

[*They all seem a little awed.* ARNIE, *however, has suddenly jumped up.*]

ARNIE: There was a young woman of Leeds
    Who swallowed a packet of seeds,
    She grew peas on her chest,
    Runner beans in her vest,
    And all round her kneecaps grew weeds.

HANSON: There was a young man of Bangkok
    Who swallowed a musical clock . . .

ARNIE: Oh, I say . . .

HANSON: . . . He could play a toccata,
    Chopin's Moonlight Sonata,
    By simply removing his sock.

ARNIE: Oh . . . This is the happiest day of my life. I want you to know that . . . Revelations are simply pouring from the skies! Sheila!

[*He goes to* JOAN *and puts his arm warmly about her.*]

HANSON: Sheila: what contribution could you make, my dear?

ARNIE: A few handstands might cause a stir. Perhaps some extraordinary gymnastic feats acquired at the hands of Miss Wilkinson?

HANSON: You can commit poetry, my dear. We – we can merely recite it.

SHEILA: You've forgotten to give sir his telegram, sir.

HANSON: Telegram? Telegram?

JOAN: Telegram?

HANSON: Ah . . .

ARNIE [*totally bemused, his arm still warmly about* JOAN]: I once read somewhere in a novel, perhaps . . .

HANSON: Scott!

ARNIE: Scott?

HANSON: That's his name! [*Points to the door.*]

MAUREEN: Whose?

HANSON: You remember Scott? A tall, lanky boy who wore glasses and dirty teeth. Won the long jump one year, I believe, by simply falling on his head.

ARNIE: Oh, Scott! ... Wasn't he the boy ...

HANSON: Could contain himself no longer during a mathematics lesson and furtively urinated out of an upper window when he presumed no one was looking.

[JOAN *giggles.*]

MAUREEN: Now that's enough!

ARNIE: Brought on a case of Thompson's disease. An hitherto unknown medical syndrome characterized by a sudden staring of the eyes, an energetic raising of the arms, and a loud, screaming sound emitted from between the teeth.

HANSON: It was first witnessed in an elderly caretaker of that name who happened to be passing beneath the window at the time.

[JOAN *breaks out into laughter.* SHEILA *giggles.*]

JOAN: Is he *here*?

SHEILA: He was. [*Attempting to conceal her laughter.*]

ARNIE: A remarkable youth, I seem to recollect. Went through all the stages of puberty by the age of eleven. Caused endless consternation amongst the younger boys.

HANSON: As we were emerging from the house a short while ago, my young companion and I, [*holds* SHEILA *firmly about the shoulders*] our course set for the hostelry, whom should we discover on the step but Scott himself attired in dark uniform and peaked cap. 'Great Heavens,' said I, 'the police.' Whereupon he indicated an insignia on his arm which suggested he was in the employ of the Post Office with special responsibility for the delivery of urgent messages. Thrusting one such into my hand he departed with an alacrity I can only assume was inspired by our past acquaintance. So intoxicated was I by the chatter of my companion that, until this moment, I'm afraid I have quite overlooked it. ... [*Finally retrieving it after a search of his pockets, reads*] Greetings!

JOAN: Is that all it says?

HANSON [*tendentiously*]: That's merely the envelope. [*He tears it open.*] Ah! This is what Scott has written. Greetings again! Here we are. . . . Regret. . . . Regret. Regret mother unwell stop cutting holiday short. Stop hope to make it some other time. Stop father.

JOAN: What's that? [*She takes the telegram.*]

HANSON [*to* MAUREEN *and* SHEILA]: Another drink?

[*Having read the telegram, however,* JOAN *now giggles.* ARNIE, *his arm still about her shoulder, gazes bemusedly into the distance.*]

JOAN: I cleaned every rotten stick in this house. [*To the others.*] I've even dusted every rotten piece of dust.

HANSON: Oh! Oh, Oh . . .

JOAN: There's not a mark not a sign of life anywhere and now they've decided not to come!

[JOAN *is very pleased, yet apparently, with her giggling, trying to hide her feelings from* ARNIE.]

ARNIE: Now. We are about to dance.

[ARNIE, *as if unaware of all this, goes to the gramophone.*]

JOAN: Here. Have you read this? Isn't it marvellous! That really is the best news I've had all day.

[*Music begins.*]

ARNIE: Sheila. Would you escort me about the floor? A limb here, a limb there. One or two gesticulations in unexpected places . . . and there we are. Ups!

[ARNIE *is unsteady, slow and mechanical, as he manoeuvres* SHEILA *about the room.*]

HANSON: Shall we form a chorus? Surround the principal players with thrashing . . .

JOAN [*to* ARNIE]: Loved one! Did you hear? Have you seen this?

[JOAN *is still giggling, despite herself; for her, now, the evening is a huge success.*]

HANSON: Arnie. Show us your armour.

JOAN: We can get rid of that too while we're at it.

HANSON: I know a secret!

MAUREEN: What?

HANSON: I know a secret!

SHEILA [*laughing*]: What is it?

HANSON: Are you ready?

JOAN: No rowdy stuff, Hanson.

HANSON: Are you ready? [*Darts to the cupboard, and with a sudden gesture:*] Woman! Behold thy. . . .
  Oh, it's locked.

JOAN: Don't look at me.

HANSON: Arnold. What is this?

SHEILA: Oh, Arnie. Can't we see it?

ARNIE: What?
  [ARNIE *has paused. He stares at* SHEILA *in consternation.*]

SHEILA [*quietly*]: Can't we see it, sir?

ARNIE: Who asked you in here?

HANSON: I did, Robin.

ARNIE [*glances at her, then moves away*]: Show her the aeroplane. There's a stuffed eagle over there.

HANSON: Aren't we going to see . . .

ARNIE: And above the mantelpiece you'll observe a Lee-Enfield rifle, a weapon of historical importance to the British nation.

HANSON: Arnold, if you'll just allow . . .

ARNIE: With that weapon we preserved . . . [*He gestures airily about him.*]

HANSON: Look, I don't wish to get impersonal, old boy.

ARNIE: And what are we now? Gropers in the debris of our . . .

HANSON: Arnold. Do I understand you are about to entertain us?

ARNIE: Tell us, Hanson. How does your mother keep her stockings up?

HANSON: Ooo! Ooo!

JOAN: I think that's enough.

MAUREEN: We better quieten down . . .

SHEILA: It's good, Miss!

JOAN: If you want something to shout about there's always this. [*She thrusts the telegram into his hand.*]

ARNIE: It's Hanson. He's an historical aberration.

HANSON: Ooo!

ARNIE: A turnip!

HANSON: Ooo!
  [SHEILA *has given way to giggles;* JOAN *also.*]

ARNIE: A sod.

HANSON: Ooo! Ooo! You heard him! [*Writes across a large imaginary blackboard*.] Tries hard: a willing worker, but effort frequently suffocated in pompous supposition.

[ARNIE *waves his arms about indecisively*.]

Ooo! You heard! [*Writes*.] Self-indulgent and tends to melodrama when opposed. Suffers from affectations, not least of which a pretension to reality. [*Bows to the room*.] Thus write I across all my reports. [*Vaguely facetious*.] Loved one.

JOAN: That's enough! [*Attempts to turn ARNIE away*.]

ARNIE: It's him. He's a propagator of untruth.

HANSON: Untruth! Why, he's a lie himself. If you measured him by any reality he'd be invisible. [*He puts his tongue out triumphantly at ARNIE*.]

ARNIE: That rifle's *loaded*.

[HANSON *pauses, then looks up. He hesitates. Then:*]

HANSON: Liar!

MAUREEN [*to JOAN*]: Is it loaded?

JOAN: I don't know. [*Giggling*.]

MAUREEN: I think we've had enough of this.

SHEILA: They're only playing, Miss!

[HANSON *lifts the rifle down*.]

ARNIE: May I? [*He puts the telegram in his pocket, first one, then the other, as HANSON fumbles with the rifle. Then ARNIE takes it from him, removes the safety catch and draws back the bolt*.] All right. A pretension to reality. [*He raises the rifle and presses it to HANSON's temple. He's still unsteady with drink*.] It's loaded.

HANSON [*pause. Then calls*]: Rubbish. [*Giggles*.]

ARNIE: I'll fire it.

[HANSON *is silent*.]

Well?

HANSON: Trouble-maker, and known disseminator of bad habits.

MAUREEN: That's far enough.

ARNIE: Are you ready?

HANSON: Yes.

[ARNIE *squeezes the trigger*.]

JOAN: No!

ARNIE: It's rusty. Hold your head still.

[HANSON *stands tensely, holding the table now, assuming some dignity.* SHEILA *has covered her face up.* ARNIE *holds the rifle more awkwardly to gain further pressure on the trigger. He squeezes again There's a click.* ARNIE *still holds the rifle there.* HANSON *laughs.*]

JOAN: Oh, God. That's enough.

HANSON: Everything you see. False all the way through. [*Takes the rifle from* ARNIE, *laughing with real pleasure. He points it at* ARNIE, *ramming back the bolt.*] Arnold: you're a falsity! [*His laughter suddenly breaks. He looks down at the rifle – examines it.*] It is loaded.

ARNIE: Yes.

HANSON [*looking up in horror*]: And you pulled the trigger?

ARNIE: Yes.

HANSON: Why . . . You madman! [*He throws the rifle down.*]

ARNIE: It was a choice you made on the evidence of your own senses, Jeffrey.

HANSON: You're mad!

ARNIE: That's not true.

HANSON [*to the women*]: He could have killed me!

JOAN [*dismissive*]: Fools! You're both fools.

HANSON: What? [*He suddenly stares at her, drunkenly distracted.*] He could have killed me!

[ARNIE, *swayingly, has meanwhile picked up the rifle. He points it at* HANSON.]

ARNIE: As a matter of fact I still can.

HANSON: No!

JOAN: Arnie!

MAUREEN: No!

[SHEILA *screams.*

ARNIE *pulls the trigger, then gazes intrigued at* HANSON's *expression.*]

ARNIE: The firing pin's removed. There's no contact with the cart-ridge. [*He lowers the rifle.*] It can never go off.

[HANSON *grabs the rifle from him.*]

HANSON: You know what I think?

ARNIE: You take it too seriously, Big John.

[HANSON *stares at him impotently, blind with rage.* ARNIE, *slowly:*] It really is unforgivable, isn't it?

MAUREEN: You better go, Sheila. Did you bring a coat?

HANSON: She's not going.

SHEILA: I don't want to go.

MAUREEN: I think you better, girl, and do as you're told this once.

HANSON: I said she's not going! [*He takes* SHEILA's *arm. Then, to* ARNIE:] God. What a deceiver. It was false, bogus, all the way through. He even makes a virtue of it.

ARNIE [*to* MAUREEN]: Shall we dance?

MAUREEN: You've gone too far, Arnold. I think we'd better go.

HANSON: Go! I think – with all due insolence to our host – that he should be compelled to open his bloody cupboard *door*!

ARNIE: Mockery ill-becomes you.

HANSON: I think he should . . .

ARNIE: *You* think? Your thoughts, Hanson . . . they're superfluous here. And your insolence undistinguished. You've been revealed as a pompous boor. Your otiose circumlocutions no longer sufficient to conceal the cringing, shivering coward within; your boldest gestures about as revelationary as a flea's. Do you really believe that I'm under any obligation to reveal *my* soul to you? My weaknesses stand higher than your greatest virtues.

MAUREEN: That's enough, for God's sake!

ARNIE: My only regret is, out of past charity, I have such weak substances on which to wreak my revenge.

HANSON [*applauding*]: Oh, bravo. Bravo.

ARNIE: I regret it all. All this. It's too puny for contempt!

JOAN: Where are you going?

[ARNIE *has gone stumbling towards the stairs.*]

ARNIE: What?

JOAN: These people: you *invited* them.

[ARNIE *comes back, takes the whisky bottle from the table and begins to go out.*]

ARNIE: Assume they aren't here. It's an easier alternative to assuming that they are.

JOAN [*casually*]: Have you read that telegram?

[*He pauses again.*]

In your pocket.

ARNIE: I heard!

[*Pause.*]

JOAN: They're not coming. As long as you realize that when you wake up. And it's just as well they aren't. You're blind drunk!

ARNIE: Do you know what you're saying? [*He snatches at his pockets, searching for then finding the telegram.*] I know what it says! I heard!

[*To* HANSON:] Did you say that Scott wrote this? He wants firing! Did *he* write this? Then sack him! He's no good. Did I tell you what he did to Thompson?

JOAN: You better go to bed.

ARNIE: I am! I am! . . . [*He stares round at them, full of threat.*] I am! [*He goes to the stairs, stumbles, regains his balance, and goes.*]

HANSON: So's friendship, if not love, repaid;
And by a graceless hand is trust betrayed.

MAUREEN Stop it! I've had enough! All this *indulgence.*

HANSON [*going to cupboard*]: Well, that comes out at least. [*He tries to wrench the cupboard door open, then kicks the thin wood open.*] Why it's empty! There's nothing here! [*He turns round, broken by his rage.*] He must have it up there with him.

JOAN: Just look what you've done . . . [*Giggles.*]

SHEILA: He's jealous.

JOAN: What?

SHEILA: It's because he's jealous. That's why he's gone . . .

MAUREEN: Sheila!

SHEILA: He is. He's jealous of Mr Hanson. Anybody can see.
[JOAN *is more disillusioned than annoyed.*]

JOAN [*tediously*]: Oh, for goodness sake. Get her out.

SHEILA: He is!

JOAN [*almost indifferently*]: Get out.

MAUREEN: Go on, Sheila. Go on. You better go now. [*To* HANSON:] Take her out.

SHEILA: He is! You're all jealous. All of you!

JOAN [*tediously*]: Take her out for goodness sake.
[MAUREEN *has taken* JOAN'*s arm as her violence grows.*]

MAUREEN [*to* HANSON]: You'd better go.
[HANSON *has taken her arm.*]

HANSON: All right. All right. But don't blame her. That camel up there. Now you just shout at him!
[JOAN *stands tensely,* MAUREEN *holding her, until* SHEILA *and* HANSON *have gone.*
Silence. Then:]

JOAN [*quietly*]: I'll have to wait for my mother. She should have been back by now. That girl.

MAUREEN: I'll stay a little longer.

JOAN Would you? Do you mind? It's very kind of you.

MAUREEN: We might as well sit down.

[JOAN *turns out of her arms and wanders about the room. Then:*]

JOAN: That girl.

MAUREEN: I shouldn't worry.

JOAN: Isn't it quiet? It must be late. [*Pause.*] She can't be long. Everything must be shut by now.

MAUREEN: Will Arnold have gone to bed?

JOAN: Oh. . . . [*She listens.*] We won't see him again tonight. [*Pause.*] I've been dreading having a scene with my mother this evening while people were here. That's why I asked her to go out.

MAUREEN: Asked her?

JOAN: I told her this evening that she would have to leave. Go and live somewhere else. . . . It sounds hard. But there was no other way of doing it. Believe me.

MAUREEN: Is that what Arnold was in a mood about? I mean, when we came.

JOAN: No. No. He doesn't know I've told her yet.

[MAUREEN *watches* JOAN *moving listlessly about the room.*]

I had to tell her to go, you know. [*Pause.*] I've never seen her so hurt. Never. She. . . . I've never seen her so hurt.

MAUREEN: Where will she go when she leaves?

JOAN: She's grown so attached to Arnie. [*Sinks into a chair opposite her. They're silent. Then:*] Don't you think it's strange? The way he's always surrounded by women?

MAUREEN: Women?

JOAN: I don't know. He can't bear to be in this house alone. Can you imagine that? Don't you think it's extraordinary? [*Pause.*] You should see the look of relief on his face when I come in. Or my mother comes in. And he's sitting here alone. I don't think he's even aware of it. [*She gets up, moves around the room again, restlessly. Then:*] I was like a wild animal when we first got married. Always smashing things. I couldn't put my hand down without knocking something over. I was never still for one minute. [*She sits down again in the same seat, facing* MAUREEN.] We were always fighting. You know, fists and things. [*She laughs into her hand.*] It's awful, isn't it? But we used to stand up, bashing each other.

[MAUREEN *laughs.*]

I think this drink's beginning to have an effect on me. [*She snorts into her hand.*] Have you heard of anybody carrying on like that? I'm glad, actually. That they're not coming tomorrow. [*She looks round at the room.*] It was all prepared. All ready. Actually, they're very nice. I don't know why. Will you have something else? I'm sure you'd like them.

MAUREEN: No. I don't think I will.

JOAN: Would you like a stuffed eagle?

MAUREEN: I don't think so. No.

JOAN: A ship?

MAUREEN: No thanks.

JOAN: It's all yours if you want it. S'all going out. Sweeping changes. Actually. You mustn't tell anybody about this, will you?

MAUREEN: No . . .

JOAN: You promise?

MAUREEN [*nods uncertainly*]: Yes.

JOAN: The fact is, Arnie doesn't give a damn for anybody. I'm exactly the same. Do you know anything about children?

MAUREEN: Well, I teach them.

JOAN: Ah, yes. [*She looks at* MAUREEN *freshly.*] Are you religious? You don't mind me asking?

MAUREEN [*pause*]: No. Well . . .

JOAN: Do you believe in God?

MAUREEN: Well, in a sort of . . .

JOAN [*lifting back her hair*]: I honestly don't know what to believe in. Is that the time? You absolutely promise?

MAUREEN: Yes.

JOAN: Well, I'll tell you. [*Looks round.*] Arnold actually . . .

MAUREEN [*pause*]: Yes?

JOAN: Is God.

MAUREEN: Oh.

JOAN: He's only assumed the identity of a schoolteacher in order to remain incognito. Inconspicuous. For a God, you see who believes in modesty and self-effacement there are severe doctrinal problems in asserting that he's God at all. Do you understand what I mean? [JOAN *watches her for a moment with some satisfaction.* MAUREEN *gives no reply at all.*] It's an enormous privilege, of course. [*Pause.*] Being married to Him at all.

[*Slow footsteps have already started on the stairs. It's only now, how-ever, that* MAUREEN *who is facing the stairs, actually looks up. She stands up immediately.*]

MAUREEN: Oh!

[JOAN *turns dreamily, slowly, as she sees* MAUREEN's *reaction.*

MRS ELLIS's *appearance is dreadful: dressed in men's pyjamas, she has a bottle in her hand. Her look is compounded of many feelings: possessiveness, triumph, greed. Her matronly breasts are scarcely con-concealed by the jacket, and as she sways at the bottom of the stairs the vision quickly changes to that of a besotted old lady. For a moment* JOAN *fails to grasp what she sees. When she does it's with a cry of denial like a child's.*]

JOAN: Mam! [*She staggers to her feet.*] Mother!

MRS ELLIS: Do you know . . .

JOAN: Mam! . . . [*She glances frantically at the hall door where she'd expected her mother to appear.*]

MRS ELLIS: It's not in there. Not in there – as we all thought. [*She indicates the cupboard.*] It's not in there at all. He's hidden it – would you believe it, the cunning devil? – he's hidden it under the bed!

JOAN: No. No.

MRS ELLIS [*to* MAUREEN]: Underneath! Well! Whoever said he wasn't cunning!

JOAN: Mother.

MRS ELLIS: It's all lies. Everything. [*Violent.*] You said he wanted me to go! You did! . . .

In fact. He doesn't want that at all.

JOAN: What?

MRS ELLIS: Arnie. [*She stands swaying, looking down at her daughter with something between consternation and triumph.*] You ask him.

JOAN: Oh, no. . . . No.

MRS ELLIS: You. . . . You. The things you told me.

JOAN: Oh, God. No. [*She sinks down, burying her face in her hands.*]

MRS ELLIS: Well. Well, then. . . . Who's sorry now? [*She collapses slowly into a chair.*] Are we having a party? Who's this, then? Another of Arnie's friends?

[*Lights fade.*]

ACT THREE

SCENE ONE

Next morning.

The suit of armour stands to one side, around it the various 'pieces'.

JOAN *is tidying the room and preparing the table for breakfast.*

She's dressed neatly and tidily, and works briskly. Bottles from the party are stacked on the sideboard.

After a while ARNIE *appears at the foot of the stairs, tousled, genial, his shirt unbuttoned.*

He stands at the foot of the stairs, yawns, stretches, smacks his lips and looks round.

JOAN *goes on working.*

ARNIE: Well. Well. Ship-shape. Someone has been up early, I can see.

JOAN: I've made coffee. Is that all right?

ARNIE: Ah, Fine. Fine. [*He comes slowly into the room, looks at the armour but makes no comment.*]

JOAN: I haven't cooked anything. I didn't think anyone would feel like eating.

ARNIE: Quite true. Quite true. [*He comes to the table, looks round at the various objects on it.*] Well, Well, Well. That was a very frivolous evening, Joan. All that booze. We shan't go through that again. Not for a very long time. No, we shan't. We certainly shan't. What? We shan't. [*He yawns. Snaps his mouth shut. Suddenly he shadow boxes, briefly, quickly. Then he yawns again, stretches.*] I've got to get down to weight. This is getting embarrassing. Last fight I ever had I only weighed three stone ten. No, was it four? [*He sits down at the table.*]

[JOAN *has poured his coffee.* ARNIE *gazes across at the armour, then, after a while, begins to sing softly.*]

Come, ye thankful people come,
Raise the song of harvest home.
All is safely gathered in
Ere the winter storms begin;
God our Maker doth provide
For our wants to be supplied;

79

Come to God's own temple, come,
Raise the song of harvest home.

Where's Edie, then?

JOAN: She hasn't got up yet. [*She has re-arranged the table and gone back to her cleaning.*]

ARNIE: The fact is, I feel in a very philosophic frame of mind. All my life I've looked for some positive reaction in people. Did you know that?

[*Pause.* JOAN *goes on with her tasks.*]

There are certain tribes in the Northern Province of Nigeria who use carrier bags for latrines. [*Abstracted, he now looks up at* JOAN *directly, waiting a moment, then:*] This man at school told me that. He worked out there once on famine relief. Saved thousands from starvation. His life was full of significance and meaning. [*Abstracted a moment.*] He said there's this enterprising man in Birmingham who sends them out regularly by post. To an agent. Who sells them at a fantastic profit. It cuts down the risk of malaria or dysentry or something. [*Pause.*] 'Hoyle's Supermarket' they've got printed on the side. [*Pause.*] It's amazing what human initiative will rise to once it sets itself to a particular task.

[ARNIE *has become quite abstracted.* JOAN *continues with her work.* ARNIE *gets up and goes on talking absently.*]

When I was a boy we had a milkman who came in a horse and trap. He wore a little bowler hat and a striped apron and came in each morning from the country with cans of fresh milk and ladled it all out with little ladles. Beautiful. They went up from one the size of a thimble to one as big as his hat.

[JOAN *has sat down casually on the arm of a chair, holding her face with her hand.*]

He ran over a boy one day. The wheel of his cart went over his head. It wasn't his fault. But he offered the boy's mother free milk for a year; you know, for goodwill and neighbourliness. She was very poor. She had eleven children. I don't think he knew that at the time. [*Pause.*] He went out of business in six months. Bankrupt. [*Pause.*] You should have seen this woman's house. Milk, there was, everywhere. Nothing but milk. [*He suddenly looks round.* JOAN *gets up and resumes her tasks: taking the coffee pot to the kitchen.* ARNIE *talks through to her.*] You know, I've always had the ambition to be a writer. The things I'd write about would be fairly rhetorical in manner.

[JOAN *re-emerges.*]

Subjects. . . . Well, it may even have caught your attention. The extraordinary mixture of hysteria and passivity one gets in society today. I mean . . .

[*While he's been talking* MRS ELLIS *has appeared from the stairs. She's carrying a small suitcase and is dressed in a coat and hat, a small fur round her shoulders.*]

MRS ELLIS: I'll send for my things when I've got an address.

JOAN: You'd better put the case down . . .

ARNIE: I thought there for a moment you know, that we were going off on holiday. God, weather like this, too. It's incomprehensible.

JOAN [*ignoring him*]: I'm heating up the coffee.

[MRS ELLIS *stands gazing irresolutely around her.*]

And do take that coat off. You'll be roasted alive. The tray's ready to fetch through. [*She busies herself now re-arranging the table.*]

MRS ELLIS: Joan . . .

JOAN: All it requires is lifting.

ARNIE: This is quite extraordinary. I've forgotten his name now. But this boy fell off the school roof on . . . Friday, it must have been. Over forty feet in height. No. I'm wrong there. Nearer fifty. Fell like a stone. Bang. Right on his head. By every right it should have killed him. But no. This should interest you, Edie. He's scarcely hit the ground than he stands up and says, 'Sir, I didn't fall. Somebody pushed me.' So damned anxious, in wandering near the parapet, to show he hadn't broken a rule.

[MRS ELLIS *has gone into the kitchen. She comes out again now, almost immediately, lost.*]

MRS ELLIS: I don't seem able to find it.

JOAN: Look for it, mother. Put the light on. Open the curtains.

MRS ELLIS: Yes . . .

JOAN: And do take your coat off.

MRS ELLIS: Yes. . . . [*She starts back, falters.*] I don't know how you can just sit there.

ARNIE: Sit?

MRS ELLIS: I can hardly stand!

ARNIE: Now, then. Now, then. There's no need to get upset.

MRS ELLIS: Upset! [*She buries her face in her hands.*]

JOAN: It's all right, mother.

MRS ELLIS [*moaning*]: I don't know what to do.

JOAN: You'll stay here, mother. It's all right.

MRS ELLIS: Oh, Joan . . . Joan.

JOAN: Now, you're all right. You're all right.

[MRS ELLIS *cries into her hands.*]

ARNIE [*brightly*]: How about some coffee?

[JOAN *has gone to take* MRS ELLIS *in her arms.*]

JOAN: Come on. You better come upstairs. I'll help you up.

MRS ELLIS: Oh, God, Joan. What am I going to do?

JOAN: Oh, now. You come up. Come on, now. Come on . . .

MRS ELLIS: I can't. I can't.

JOAN: I'll bring you something up. Now, come on. You'll be all right.

[*She leads her mother to the stairs. They go out.* ARNIE *has stood up. He walks about. Puts his hands in his pockets. Whistles.*]

ARNIE: This is quite extraordinary. [*He touches the armour confidingly.*] About two days ago the Director of Education came up to me and said, 'Bancroft,' he said – I mean it's not as if my name was Bancroft – 'Bancroft, I don't know quite how to tell you this, and I should hate it to get around. But the fact is, Bancroft, my wife has recently begun to manufacture money. The thing is, that periodically she lowers her knickers and from inside takes a miscellaneous collection of coins. The process, as far as I am aware, Bancroft, has completely taken over her excretory organs. And it's mostly silver. The coins, I mean.'

You know – would you believe it – the only comment he made after telling me all this was 'Pity it isn't gold, Bancroft. Just like that rotten bitch to produce second best.' [*He laughs.*] Anyway, I thought you'd like to know.

[JOAN *has come in as he finishes this.*]

Oh, how is the old bird?

[JOAN *begins her preparations of making a glass of warm milk.*]

You know, this unnerves me. I'm looking for some sort of constructive attitude from you, Joan. Something a bit bolder. To generalize about one's misfortune is invariably a sign of moral recovery in my book. If you could work something up on those lines I'd be immensely grateful.

JOAN: Yes. [*Goes on with her task.*]

ARNIE: I think I need to feel degenerate.

JOAN: I'm taking my mother up a glass of milk.

ARNIE: You see. Those are not the sort of remarks I'm looking for, Joan.

[JOAN *has now gone into the kitchen.* ARNIE *talks through to her.*]

The sort I'm looking for only you can provide. There's no one else. My only other opportunity for being punished lies immobilized, apparently, upstairs.

[JOAN *returns to collect the sugar from the table.*]

JOAN: There's an old woman up there, broken in two.

ARNIE: Well, at least she has that reassurance. What have I got? Nothing. Nothing. I don't understand it. I don't. I get no crumb of consolation from this at all. I feel I should get something. I deserve to suffer something, Joan. Even if it's only retribution.

[JOAN *hasn't answered.*]

These silences unnerve me. At any moment I'm going to suffer a relapse. I think I should warn you, Joan. You know what that might lead to.

[JOAN *still offers no answer.*]

[*Suddenly.*] I should also like it to be known that this sudden and alarming capacity to behave like a frog . . . to bespatter detachment on every side, to spawn ill humour, to sit for hours on end on a pad of disaffection . . . that all these qualities, while adding conviction to your image as a woman, *in no way*, in no way, improve your image as a man!

[JOAN *still makes no sign. Silence. Then* ARNIE *indicates the armour.*]

I don't understand. Some blame for my predicament attaches itself to you. I lie here, caught up in a million abominations, attributes, some of them fed in long before conception. And some of them, *some of them*, fed in by you! In that clammy little hand lie parts of me I don't think, in all honesty, you understand.

[ARNIE *follows* JOAN *to the kitchen door.*]

Guilt and austerity are not necessarily compatible, Joan, I mean . . . effusiveness could make your message just as clear.

JOAN: You've behaved like a dwarf. Everything in your life is like that. Dwarfish.

ARNIE: Well. Yes. That's something.

[*He talks through to her in the kitchen.*]

A dwarf. [*Pause; reflects.*] I don't like that somehow. [*Half-laughs.*] You know I object to that, Joan. I don't feel like a dwarf. [*He looks at his hands.*] I wouldn't describe them particularly, for instance, as dwarfish.

[*Silence.*]

Haven't you anything else to say?

[JOAN *re-emerges with the glass of milk.*]

JOAN: What are you going to do, Arnie?

ARNIE: I don't know. [*Pause.*] I'll do the only decent thing, I suppose.

JOAN: Yes.

ARNIE: That's all there is to do.

JOAN: Yes.

ARNIE: I'll marry her.

[*They're silent. Then:*]

JOAN: Why don't you leave, Arnie? And rid yourself of all this torment?

ARNIE [*abstracted*]: I don't know. Life has no dignity, Joan. No, I do agree with that. [*Pause.*] And death hasn't a great deal to recommend it, either. [*Pause.*] Both of them, when you look at it: they're pretty anonymous affairs. I don't know. I feel I should be able to do something. I feel . . . the moment's come . . . it's actually arrived. [*He grasps the air.*] And yet it refuses to . . . emanate. [*Suddenly looks round at the room.*] Anyway, I couldn't leave all this. My own fireside. I've worked hard for all this. I have. It's mine. This is my situation in life.

[JOAN, *after watching him with some attention, has turned away at this towards the stairs.*]

Perhaps I could go mad. Insanity, you know, is the one refuge I've always felt I was able to afford. The insights that irrationality brings. Well, in the end, that's what we're looking for. Cleavages. Cracks. Fissures. Openings. Some little aperture of warmth and light.

[JOAN, *after some hesitation, goes with her glass of milk.*]

Look, this is a very poor arrangement. I haven't got your attention at all. [*He turns away.*] I don't know. I might as well be talking to the wall. [ARNIE *goes to the armour: examines it sadly. Then he goes to the wall. He moves from one patch to another on the wall as if carefully selecting the right one for his task, rubbing his hand over its surface, then finally choosing one spot and taking up a stance before it.*]

When I was young, my mother said to me:
'Never drown but in the sea –
Rivers, streams and other dilatory courses
Are not contingent with the elemental forces
Which govern you and me – and occasionally your father –
So remember, even if the means are insufficient, rather
Than die in pieces subside by preference as a whole,
For disintegration is inimical to the soul
Which seeks the opportunity or the chances
To die in the circumstances
Of a prince, a saviour, or a messiah –
Or something, perhaps, even a little higher –
You and me and several of your aunties,
On my side, though working class, have destinies
Scarcely commensurate with our upbringing:
I hope in you we are instilling
This sense of secret dignities and rights
– Not like your father's side, the lights
Of which, I hope, we'll never see again,
Who have, I'm afraid, wet blotting-paper for a brain!
   [*Pause.*]
'Please, please my son,
Don't fail me like your father done.'
   [ARNIE *stands for a moment regarding the wall, expectantly, tensed. Then slowly he relaxes. His head sinks, his shoulders droop. His forehead leans against the wall.*]
Oh. Oh. Oh.
When I was young, when I was young,
There were so many things I should have done.
   [*Fade.*]

SCENE TWO

Evening, a few days later.

The room has been cleared of all ARNIE'S *possessions. It's clean and immaculate. A large vase of flowers stands on the table and another on the sideboard.*

From the hall comes the sound of voices.

HANSON [*heard*]: Arnie? [*Pause.*] Arnie? Arnie! [*Pause.*] He can't be here. [*Whistles.*]

MAUREEN [*heard*]: Arnie? [*Knocking on outer door.*] Can't hear anybody.

> [*The calling has been tentative, apprehensive. Then, finally, the door opens and* HANSON *puts his head round.*]

HANSON: No. No one here. [*Whistles.*] No.

> [*He and* MAUREEN *come in.* HANSON *carries a parcel.*]

MAUREEN: Goodness.

HANSON: I say. [*They look round at the changes.*] Drastic renovations, what?

MAUREEN: Joan?

HANSON: I say . . . [*Whistles a tune to himself as he looks round, tapping furniture and empty spaces with his stick.*]

MAUREEN: Joan?

> [MAUREEN *has glanced in the kitchen.*]

No: no one.

> [*Shrugs.*]

HANSON: Well, then . . .

MAUREEN: I suppose we better wait.

HANSON [*looks at watch*]: I don't know. What? Arnie! [*Then distracted*] I say. Cupboard restored. Would you believe it?

> [*Goes to look, then, in the kitchen. Comes back. Sets parcel he is carrying on the table.*]

Ship deserted, what? Oh . . .

> [*Sounds of the outer door opening, etc.* HANSON *hastily composes himself, tie, etc.* MAUREEN, *who has sat down, gets up.* MRS ELLIS *comes in, carrying a basket.*]

MRS ELLIS: Oh . . .

MAUREEN: Mrs Ellis . . .

HANSON: We . . . Oh, allow me . . . [*Offers to take her basket.*]

MRS ELLIS: No . . . It's all right.

MAUREEN: We found the door open. We knocked, but there was no one here.

MRS ELLIS: Oh . . .

MAUREEN: Is Joan out, too?

MRS ELLIS: Yes . . . I've just been . . . She . . . I'll just put these in the kitchen.

HANSON: Please. Allow me.

   [*Offers to take basket.*]

MRS ELLIS: No. No, it's all right.

   [*She goes into the kitchen.*]

HANSON: Well, well . . .

   [*He whistles a tune again, glances at his watch, at* MAUREEN, *wanders round the room.*

   MAUREEN *goes to the kitchen door.*]

MAUREEN: How is Arnie, Mrs Ellis?

   [*After a moment* MRS ELLIS *comes out.*]

MRS ELLIS: Oh, he's . . . all right.

HANSON: Fine. Fine. We . . . popped round. He hasn't been to school: The past few days.

MRS ELLIS: No.

HANSON: We . . . ah . . . thought we'd pop round.

MRS ELLIS: Yes.

HANSON: Fine. Fine.

   [*She's taken off her coat and goes through to the hallway to hang it up.* HANSON *and* MAUREEN *exchange glances.* HANSON *whistles a tune.*

   Outside in the hall the sound of Joan's arrival: 'Oh, it's you.' 'Visitors.' 'What?' 'Mr Hanson . . . schoolteacher . . .'

   HANSON *re-composes himself. A moment later* JOAN *comes in.*]

JOAN: Oh, hello.

HANSON: Joan.

MAUREEN: And how are you?

JOAN: I'm well. Fine. And you?

MAUREEN: Yes. Fine.

HANSON: Fine. Fine.

JOAN: Isn't Arnie in?

MAUREEN: We knocked, and shouted.

HANSON: Found the door ajar. What? No answer.

MAUREEN: No.

JOAN [*taking off her coat*]: If the door was open he can't be far away.

HANSON: Well, then ... [*Silence.*] Everything in order, then?

JOAN: I think so. More or less.

HANSON: Well, then ... [*Glances at watch.*] I suppose we better ...
be making tracks.

[MRS ELLIS *has come in and gone through to the kitchen.*]

JOAN: Stay and have some tea if you like.

HANSON: Yes. Fine. Well.

JOAN: My mother will be making some.

HANSON: Fine. Fine.

MAUREEN: How is Arnie, Joan?

JOAN: I don't know. All right. [*Shrugs.*]

HANSON: We were just remarking. Several days since he put in an
appearance, what? At school.

JOAN: Yes.

HANSON: Nothing to worry about, then?

JOAN: No. I don't think so.

[ARNIE *has appeared behind them, from the stairs. His head is done up,
turban-fashion, in a towel. In his hand he carries the sword.*]

HANSON: Good. Good. We were just remarking. Vast changes.
What?

JOAN: What?

HANSON: The room.

JOAN: Ah, yes.

HANSON: Flowers! [*Smells them.*] Beautiful.

JOAN: Yes.

HANSON: Altogether. [*Indicates room.*] Lighter.

JOHN: Yes.

[*In glancing round they become slowly aware of* ARNIE. *Silence.
Then:*]

ARNIE: The King, though broken by his plight,
    Shall rise again to set things right!

HANSON: Oh ...

MAUREEN: Arnie ...

ARNIE: Well, well, well. How are we all? Jeff?

HANSON: I'm fine. Fine.

ARNIE: And Maureen. How are you, my dear?

MAUREEN: I'm well, Arnie.

ARNIE: Just arrived, eh?

HANSON: Yes. Yes. Just about.

ARNIE: Thought I heard sounds. Couldn't be too sure. Got both my damned ears fastened up.

MAUREEN: And how are you, Arnie, yourself?

ARNIE: Oh, not so bad. Not so bad. Can't grumble. Can't complain.

HANSON: The Head sends his felicitations, Arnie ...

ARNIE: Fine. Fine.

HANSON: And the staff and pupils likewise. Looking forward, needless to say, to your early return to duties.

ARNIE: Ah, yes.

HANSON: Brought a few essentials here, Arnie.
    [*Indicates the parcel.*]
 Keep the system mobile, mind alert.

ARNIE: Ah, yes!
    [*Silence.*]

HANSON: We were just remarking.

ARNIE: Yes.

HANSON: Vast changes since we were last here.

ARNIE: Changes.

HANSON: The room ...

ARNIE: Gave them all to the refuse-man, you know.

JOAN: I'll just see about the tea.
    [*Goes to kitchen.*]

ARNIE [*to* MAUREEN]: And how are you?

MAUREEN: I'm well, Arnie.

ARNIE: I suppose you've seen their lorry? They have a blade in the back which crushes them all up.
    [*Suddenly, hugely:*]
 Crush! Crush! Crush!

HANSON: What, all of them, old boy?

ARNIE: Absolutely. [*Gestures at the room.*] The lot.
    [*Then, after a moment, swinging the sword:*]

'Cept this, of course.

HANSON: Yes.

ARNIE: I kept it back.

[*Whistles then between his teeth as, in demonstration, he slashes it about him.*]

HANSON: Ah, yes.

ARNIE: Bound to come in useful.

HANSON: Yes.

ARNIE: At least, so I thought.

HANSON: Ah, yes, old boy.

ARNIE: Arms, hands, feet, legs, abdomen. The lot.

[*Mimes the lorry's blade.*]

Head!

[*Gurgles, hand across his throat.*]

HANSON: We spoke to Sheila, by the way.

ARNIE: Yes?

HANSON: Had a little word in her ear.

ARNIE: Ah, yes.

MAUREEN: I think she'll show a little discretion.

ARNIE: She will?

HANSON: I think so, old man.

ARNIE: Good, good. I could do with a little bit of that myself.

[*Laughs.*] Joan?

[*Looks round. Then he gestures towards the kitchen.*]

She has a job.

MAUREEN: Oh.

ARNIE: Out to work each day.

HANSON: Yes?

ARNIE: Perhaps she mentioned it?

MAUREEN: No. [*Shakes her head.*]

ARNIE: She acquired her credentials, I'm glad to say, long before I married her. In a secretarial capacity, of course.

HANSON: Ah, yes.

ARNIE: Type. Type. Type. You should see her fingers. Flexing. Even in bed.

HANSON: Ah, yes, old boy.

ARNIE: On the other hand . . .

HANSON: Yes, old boy?

ARNIE: Absolutely nothing to worry about.

HANSON: No, no . . .

ARNIE: The doctor recommends a long sea-voyage.

MAUREEN: Sea-voyage?

ARNIE: And a complete change of air.

MAUREEN: I see.

ARNIE: I would have thought, myself, that the two of them were perfectly synonymous.

HANSON: Absolutely.

ARNIE: I'm overworked.

HANSON: My dear boy . . .

ARNIE: My nerves, Jeff, are stretched beyond endurance.
   [Glances round with some exaggeration to see that he is not overheard.]
   I'm afraid I should have warned you. Joan . . . [taps his head.] You will find her, I'm afraid, considerably changed. Her work – the contingencies of high office, the flow, the rapid, reckless inter-change of ideas which has been her lot now [dramatically consults his bare wrist] for the past six hours, leaves her – I'm very much afraid – prostrate.

HANSON: Ah, yes.

JOAN [entering]: My mother's bringing in the tea.

HANSON: Oh, that's very kind of you, Joan.

MAUREEN: Shouting at the devils all afternoon. Just one of those days. When you want a bit of peace you can never get it.

ARNIE: What do you really think, Jeff?

HANSON: Think?

ARNIE: Feel, if you like. What do you really feel?

HANSON: I feel we're completely out of touch with one another, if you really want to know.

ARNIE: I'm not out of touch with you. I can see, for example, that you are embarrassed at being here, anxious to conceal it, and look-ing forward to the moment when you leave and can tell people outside how I am looking and behaving, and what things I say. And as for Maureen – I can see how my behaviour has licensed what was previously impossible. Does that sound like someone out of touch with you?

HANSON: You take to insanity, Arnold, like other men take to drink.
   [A silence. Then:]

ARNIE: You have insufficient innocence to be a fool, Jeffrey.

[ARNIE *watches him a moment. A pause, then:*]

MAUREEN: We're still struggling along, by the way, Arnie, with rehearsals . . .

HANSON: Oh, yes. I'm afraid your absence, old man, has been severely felt. And, somewhat ineffectually I must confess, I have been obliged to take your place . . .

ARNIE: Robin Hood!

HANSON: Ah, yes!

ARNIE: Jeff. You must have discovered it for yourself.

HANSON: Yes?

ARNIE: A usurper. An outlaw!

HANSON: Ah, yes.

ARNIE: Always on the outside of things. Maureen! – cynical of the established order: disenfranchised, dispossessed. A refugee, if you like, from the proper world.

MAUREEN: Yes.

ARNIE: I hope you've kept them to it, Jeff!

HANSON: Well, as a matter of fact . . .

ARNIE: *Kings.* [*A dramatic self-gesture.*]

JOAN [*to* ARNIE]: Why don't you sit down?

ARNIE: They're a sort of receptacle, if you like. Into which flow all the goodness and intentions of mankind: and out of which in turn flow benevolence – and decisions. Authority. Rule. One becomes a king, not by chance – but by right: attributes fed in long before conception. Pre-ordained.

HANSON: Well, we weren't making it that complicated. [*To* JOAN] Robin stood on his bow yesterday afternoon and nearly guillotined his ear.

ARNIE: You think kingship's something foreign to me, Jeff? Let me tell you – I've studied it all my life. It's my profession. History! . . . You think I come from an age sentimental about its motives. You're wrong. My ancestry is rooted in action, in events, not causes. It's only fools who worry *why* they are. [*Pause.*] Do you know what goodness is?

HANSON: Goodness? [*Glances at the others.*]

ARNIE: Do you know what evil is? [*He looks round at them; they don't answer.*] Look. A simple arithmetical problem – set in all the schools.

[*He pulls up a chair and sits facing them.*] Take what we are from everything, and what remains?

HANSON [*pause*]: I don't know.

MAUREEN [*as ARNIE looks to her*]: No.

ARNIE: Goodness and Kings. [*He studies* HANSON *a moment. Then:*] Kings rise above themselves. They become . . . inanimate. Formed. [*He shapes it with his hands. Then he looks up at them; sees their looks.*] Do you know what the greatest threat to the present century is? [*Pause.*] The pygmies. [*He smiles at them.*]

HANSON: Yes.

JOAN: Arnie . . .

ARNIE: So small, so inconspicuous, they infiltrate everywhere. Not only out there, but into seats of government and power. And, of course, they're disguised. Not as men. Not even as small men. But as conditions of the soul. [*Relaxes.*] You think that's a conspiracy? No. We *choose* the lesser men.

HANSON: Yes.

ARNIE: Napoleons – they have their day. Usurpers, whether for good or ill. But the king rules not by revolution but by constitution. He is *born*: he is *bred*: he is created king *inside*. [*Pause.*] His *constitution* makes *the* constitution which makes him king. Joan, I don't like you standing behind me.

JOAN: It's my mother. She's bringing in the tea.

[JOAN *has gone to hold the kitchen door:* MRS ELLIS *enters with a laden tray.*]

HANSON: Ah, grand. Lovely.

[MRS ELLIS *nods without looking up.*]

ARNIE: Isn't that a miraculous sight? A tea-tray elevated through the air entirely by its own volition.

JOAN: Arnie, I'm afraid, has taken to assuming my mother doesn't exist.

[MRS ELLIS *puts the tray on the table. She serves the tea according to instructions.*]

JOAN: Maureen. Milk and sugar?

MAUREEN: Thank you. We ought really to be leaving fairly soon. [*She looks to* HANSON.]

ARNIE: Oh, don't stay on my account, Maureen. I can perform miracles any time for your amusement. If you wish, I can make that

93

tea-tray depart to where it came from entirely under its own resources.

JOAN: Milk and sugar, Jeff?

HANSON: No sugar. I've decided I must slim.

ARNIE: Or sugar transfer itself, unsolicited, from bowl to cup.

MAUREEN [*to* HANSON]: Ay, now ...

HANSON: That's to say, someone has decided for me.
    [ARNIE *has been overlooked.*]

ARNIE: What's that!

HANSON: My dear Arnold.

ARNIE: *What?*

HANSON: You don't have to play these games for *us.*

ARNIE: Oh?

HANSON [*taking the bull by the horns*]: We're your friends. Whatever
    you do, you're a friend, and we're concerned for you. [*Looks to*
    JOAN *and* MRS ELLIS.] Look, I don't wish to embarrass you, Joan.
    But you understand?

JOAN: Yes ...

HANSON: So there's no need for this eccentricity, Arnie.

ARNIE: What are you trying to do, Jeff?

HANSON: I'm trying ...

ARNIE: Hoping to *ingratiate* yourself with me?

HANSON: I hope there's no need for me to do that.

ARNIE: You're being very foolish. Do you know *anything!*

HANSON: It seems not.

ARNIE [*carried away*]: Scars. ... [*He holds out the palms of his hands,
    looking at them.*] They inhabit the skin. They grow there after a
    while like natural features. Deformities actually acquire that author-
    ity. [*Looks up bitterly at* HANSON.] Did you know? [*Pause.*] Remove
    them – and you remove life itself. Well?

HANSON: I don't know what you're talking about actually, Arnold.

ARNIE: I'm talking about ... alternatives.

HANSON: Alternatives. I see.

ARNIE: To kingship. [*Stares fixedly at* HANSON. *Then he smiles. A
    moment later he relaxes completely.*] Oh, Jeff. [*Laughs.*] You looked
    positively embarrassed. Didn't he? Pompous, if I didn't know him
    better.

MAUREEN: Well ...

ARNIE: Ah, come on, now, Jeff. Fair's fair. 'A friend.' You old prigster!

> I know a man with two left feet
> Who'd rather be dead than be seen in the street:
> Yet the fellow would hardly have seemed such a sight
> If he hadn't have had two more on his right.

[*He laughs, spreading out his hands.*] I shall now tell you a dirty history.

HANSON: I honestly think, Arnie, we've had enough.

ARNIE: History has always had a certain fascination for me.

MAUREEN: Joan. I really think we should go.

ARNIE: The raising of Lazarus as a permanent act of restitution. Kings, queens, emperors. Saints! Inhabited by one's own domestic soul!

  [*They're silent.*]

[*Getting up*] Everything has to be defined. Yet how can you define anything except by its limitations? Why! – my limitations are limitless!

MAUREEN: I really think we ought to be going, Joan, you know. We can pop in again, later in the week – if that's convenient.

JOAN: Yes. Any time you like.

HANSON: Well...

ARNIE: Do you remember Scott? ... Scott!

HANSON: Arnie. I'd like...

ARNIE [*direct to* HANSON]: Certain things can't be destroyed, however much you try. Rifles rust, erode, and fall apart. They become mechanically defunct. But swords – while rusting too, preserve down to their last grain an emblem of the truth. Instruments of honour, which the world is a feebler place without! ... Dignity. [*Draws himself up.*] The past brought down to us in swords!

HANSON: Arnie, we have to be going.

ARNIE: Ah, yes.

HANSON [*to* JOAN]: If there's anything we can do, Joan. .... You will let us know?

JOAN: Yes. Thank you.

MAUREEN: Bye, Arnie.

HANSON: Goodbye, Arnold.

ARNIE [*cheerfully*]: Good-bye. Good-bye. It's been very good of you to come.

MAUREEN: Good-bye Mrs Ellis.

[MRS ELLIS *nods and, having collected the cups, etc., carries the tray out to the kitchen.*

ARNIE *nods cheerfully, standing to one side as they leave. Left alone, he walks up and down a moment, then goes to the fire, gazing down. There are sounds of farewell from the hall, then* JOAN *enters.*]

JOAN: Do you want some more tea?

ARNIE: What? I don't know.

JOAN: Soon, there'll be nobody coming here at all.

ARNIE: No. No. That's quite true.

JOAN: Where did you manage to find that?

ARNIE: I extracted it.

JOAN: Yes?

ARNIE: From the dustbin.

JOAN: My father had a sword.

ARNIE: Yes?

JOAN: When I was young. [*Pause.*] He could hold it at full stretch, in one hand, without the tip even quivering, and count slowly to a hundred.

ARNIE: I look behind me, Joan.

JOAN: What?

ARNIE: I live. I go along. I look behind. ... And I see ... not achievements towering in my path.

JOAN: No ...

ARNIE: Ruins. I can see ... wonderful.

[*A vision rises before his eyes. Finally, slowly, he sits down.*]

If I raise you to the status of a queen, do you think you could be realistic?

[JOAN *takes the remainder of the things into the kitchen.*

ARNIE *sits alone, abstracted, still, the sword in his hand.*

After some little while JOAN *comes out followed by* MRS ELLIS.]

JOAN: Arnie ...? Is there anything else you want?

ARNIE [*pause*]: What?

JOAN: My mother has something to tell you.

ARNIE: What?

MRS ELLIS: Arnie ... [*Looks concernedly at* JOAN, *then clenches her own hands.*] I ... we've ... I'll be leaving tomorrow.

ARNIE: What? What? Who said that? Who!

MRS ELLIS: Arnie. I'll be going tomorrow. I've found a room.

ARNIE: I could have sworn . . .

MRS ELLIS: It's a small flat, really.

   [ARNIE *looks up.*]

   The place I've found.

ARNIE: It's you! It's you!

MRS ELLIS: Joan helped me to find it. And . . .

ARNIE: Look. You are, or are you not, *positively speaking*?

MRS ELLIS: I . . . It's already furnished.

ARNIE: Well . . . at least that's clear. It would have been alarming, Joan, at this late hour, to have discovered . . . of all things . . . that I suffered from hallucinations.

MRS ELLIS: I think it's the best for all of us.

ARNIE: I'm sure. Yes. Yes. I'm sure. I'm sure. [*Suddenly.*] We've had a good time, Edie.

MRS ELLIS: Yes.

ARNIE [*taps side of his head*]: I had something then on the tip of my tongue. No. No. It's gone. It's gone.

MRS ELLIS: It's not so far away . . . that I can't pop in from time to time.

ARNIE: No. No. I'm sure. We have, after all . . . what have we? . . . What? This is extraordinary. After all these years.

JOAN: Yes.

ARNIE: I'd say . . .

JOAN: Yes?

ARNIE: That that was a revolution.

JOAN: Yes.

ARNIE: Or a revelation. I'm not sure which. [*Pause.*] Ahem! [*Pause.*] I better make a speech. A moment like this . . . Can scarcely go by. Unacknowledged.

JOAN: I don't think it's necessary, Arnie.

   [ARNIE *has stood up.*]

ARNIE: No? [*He puts down his sword.*] This is a very heavy sentence, Edie.

MRS ELLIS: I'm not sure . . .

ARNIE: On us. On us. I might well have to make amendments. To the constitution. To accommodate that.

   [*He holds the top of his head.*]

It had been my intention . . . to leucotomize my wife.

MRS ELLIS: Yes . . .

ARNIE: Amongst several other . . . As it is . . .

[*Gazes up at them from beneath his hands.*]

We better have a party.

MRS ELLIS: After I've gone.

ARNIE: Yes. Yes. After you've gone.

MRS ELLIS: I'll . . . go up. I've still some things to finish.

ARNIE: Yes. Yes.

[*She goes.*
Silence. Then:]

Back to school. Monday!

JOAN: Yes.

ARNIE: Rest. Recuperation . . . Work!

JOAN: Yes.

[*Silence. Then, suddenly:*]

ARNIE: Oh! [*Cries out.*]

JOAN: Arnie!

ARNIE: Oh! There's something coming out!

JOAN: Arnie . . .

ARNIE: Oh, dear, Joan.

JOAN: Arnie . . . It's all right.

ARNIE: Oh, dear, Joan. There's something here . . . that's very hard . . . Merciless.

JOAN: Arnie . . . It's all right.

ARNIE: Oh, dear, oh!

[*He covers up his head.*]

JOAN: Arnie.

ARNIE: Oh, dear. Oh, dear. There's something. What? Oh, dear. There's something coming out.

JOAN: Arnie.

[*He looks up, still holding his head.*]

Come on, now.

ARNIE: Oh. Oh.

[*His hands are clasped to the top of his head.*]

What am I to do?

JOAN: Here.

[*She holds out her hand.*]

ARNIE: Oh. *Now*. [*Screams, hugely. Then:*]
JOAN: It's all over.
ARNIE: Oh, dear.
  [*After a moment he lowers one hand.*]
  Oh I'm sure . . . I think.
JOAN: Yes.
ARNIE: In all sincerity.
  [*He calms. He looks slowly round.*]
  Nevertheless. I'm assuming that I can come out. The assumption is merely based, you understand, on a generality of feeling.
JOAN: Yes.
ARNIE: Oh.

> Oh, lovely woman . . . feel no obligation;
> Beauty is its own salvation.
> The rest is meant to burn.

  I can't hear a thing.
JOAN: Are you coming up?
ARNIE: Up?
JOAN: Yes.
ARNIE: Have I finished?
  [*He looks around.*]
JOAN: Yes.
ARNIE: I've finished?
JOAN: I think so.
ARNIE: Are you sure?
JOAN: Yes.
  [*They stand facing one another, still some distance apart.*]
ARNIE: Oh. Joan. Thank God.
  [*Fade.*]

PETER TERSON

The Mighty Reservoy

The Mighty Reservoy was first produced at the Victoria Theatre, Stoke-on-Trent, on 29 September 1964, with the following cast:

DRON	Bernard Gallagher
CHURCH	Gordon Reid

Directed and designed by Peter Cheeseman

The action of the play takes place on top of the Reservoir and inside DRON's Shed.

ACT ONE

On top of the Reservoir.

DRON: Now, careful, we're up.

CHURCH: Yes.

DRON: Now steady on there. See how it is?

CHURCH: Magnificent.

DRON: Big ent it?

CHURCH: It's like some huge tortoise.

DRON: It's like a pig's belly upside down ent it?

CHURCH: Yes. A huge static tortoise. Very impressive.

DRON: Bloody big thing tho', ent it?

CHURCH: Big indeed.

DRON: Now, careful on. Hey. – What's that bloody stink? Get the muck off your boots. Slip from here and you'd slide to your severe injury man. Straight over the edge you'd go.

CHURCH: My goodness. Up here. What a sight. I'm glad I met you. I've often seen this from the walk.

DRON: Told you I'd show it to you didn't I now? Told you. Nobody else could have showed you this reservoy you know. Nobody else.

CHURCH: I highly appreciate it.

DRON [*sniff*]: Have you cleaned them boots yet? All the muck off?

CHURCH: Yes. I think so.

DRON: Christ, you're not cleaning your dancing slippers you know boy. Get 'em cleaned like this.

CHURCH: Yes. I see.

DRON: Pull the muck off your boots when you come to the top of this reservoy, there's my rule plainly stated. My number one rule.

CHURCH: Yes. Quite. I see. Very wise.

DRON: Even if my own father came up here; my own flesh and blood. I'd say to him, 'Father,' I'd say, 'Scrape the muck off your boots afore you come to the top of this reservoy.' That's what I'd say. First rule.

CHURCH: *Very* wise indeed.

DRON: Wise?

CHURCH: A very wise precaution.

DRON: I'm glad you say wise. Would you say as how it's intelligent?

CHURCH: I would indeed.

DRON: I mean you are a man as what you would say was educated. I mean, I've heard it said, actually heard it, the actual words, I've heard it said, 'That Churchill, the new feller, is an educated man.' I've heard them very words so what I say is true. But you've just said as how my rule was intelligent.

CHURCH: Yes. Quite definitely.

DRON: Well, if you, an educated, intelligent man yourself, says my words is intelligent then that must of natural fact make me intelligent in your eyes in my sphere as it were all taken as all.

CHURCH: Yes? I think it a very intelligent rule.

DRON: Not 'very'. I aint pushing it.

CHURCH: Well, intelligent rule.

DRON: *Right*. Muck off your boots. Now, if you're ready. I'm going to mount up this ... this ... er ... don't tell me. The bit that curves on a building ... like ... like a roof ... no ... don't tell me. . . . Like St Paul's. You know. The top. The curve bit. Like this. I got it ... it's coming to me ... it's ... you know ... yes ...

CHURCH: Dome.

DRON: Dome. I got it. It's like a dome. We're going to the top of the dome. I knew that you see. I worked on the building of this last year.

CHURCH: How interesting.

DRON: Yeah. Yeah. I was on it. There was an engineer on it. Scotsman lived on the site. On a caravan. Family up in Glasgow. Never bothered with them much though. When a thing as big as a reservoy claims your life that's it mate. Minor things go by the board I'm telling you. Good man. Drank though. Whisky you see. Good man on reservoys though. Very very good on reservoys! Anyway, he used to say, in his Scottish voice, like, I can't make it out very well like, but he used to say, 'We'll soon be at the dome.' That wasn't very Scottish was it?

CHURCH: It was alright.

DRON: I cannot make on Scotch very much. But that's what he used to say. 'We'll be on that bloody dome soon Dron,' he'd say to me, 'That's the killer Dron,' he would say, 'The bloody dome's the killer. Och,' he'd say, 'Any sod can build the bottom of a

reservoy but it's the dome that tells the men from the bloody boys.'
He was a sod. Lived here in the caravan all on his pat. They reckon
he made eighty a week.

CHURCH: *God*, eighty a week. How puny that makes my salary.

DRON: You're alright tho' aren't you? Nice office job. In the dry.

CHURCH: There is no eighty a week.

DRON: Well – he made eighty a week. Mind you he was the top man
at his job. Left Scotland you know. Built reservoys all over the
world. Birmingham, London, Cardiff, places like that. He's been
all over. Built one for the blacks once I think. But then, he was a
top man. Is that muck off your boots?

CHURCH: Yes.

DRON: You'll see the village from up here.

CHURCH: *Really?*

DRON: Yeah. See it all? Roofs like. Not wall, it's so high you see
roofs. And the smoke is sort of coming up at you. Like, slanting.
Now, go bloody careful. 'Cos I'm responsible for you.

CHURCH: I suppose you are.

DRON: Bloody am mate.

CHURCH: *To* you then.

DRON: All the muck off your boots?

CHURCH: Yes.

DRON: What nice boots. Where did you get them?

CHURCH: Town. Smythes.

DRON: Them bloody twisters? They're no good! If you want a pair
of boots you should have gone to the Growers' Co-operative see?
Cheaper see. For the Growers.

CHURCH: I thought the Growers' Co-op was just for the growers
themselves?

DRON: Hell! No. Anybody can go there. Not know that?

CHURCH: No.

DRON: Anybody can go to the Growers' Co-operative for a pair of
boots. For anything come to that. Don't care who you are. Don't
care if you're a bloody chorus girl you can still go there, money
down, 'Pair of boots please and no messing.' Bloody vicar could go
in. Now they'd know he wasn't no grower in his collar but they
couldn't refuse him. You were a daft sod going into town. There's
a shilling bus fare for a start.

CHURCH: I hadn't thought.

DRON: Ah well, you've heard what happened to the man who didn't think haven't you?

CHURCH: No.

DRON: He messed his pants.

CHURCH: Ha. Very witty.

DRON: Now, careful. There should be a ladder up here but they aint got it yet. That's why these planks is still here. Be safe with a ladder.

CHURCH: Yes, a ladder would be useful.

DRON: Never mind useful. There should be a ladder up here. But there aint. We should not be on here without a ladder. It says so in the book of rules. 'Man will not go on dome of reservoy without ladder being thereon.' It says in black and white. If we were to fall off there'd be no insurance you know. Oh no. No insurance. The company would take one look. 'No ladder,' they'd say. 'That's your lot. No insurance. Get stuffed.'

CHURCH: I suppose they would.

DRON: Bloody would mate. Too big a risk. Smooth. Feel it. Just feel it. So smooth man.

CHURCH: It is remarkably smooth.

DRON: You'd slide off that like off a kipper's arse. That's why I'm holding myself responsible for you.

CHURCH: Oh I'm sure I will be alright.

DRON: Smooth as a billiard ball this is mate. Mind you, mind you, the Scotsman would have had a ladder on. 'Right, Dron,' he'd have said, 'Whip up there and get a ladder on afore you take your friend up.' When he went things just fell to pieces. Look, they ent tidied up the mess yet. Not tidied up a drop of it. He would have had this lot shiften. I tell you. And a ladder up.

CHURCH: But why did he leave?

DRON: Leave? I'll tell you that tale later. It'll keep. Do you take a drink? It'll keep for a drink. Do you take a drink?

CHURCH: Occasionally, but we don't budget for drink in our house really.

DRON: Budget my arse. Not asking you to pay for it. I got a little bit of drink on tap in the shed. Drop of plum wine. Not a lot you know. Just a drop for when I get a sweat on. Or I like to eat with a friend and have a drop. In fact I'm expecting a friend up tonight.

Very good man he is. He'll be up. He as good as promised. Said he'd
be up. Top grower he is. Now he'd tell you you could go into the
Growers and get yourself a pair of boots any time and he knows,
cos he's not just a bloody swede man he's a top grower. The best.

CHURCH: Really?

DRON: Oh yeah. Perce. Top Grower. Yes, he'll be up for a drop of
wine. We'll probably see him from the top here.

CHURCH: Don't let me butt in.

DRON: Butt in be buggered. No he'll be pleased to meet an educated
man like you. Good talker he is. Chairman of the Glasshouse
Growers' Association. Wears a bow tie for 'do's'. He'll be up here
for a drink.

CHURCH: I'd like to meet him.

DRON: You will. Hey – have you got a head for heights?

CHURCH: Quite good thanks.

DRON: Hell. Nearly forgot to ask. Well never mind the view. Keep
your eye on me. Just watch my arse all the way up. I didn't mean
that dirty. Just an expression. . . . You alright then?

[*They climb up to the top.*]

CHURCH: Yes. Made it.

DRON: *Here* we are then. Top of the world this is. Top of the world.
Tibet is second.

CHURCH: The view is glorious.

DRON: Better than the pictures isn't it?

CHURCH: Yes.

DRON: Better than the telly anyways.

CHURCH: Much, much better than the telly.

DRON: Well you couldn't get a patch of this on telly. . . . Clouds and
that . . .

CHURCH: It's marvellous. They're the Malvern Hills aren't they?

DRON: Yes, and that's the wireless tower where we gets all us wireless
from. The Archers comes from there mate. Not many folks as
knows that is there?

CHURCH: The Malverns look so beautiful.

DRON: Yeah, you should see the mast in the dark with its aeroplane
lights on, real beautiful as you say.

CHURCH: And surely they're the Cotswolds?

DRON: Oh them's the Cotswolds alright. And up there mate is

another water reservoy. Not as big as this though. At Blockley. Famous reservoy, Blockley be and I'll tell you for why not long from now.

CHURCH: The Cotswolds roll away don't they?

DRON: That one at Blockley was famous afore they built this one. Well, still is famous like, but, them Blockley fellers don't half get mad when I tell them I'm in charge of this 'un. That shuts them up.

CHURCH: Look at the Vale. Look, the wind of the river. With mist beginning to cling to it. Like a snake in the haze.

DRON: They don't get no snakes round these parts. But that stinking putrid river. Believe it or not, provides drinking water for the Army Camp.

CHURCH: Look at the Vale towards Evesham. Look at the glass.

DRON: Fields of glass down there man. Fields of it. Why in my old feller's day (and that wasn't so long ago if you count seventy young enough) there weren't a pane of glass down there, now, it's fields of it.

CHURCH: Yes. They must do well.

DRON: Look, I'll show you my friend's place. Perce. The man as said he would drop up. See, now, follow the road, yes. Past the pub. Over by the river, now come up, no too far, yes, back a bit. Now. See that bungalow? With all them straw bales there? Now all that glass and all that land is my friend Perce's. You might see him. See him? No? He might be in one of the glass houses. He's got glass man. Acres of glass. You couldn't find enough soil for a worm to turn in as hasn't got a piece of glass over it. He's the best. I'm expecting him up tonight. Percy his name is. I'll introduce him. To, er, Mr Churchill eh? To Perce?

CHURCH: Oh, Church, make it Church.

DRON: I'll introduce him then. Good feller Perce is. Very go ahead. Very enthusiastic. Wires his tomatoes up on the trot. On the trot he does. He said he'd be up for a drop so we'll be alright, Church.

CHURCH: How interesting. What are all the bales of straw for?

DRON: Makes glasshouses out of them.

CHURCH: How does he make glasshouses out of straw then?

DRON: New method. Perce's method. Shouldn't be telling you really.

CHURCH: Oh well, please ... you know ...

DRON: Well Perce won't mind, he's a good friend. See, he gets his
straw bales you see, makes a couple of high walls out of straw and
lights across the top. You know lights? Big sheets of glass lights is.
They call them lights. Just for a name. Lights. They's just big
sheets of glass but they calls them lights. Puts them across, these
lights, these big sheets of glass, he's got a glasshouse, out of straw.
Straw keeps the tomatoes warm. Heat off the straw see? Did I say
tomatoes? Footballs. They are, footballs. The race to market hasn't
even started when Perce gets there.

CHURCH: I'd like to meet him.

DRON: You will do. I'll take you down for a little drink in the shed
and Perce will be up. You and him will get on well. He'm bloody
Chairman of the Glasshouse Growers' Association. Ole Perce. Not
that he's old. He's in his prime. 'Bout my age. No older. Man in his
prime. Strings his tomatoes on the trot. Beautiful eating tomatoes.
Beautiful.

CHURCH: I'm glad I've met you tonight. I've lived here for three years
and not got the touch of the country really.

DRON: Pleased you came. I think the village should know about its
civic amenities. But they're not interested. Beautiful it looks this
from Blockley hilltop. Beautiful. You can see it from right beyond.
But they don't care. They don't know. You know where Blockley
is do you?

CHURCH: I know the village. Has a Norman Church hasn't it?

DRON: Don't know about Church but it has a famous reservoy I
tell you. Now, look, see that tower there. Where? Where is it?
Where you gone you bugger? Broadway tower. Where is it hid?
It should be there. Well, ah, yes. It's in them trees. Funny how
things change from up a height ent it? It is though ent it? Funny how
things change from up a height? I mean, from down on the floor of
the vale there that tower stands out a mile don't it? But from here,
Christ, you lose it in the trees. But that's life ent it? Now, you see it?

CHURCH: I see Broadway Tower yes.

DRON: Well, over behind there is Blockley Reservoy. Now from
the Reservoy there you should see this. Beautiful it do look.

CHURCH: One would never realize.

DRON: Well you wouldn't would you? You talk about the Malvern
Hills mate, you should see this. But the village don't know.

CHURCH: I've often walked past it. But never been right up.

DRON: Any time. Any time you want to come up, just call on me. I'm here all nights. I'm here. Where was you going tonight when I saw you?

CHURCH: Just walking.

DRON: Just walking. What do you want to walk for?

CHURCH: Exercise.

DRON: Bloody hell. You mustn't work hard enough mister. I'm damned if I'd walk in the country for exercise. Or anything else. Just come up here to work.

CHURCH: There's a lot to be said for that. Walking is rather aimless. I find it so. I would like to come up here for a purpose I suppose.

DRON: That's up to you ent it? I come up here every night, to work, work, and look after the reservoy.

CHURCH: You have land up here?

DRON: I have a piece yeah. I had a piece down in the vale too as my old man had in his day: but, you know, I got rid of that, and I just come up here now. That's my bit see? Where them barrels is outside the shed. That's mine down to them plum trees. Them's mine and all.

CHURCH: It's a bit overgrown isn't it?

DRON: Overgrown? Time of the year. 'Sides I'm a busy man. 'Sides I've got the Waterworks job see. 'Sides, it's the time of the year. 'Sides it might look overgrown to you like, but to the expert eye, there's purpose there you see. Plan. 'Sides, this Waterworks job is a big job in itself.

CHURCH: Oh yes, what do you do on the Waterworks?

DRON: I move all around the area mate. Diggin' mains, settin' in pipes, tappin' and drillin'. As far as the eye can see from here is my territory. Blockley, and beyond, the Malverns, up there into the smoky Midlands, mine, all mine.

CHURCH: And at nights you are in charge of the reservoir?

DRON: I am. I am indeed.

CHURCH: A responsible job.

DRON: Responsible? You tell them down there that, not me. I'll say it's responsible. Oh they think I just sit up here on my arse watching the bloody water.

CHURCH: But they're wrong?

DRON: Oh, they're a set of twerps. Sitting down there. Watchin' telly. Goin' to church. But it's not every man as could look after a reservoy this size. Do you know there is over 500,000 gallons of water in here?

CHURCH: 500,000 gallons? That's a lot.

DRON: That's a lot of water. Well, what's going to happen if there's a burst?

CHURCH: It's very well made.

DRON: Don't tell me it's very well made. I know it's very well made. I helped to mix the concrete to make it. But what if there's a burst as you can get in the very best of structures? It would sweep that village down. It would rush down that path you came up, like a river, a torrent, sweep them away, women and children in their beds. Babies asleep. Sweep them away. But it's me as sits here and gives the alarm. There's an alarm here you know.

CHURCH: Is there really?

DRON: Oh yes. Oh yes. An alarm. For which I have the key. There it is. Alarm in that box. It's me as looks after that as well. You and your well-built. What would they have an alarm for if it wasn't going to burst? Eh? Now you tell me that. What would it have an alarm for if it wasn't going to burst?

CHURCH: There's truth in that. But perhaps it's a laid down procedure.

DRON: They don't lay down procedures for nothing do they? Eh? Now you tell me a procedure that's laid down for nothing. Go on. I'll give you a minute to think on it. Give me a procedure that they lay down for nothing and I'll give you a quid.

CHURCH: Well, I must say.

DRON: No. Uh. Let's be fair. I'll give you a minute. You give me a procedure that they lay down for nothing and I have a quid waiting to be claimed. It's got your name on it.

CHURCH: Well, one could think of the sand bucket in huge buildings.

DRON: Don't know what you're on about.

CHURCH: You know, in some huge buildings they have sand buckets for fire precautions but they wouldn't do any good at all.

DRON: Ah, would they not though.

CHURCH: Not effectively. We have a set in our office blocks.

DRON: What? Sand?

CHURCH: Buckets.

DRON: Full of sand?

CHURCH: Yes. And I'm sure if a fire broke out, they'd be no use at all. The office would go up like tinder.

DRON: Depends on the size of the fire don't it? I mean, if you dropped a cigarette end, you could nip it out with sand afore the building caught alight. Couldn't you?

CHURCH: Yes. But surely.

DRON: Surely nothing. I'd say that was a very wise procedure. I would.

CHURCH: But a fag end, you could stand on it.

DRON: Ah yeah, but folks isn't going to go round standing on fag ends with their best shoes on is they? I mean, if you put yourself in their place. What right has anybody to ask you to put out a fire with your shoes?

CHURCH: Well, yes. I see that. But a fag end is nothing.

DRON: No, it's a matter of correct procedure you see. You put sand buckets up and say, 'In case of fire, chuck sand on it.' It's correct procedure. But if you put a notice up; 'In case of fire, stand on it.' That's a liberty. No. No. No. Now listen. That is correct procedure. Same as the alarm up here.

CHURCH: Well, perhaps I'll give you that.

DRON: I'm bloody sure you will mate. I mean, just because it's made of concrete means nothing. That's what them down there in the village think; 'Oh,' they think. 'It's made of concrete, it'll be alright.' But even the strongest of things can go astray. I mean, the Leaning Tower of Pisa, nobody expected that bugger to lean, but it did. The Bridge of Sighs, nobody expected that to go round sighing, but there you are. The Titanic. Dunkirk. I could name you a hell of a lot. The Shifting Sands. There's no telling the forces of Nature.

CHURCH: Yes. Quite so.

DRON: Well. But they never know that. They just don't EVEN THINK. I bet you've never thought of the matter?

CHURCH: The Reservoir?

DRON: The reservoy, the whole system of water supply, the lot. All the implyings.

CHURCH: Oh yes. Yes.

DRON: You don't mean to tell me that when you turn your tap on you think to yourself, 'that water's nice tonight', or 'it's coming out well'?

CHURCH: Oh, I think I'm well aware of it. You know. I remember when we first got the supply, it was much better than previously.

DRON: Ah well, that's pleasing news.

CHURCH: I often remember us having to fill bathfuls during the day because they turned it off at night. But they don't do it now.

DRON: No. No. Oh good. You're a good feller. Course you're not a native though are you? That's it. You're not a native.

CHURCH: No. I've just moved in in recent years.

DRON: That's it you see. The natives don't give a damn. Why, the drought was caused by them watering their land. I've seen them water grass. I've seen them water grass. My heart wept.

CHURCH: Don't *you* use water on the land?

DRON: Nah. Not good soil for water up here. Too high. Down in the vale you want to water. There's fellers down there making gold out of water.

CHURCH: But the land you sold. Wasn't that good with water?

DRON: That was before the reservoy. Water wasn't used like that then. Course if I had it now it would be different. I'd be worth gold. But I'm attached to the Waterworks now. I'm happy with the kit I've got.

CHURCH: Yes.

DRON: I'm glad you saw that about the water supply. It shows you're not a native.

CHURCH: Oh no. I'm not a native.

DRON: How do you like it here then? Alright be it? Here?

CHURCH: Quite nice thank you.

DRON: Course you got one of them new houses outside the village haven't you?

CHURCH: They're very comfortable.

DRON: Got all the convenience and that have they? Fridge and that?

CHURCH: Oh yes. Yes.

DRON: Electric good is it? All electric?

CHURCH: It's a very good supply.

DRON: Very neat little row of houses. Make the rest of the village look a bloody shambles.

CHURCH: They're very trim.

DRON: Nice bit of garden?

CHURCH: Yes.

DRON: Not too much and not too little?

CHURCH: That's it.

DRON: Enough to potter about in that's what you want.

CHURCH: Yes.

DRON: Not too much and not too little. A bit of veg. Eh?

CHURCH: Fresh veg is nice.

DRON: Oh yes. There's nothing like a bit of home grown. And a patch of lawn at the front?

CHURCH: Yes. My wife does that.

DRON: Keeps you busy nights?

CHURCH: Oh yes. It always needs trimming.

DRON: Just keeping down. That's the thing. Just keeping down.

CHURCH: Yes.

DRON: And you travel to Cheltenham to work?

CHURCH: Yes I do.

DRON: But it's nice to live in the country?

CHURCH: Hoh yes, my wife and I fancied a house in the country.

DRON: Well, if you got what you fancy there's a lot in it.

CHURCH: Well indeed, precisely.

DRON: You'll have a little car to take you in? To Cheltenham like?

CHURCH: Yes. It doesn't take an hour.

DRON: Bit of upkeep on it though?

CHURCH: Oh yes, keeps you stretched.

DRON: Your wife goes in with you does she? To help out a bit?

CHURCH: Well . . . yes. Yes. She does.

DRON: Well that's the way to do it isn't it? Both pull a bit like.

CHURCH: Yes.

DRON: You have to haven't you? I mean, like, fair's fair. Works near you does she?

CHURCH: In the same office actually.

DRON: Hah. Yes. Well, there's some fellers as likes to see a lot of their wife. Very nice if you're built that way.

CHURCH: Oh yes. It's, you know . . .

DRON: No kids then?

CHURCH: Well, you know how it is. Best to get a little house first, and the car paid off.

DRON: Very wise. Long as you don't leave it too late.

CHURCH: We're trying now though.

DRON: Oh. Good luck.

CHURCH: Thank you. We thought we'd start one before it's too late.

DRON: That's your house there, isn't it? Middle one in the row?

CHURCH: Yes. That's it.

DRON: That your wife in the garden? Just a speck?

CHURCH: Yes. Yes it is. I thought I'd have a night off you know.

DRON: Nice pretty gel, must have looked nice when she was younger.

CHURCH: Thank you.

DRON: Well then. It is getting chilly here.

CHURCH: Yes. The sky looks glorious. The Malverns are fading.

DRON: I wish them lights would come on the wireless mast.

CHURCH: And look at the Cotswolds. How magnificently they roll away.

DRON: You should see the reservoy up there.

CHURCH: And the Avon. The mist is climbing on it isn't it?

DRON: Bloody army camp drinks that muck.

CHURCH: It's a most beautiful sky.

DRON: Wish there was an aeroplane in it. With its lights on.

CHURCH: The village looks ancient, and indestructible down there.

DRON: Bloody dark hole. Got woodworm from the Church to the Manor House. They ought to have the lot down. Bulldozers on the job and make nice bungalows like yourn. Can't see Perce anywheres, can you?

CHURCH: No.

DRON: He's a great worker. He likes working while there's light. He'll be up though – he said he'd be up. Now wait a minute before you go. I'm going to show you something. Something as I don't readily show people.

CHURCH: Oh. What is it?

DRON: Inside. In – side. The water. It's a beautiful night.

[DRON and CHURCH *climb down to where there is an iron trapdoor in the reservoir.*]

This door is heavy. I want you to watch this. Now, stand there and you'll get the best view.

[DRON *heaves open the hatch. Metallic clanging echo roars out round them.*]

CHURCH: Goodness.

DRON: Looks impressive, like. Don't it?

CHURCH: Yes.

DRON: 500,000 gallons there. Lot of water for a man to look after I tell you. Lot of water for a man to look after.

[DRON *lowers hatch. Roaring again.*]

What if it should crack eh? They never ask themselves that. If it should crack. Oh, no. Wash away the village it would. There's a natural channel down there, whoosh, church first thing hit, no respecter of religion water isn't. Water must find its own resting. There's a thought. Water must find its own restin'.

CHURCH: Yes indeed.

DRON: And it don't matter what's in the way it'll take it. No messing. Water, must find its own restin'.

CHURCH: What were those things down there?

DRON: I'll show you in a minute and you'll see. I'll show you again. Right. [*Opens hatch. Roar.*] Up it comes. See, measurement.

CHURCH: Yes. I see the measurement thing.

DRON: See that thing like a ruler? Measurement. Look, read, it's at nineteen, nineteen. That's the measurement then you see? Nineteen.

CHURCH: Yes, but those float things. What are they?

DRON: All to do with measurement you see. It's all measurements.

CHURCH: How *do* the floats work?

DRON: They works with that ruler thing. You see? Measurement. It says nineteen. That's measurement. See.

CHURCH: Yes. You don't know how exactly?

DRON: Of course I know how exactly. It's to do with measurement. Them floats, although you can't see, is to do with that ruler thing. Nineteen feet. I was there when they put them in. The Scotty did it. Course I know it. Measurement.

CHURCH: Yes.

DRON: Beautiful though eh? Before I put it down. Beautiful ent it?

CHURCH: It's very nice.

DRON: I could come and watch that every night. Pure water you know. 500,000 gallons of it standing at nineteen. Isn't it bloody amazing eh? This beautiful mass of water, looking solid there's so much of it. And they don't know. There could be a crack in there, and they'd be gonners.

CHURCH: Indeed.

DRON: There was cracks in it when they first filled it you know.

CHURCH: Go on. Never?

DRON: There was cracks in there when they first filled it. Oh yes. That's how I got this job. Because when they first filled it I was detailed, seeing as how my land was near, to come and watch it. Give an alarm to the engineers see if anything went wrong. Not to the village. 'Cos it was just filling. But to the Scotsman and his fellers. He used to live up here with a van, as I might have said.

CHURCH: Did the crack fill up then?

DRON: Oh yes. Yes. We saw to that. They allus get cracks in when they's first filled in see. It's er, wetness of the water, and the new concrete see and one goes ... and the other ... forces and that. Cracks. I sat and watched them cracks. Nights. But they filled in alright.

CHURCH: Wonderful.

DRON: Of course if it happened now it would be serious. Now it's dry. Terrible man. Sweep the women and kiddies from their beds it would. Torrent. You know Frejus? When a dam burst? Frejus. Bloody disaster it was. Oh yes. That's what it would be down there. Just wreckage, and people scratting about after looking for their few belongings and loved ones. Yes sir. Just devastation in the wake of the flood. That's how they puts it. Devastation in the wake of the flood.

[DRON *closes hatch. Roar.*]

CHURCH: So vast a natural thing is frightening isn't it?

DRON: 500,000 gallons.

CHURCH: I was brought up, living on a coal field. My father was a miner.

DRON: A miner. Now there's good. I thought perhaps he'd be a clerk or a doctor or something.

CHURCH: A miner. We kids were brought up on a coal seam, and this is the same feeling. A natural force working below. It was like living on an underground mountain.

DRON: Do you realize that we are standing on a mountain of water? A great lump of water. It's a killer all that water. But it's contained. You see? Contained. Like. Controlled. And I'm the man as looks to it. Christ, if that measurement ever left nineteen man this damn reservoy could kill. The pressure would crack it and then, the torrent. Look at that damned view.

CHURCH: It looks beautiful in this half light.

DRON: You can't see the Blockley reservoy in this light.

CHURCH: Look at the steel blue of the sky before the dark creeps up over the Malverns.

DRON: The lights will be going on over them aerial masts soon.

CHURCH: See, how the Cotswolds are shadowed already.

DRON: Later on you will be able to see them orange lights on the motorways. A great line of orange lights. We have our big sifting beds over there. Beautiful sight.

CHURCH: The village, wraps itself in a mist. The church, like a slimy snail drawing in its horns for the night. (Dylan Thomas.)

DRON: Who's he?

CHURCH: A writer. He said something like that. The church like a snail.

DRON: You read much?

CHURCH: I like . . . poetry. A bit.

DRON: Perce writes for the Glasshouse Growers' Gazette. He's a writer. How to bring the tomatoes on and that. Real poetic. You'll meet him when he comes up.

CHURCH: Ha.

DRON: Can you see your missus? Still pottering is she?

CHURCH: Yes. I can see her.

DRON: Nice woman. Must be nice working with her all day? Is it?

CHURCH: Yes.

DRON: Does she let you out at night?

CHURCH: Oh yes. Yes.

DRON: Course you fellers do a lot of that sort of thing don't you?

CHURCH: What sort of thing?

DRON: You know. Being with your wife a lot and that.

CHURCH: Yes.

DRON: You never sort of hit them about, or any of that do you, youse office fellers?

CHURCH: Oh no. We live well-ordered lives.

DRON: Mind you, I got nothing against wives. I mean. I got a wife, you know? Suppose it's nice to be with them a lot like is it? I mean I'm not in a lot.

CHURCH: Oh I like it, quite nice.

DRON: When I pass your place and see it all like a new pin and that house all neat like, I think to myself, I think, 'Lot of time spent on there together.' Like.

CHURCH: It's very nice. But a little limiting.

DRON: Limiting? What's that then?

CHURCH: Well, it's sort of confined you know? You feel after a few months on your garden that perhaps it's an awful lot of time on a little thing.

DRON: I see.

CHURCH: I mean, my wife likes it, she has nice flower beds with geraniums and asters and delphiniums and aquilegias and all sorts of things that I can't even say; and plastic gnomes around a plastic pool with stones and a painted mill.

DRON: I saw that, very bonny.

CHURCH: But I, I, sometimes . . . I, look around; and the rest of the men are *doing* things . . . they're working on their land till last light . . . rotovating, tilling, picking, hoeing, planting. Working up tremendous thirsts then going to sit in the pub and drink sharp cider till dark. Whereas, I . . . you know . . . I never get more than a very dry sweat on in the garden and cocoa can cool my thirst.

DRON: I don't get you like. Who the hell wants to work till dark I'm asking?

CHURCH: You know I, one gets a bit fed up. I don't get out a lot.

DRON: I'm not getting you wrong am I? Keeping you out?

CHURCH: No. Oh no. It's not like that.

DRON: She won't tell you off will she? I mean, I don't want her down my neck.

CHURCH: No, that'll be alright. I. I, we had a bit of a row as a matter of fact.

DRON: Oh oh ho.

CHURCH: Not a big one. We never get sort of nasty with it, or worked up, but, I just said, 'I'm a bit fed up tonight,' and she said, 'Fed up? But there's plenty to do in the garden,' but I said, 'Yes, but I don't want to fiddle about in the garden,' and she said, 'I thought you liked us both working in the garden together? You in the back, me in the front?' and I said, 'Yes I do dear. But, you know, I feel I don't want to do it tonight.' And she said, 'Alright then, neither do I. What shall we do? We can't afford to go out, that's for certain, not this month.' And I said, 'I fancy a walk,' and she said, 'Well, that suits me.' Because she likes walking too, we walk miles together, and so, she tripped up the path, saying, 'I'll get my sandals on,' but I said, 'No. Don't. I want to go . . . alone.'

DRON: Then the row?

CHURCH: That was the row.

DRON: You do live a stormy life son don't you?

CHURCH: This is it isn't it? It's all substitution. Gardens for land, innuendoes for rows, tremors for earthquakes.

DRON: Hah. You talk very cleverly. I'm glad you're up here. When Perce gets up you can have some nice talk the two of you. I'll listen.

CHURCH: What I'm trying to say is that . . . well . . . somehow, everyone else is alive, concerned with the land, but I, I am just fiddling. I tell you, I'd like to *do something real and earnest*. I mean, keeping the plastic gnomes nice and clean isn't exactly life and death.

DRON: Them gnomes of yours looks nice.

CHURCH: Oh, but what I mean is . . . life must be more real. As it is to the men of the land. You don't know what life's about in an office in Cheltenham. 'Good number.' When my father came up at night there was a sense of . . . of communion about him. He'd been down there in the bowels, he'd wrestled with Nature that man had. Whereas me, ha, when I come home at night the most I've wrestled with is a traffic jam on the Cheltenham–Winchcombe Road. Man, he came home like a toiler. Life has got to be real again. More earnest. Man I'm only half living compared with my father. He would laugh at my life. He wouldn't call it a man's life. He would call it a boy's life. A boy's existence.

DRON: You're alright. You got a good number haven't you?

CHURCH: Huh. Good number.

DRON: You're all right. Nice spot in Cheltenham, dry in the winter, what more do you want?

CHURCH: Hah, never mind. Perhaps I ought to take land, land, do a real job of work, get with it. Take to the land.

DRON: There's one thing, you'd be a bloody nut to go down the pit, father or no father.

CHURCH: I see it in the land men Dron, these men know it. They're of the soil, the same as my father was of the coal. They know it still.

DRON: I'd like you to meet Perce. I would. I would like you to meet Perce. He'd put you right.

CHURCH: I don't think you've followed me.

DRON: Perce is the best grower in the district. He made that patch of land of his into a goldmine. He made it pay. Now he has a field of glass and them like bloody diamonds. That's Perce. That land was ash. Ash. But you'm made it pay. Any time of the year you'll see Perce with his village women a picking onions or strawberries or radish or tomatoes or lettuces; why, he beat the Channel Islands to the tomatoes this year. PERCE THE GROWER. He'll be up here. He said. 'Hi Dron,' he said, 'I'll be up there to have a bit of your damson wine tonight.' And he will be. Can you see him?

CHURCH: No. I can't see him.

DRON: No. It's getting dark. Here – I want to show you something else. [*He lifts up the hatch to the reservoir.*] See that? See how black and still it goes when the light is off it?

CHURCH: Yes.

DRON: It's like a living thing see? That's how I see it. A living thing. A giant, as could drown a village. And you know what?

CHURCH: What?

DRON: It's got needs, needs as must be settled. Appeased.

CHURCH: Yes?

DRON: Aaah, you wouldn't know. You'm 'll think I'm talking daft.

CHURCH: Go on, go on, these needs.

DRON: You'm know what it's after? You'm know what it needs?

CHURCH: No, go on.

DRON: You know, you can hear her talking? A nights. If you listen hard enough, you can hear her talking?

CHURCH: Yes. I understand. My father used to say the coal seam talked.

DRON: You'm do know don't you a bit? You'm know feller?

CHURCH: Tell me, what it talks about? What it needs?

DRON: Her talks about her needs, mumbling, talking. You know her needs?

CHURCH: Tell me.

DRON: Have you ever heard of what happened at the Blockley reservoy.

CHURCH: No. What happened at the Blockley reservoir?

DRON: Her had a man.

CHURCH: A man? Was it? A man?

DRON: Her had a man. It was a few months after her was made. Her was heard, like, the locals still talks about it. Her was heard a-groaning and moaning, settling down like. Reservoys must settle. Then one morning, the man in charge, like myself only a Gloucestershire man, went up and had a look in her cos she was mortal quiet like, and there, in the water like this, as if hanging, like this, a man.

CHURCH: Drowned?

DRON: Her had killed him more like it. Oh, the coroner said drown but they all reckon as how had drawn him up there and had him. Her must have her man. Her was satisfied after that. Her had had her man. She allus sounded happy after that. No more grumbling and mumbling. Just sort of like a woman with a baby. Content with it.

CHURCH: Yes I understand. My father always said that the coal seam had life. He knew. I like your reservoir. It's a Mighty Reservoy this one Dron. A mighty reservoy.

[DRON *drops the door.*]

DRON: Now look – no coming up here with muck on your boots. And lissen feller. Never come up here on your own, do you hear boy? And no liftin' this hatch ever, without me. I'm the only hatch lifter. I know this gel. She'm can't have me, she'm wary of me, but you . . . she'd have you in a flash . . .

CHURCH: I was a boy on a coal field. I respect her, Dron.

DRON: Come on, I'll give you a drink of damson boy. Bet your father would have liked that.

CHURCH: He would have liked you Dron. He would have liked you.

DRON: Come on. Not take a minute. Expect your wife wants you back.

CHURCH: I'm wanted back for the news and the play.

DRON: Look, the lights on the aerial mast. Look.

[*They go down.*]

ACT TWO

The Cabin of DRON. *Three large barrels.*

DRON: This be it.

CHURCH: I'm just having a glance at the land.

DRON: Don't glance too hard. It's a bad time of year.

CHURCH: It's terribly overgrown. Nettles and thistles, rhubarb run to seed and everything.

DRON: Bad time of year see? Course it doesn't do no harm to have it lying fallow for a time. Here, a drink. Just one glass, you ent fussy is you?

CHURCH: No. I'll share a glass with any man. Ha ha.

DRON: Red wine or white?

CHURCH: Eh?

DRON: Now I'm asking you, red wine or white. We're not pigs you know, as some folks in the village might be thinking.

CHURCH: But are these the barrels? They're so big.

DRON: Red wine or white?

CHURCH: They must hold fifty gallons surely?

DRON: They did, I've had them a few months. Now, red or white?

CHURCH: How much wine is there here then?

DRON: Well, I'm having bloody red. And there's only one glass.

CHURCH: Oh yes. The red will do me too. Thanks.

DRON: Aha, this is how they do it in hotels see? Red or white. I mean, the best folks do it like this you know. Bishops, and lawyers and earls and that. All have red wine or white wine. We're not pigs.

CHURCH: I say, it looks good.

DRON: Taste that mate.

CHURCH: Phew. Strong.

DRON: Damson. Nice drop of damson that? Nice would you say?

CHURCH: Very nice. It's so strong and sharp.

DRON: Well, damson is strong and sharp. That's the characteristics of damson. You know your wine mate.

CHURCH: I made some when I first came here. Dandelion, cowslip and rose petal.

DRON: God Almighty. Maiden's water.

123

CHURCH: Ha ha. That's just what my father would have said. He would have liked this though. This would have set him going.

DRON: How much did you make?

CHURCH: A gallon of each.

DRON: Ha! Go steady man. You'll get the cat drunk.

CHURCH: But this is such a huge amount.

DRON: Not really, I got friends. Here, drink up.

CHURCH: After you.

DRON: Well, you go half way down. Then I'll finish.

CHURCH: It's very nice. But I thought that you shouldn't drink home made wine in tumblers? Just in wine glasses.

DRON: Wine glasses my arse, they'm cut your lips them's so fine. Know what's the best thing for drinking wine out of? Shall I tell you what's the best thing for drinking wine out of? . . . *jam jars* is the best thing for drinking wine out of.

CHURCH: You don't say?

DRON: Yes. It's the best thing for drinking wine out of, jam, bloody jars. Of course, I got a guest here tonight, so I won't drink out of them jam jars.

CHURCH: Please do Dron. Forget this manners thing man.

DRON: Oh no. I'm not a bloody pig you know. I mean, the village down there's a set of bloody prudes. Cussing a man cos he likes a drink.

CHURCH: But you haven't a bad name in the village have you?

DRON: Bad name? No. Oh no. My father had land in the vale once. No. But they just don't understand. Oh I mean I *care* for them folks down there you know. I *worry* about them. I mean if that level got over nineteen, where would they be? Oh they think highly of the school teacher, 'cos he devotes his life to the kiddies, but what I'm saying is *what about me*? I worry about the kiddies. Water is no respecter and needs a man of high calibre to tend it. But they don't know that.

CHURCH: They're narrow minded Dron. I don't think they even think about the larger issues of life.

DRON: Another thing. They say I sit up here like a pig, but I got red wine haven't I? I got white wine? Is that pigging it?

CHURCH: It's the correct way.

DRON: We'll have another. Now. I think we'll have a drop of white wine. You liked the red wine?

CHURCH: I thought it was like Beaujolais.

DRON: Now that's interesting that. You are a man of perception in drink. I have often said 'What is the difference between my damson and Beaujolais. Why should there be a difference: they're both red ent they?'

CHURCH: Yes. They're both red.

DRON: Shall I tell you the difference? Shall I tell you the difference what them down there, in the Mothers' Union and that don't know? The difference is purely, that Beaujolais is made in France. That is all the difference between the two, but because this is made on Reservoy Hill they don't want to know.

CHURCH: But surely, Beaujolais is made with grapes?

DRON: So what? A grape is just a small damson. That's all; and a white grape is a small plum. In France, grapes is as common as plums is here.

CHURCH: You're quite a philosopher aren't you?

DRON: I been around, I been to France. The bloody Mothers' Union ain't been to France, but I been to France. I fought in France.

CHURCH: My father fought in France in the First World War.

DRON: And I fought in France. That's what them fail to remember. Oh, the Mothers' Union likes the nice fellers who put flowers on the altar and cut the lawns of the green and put stalls up for the fête. But, if it hadn't been for me and your father they'd all be sleeping with Germans now. And not so much of the bloody sleep either. How's that for a white wine?

CHURCH: Should we mix it?

DRON: Course you should mix it. They'm mix well. In hotels and at these big dinners like banquets they mix it; bit of red with the meat, then a bit of white with the fish, then port before and whisky after. Oh it's all right mixing. Don't mind mixing.

CHURCH: And so you were in France in the war?

DRON: France, Germany, the lot mate. Right up there. Always under the bullets. I wasn't one of your home lads or ten miles behind the lines. I was with them.

CHURCH: They called my father up. And as a miner they tried to get him digging trenches, but he deserted and joined up again as an infantryman under a different name.

DRON: What was he in?

CHURCH: The Buffs.

DRON: Up the Buffs. No. Steady the Buffs.

CHURCH: That's right. Happy sound. Steady the Buffs. He was always laughing and saying 'Steady the Buffs'. He was a tough nut. When he was out of work, and things were real hard, he would go walking miles and miles, scratching round the slag heaps for coal and then pushing it into Newcastle on his bike to sell; then he would come home, whacked, grin, and say, 'Steady the Buffs'.

DRON: I was with the Buffs.

CHURCH: You were with the Buffs?

DRON: I was with the Buffs, I was with the commandos.

CHURCH: You were with the Buffs and the commandos?

DRON: I was with the commandos and the Buffs and the para-troopers.

CHURCH: You fought with those?

DRON: I was allus under fire. That's what the women down there don't realize. That I was under fire with the Buffs, the paratroopers and the commandos. They don't, or won't realize that.

CHURCH: You were with them?

DRON: All the time. From France to Berlin. Don't give me nothing about grapes. I know grapes. They're just small plums.

CHURCH: What were you in?

DRON: Oh, I was attached to them you see.

CHURCH: Yes. But what were you in?

DRON: It's a long story as a matter of fact. Drink up. You like that white wine?

CHURCH: It is a quality wine.

DRON: Quality wine? You think so? Quality eh?

CHURCH: It's not quite so clear as the red.

DRON: You noticed eh? You're a bloody connoisseur. I know a connoisseur when I see one. Not many fellers as would notice how the white was a bit more bodier than the red.

CHURCH: Oh yes. I had noticed. Hmm, this is quite a distinct taste. Quite distinct. It has the quality of gin.

DRON: Do you think so? You know, I'm glad you said that. It's made out of magnum plums. You know? The yeller ones. The equivalent of white grapes really.

CHURCH: Is it really? It's good.

DRON: You know your wine.

CHURCH: It's in my blood to know drink. Must be coming out.

DRON: Your father would have liked this white. He would have liked the red too, but he would have liked the white. I met a lot of the Durham lads. The miners.

CHURCH: Northumberland, he was. Ashington. Northumberland.

DRON: I met a lot of them lads. I fought with them.

CHURCH: You were saying. You were with them.

DRON: Oh yes. Well, I was with the Pioneer Corps at first, you see. Being a land man. Digging and that. But one day, I was sick, so I beefed around the cookhouse, and did a bit. Now I was allus a good cook; specially with a frying pan or an oven made out of an oil drum. So I got attached to the Catering Corps. And because I was so good with oil drum stoves and frying pans they put me on field kitchens, well, there you are. Field kitchens, means up with the lads. I was with them, through France, and Germany, and Berlin. *I've cooked under enemy fire*. I've given a lad a fried egg in the morning then he's died with it still in him. But *they* don't know that. Why doesn't *she* tell them?

CHURCH: She?

DRON: Her. The wife. She's gone and joined the Mothers' Union. Telling them tales about me, how I'm not at home nights and things like that. She doesn't tell them about the bloody front though does she? It's all one way traffic when she's on about me. But there's another side you know. It's not all fun for me being on watch all the time. Sure I never see her, sure I never gets in for tea. But by the time I get from work, come up here, check for cracks, have a little drink, check for the height of nineteen on the measuring stick, have a little drink, mebbe have somebody in like Perce, or yourself, the night is gone. The night is gone. 'Oh,' they say. 'Poor Olive, doesn't see much of him. Poor Olive.' Poor bloody Olive, but it's not her as has the responsibility and the worry of this reservoy. Yes. [*Shouting*] Poor bloody Olive is it? But a wife should stick by her man in his worries and responsibilities and not go talking about him to the old hens. That's in the marriage vows you know bloody Olive. Woman will be faithful to her man and not go cracking about him to the whole bloody force of mothers in the bloody vale.

CHURCH: She tells them about you?

DRON: Boy, you don't know. They've taken her to their bosom. And they've got plenty of that. Hi, wait till your wife's eligible. They'll have her in. You think you lead a quiet life now. Wait till she gets with them son. One kid, that's all it needs. One kid and they call themselves mothers. Mothers.

CHURCH: Yes. We've waited for a child. Eight years wait. Then we'll have *one*. How sensible. How well planned. Ye Gods, I'm thirsty. My father had five by now.

DRON: And still going strong I'll bet he was?

CHURCH: He was. He was. This wine is *great*.

DRON: Drink up, we'll have another.

CHURCH: Look at your reservoy against the night sky.

DRON: Still there be she?

CHURCH: Still there. Looming with menace.

DRON: Go to sleep my beauty. You'm stay a bloody virgin will you. And don't get spiteful and go a splitting and cracking. You know, we'd be the first to go here?

CHURCH: Yes. That's what my father would say of the coal. 'You're sitting on a giant,' he would say, 'an underworld giant,' and laugh. *He knew the forces of life.*

DRON: It would take your house away as well you know.

CHURCH: And welcome. And welcome.

DRON: Them plastic gnomes and white stones. It would settle them.

CHURCH: Yes. It's her little hobby, the front garden. I'm the man of the house, I do the vegetable garden. It's about as big as a twopence-halfpenny stamp.

DRON: She does the front eh? She must have got you to paint them stones white though and that rope yellow.

CHURCH: Oh yes, yes. Er, you don't think it's a bit much do you?

DRON: Bit much? It's smashing mate.

CHURCH: I thought perhaps it was a bit neat.

DRON: Smashing, can tell there's a lot of time spent on it.

CHURCH: Lot of time? A lifetime.

DRON: I think them plastic gnomes of yours are nice. They're the highlight of the village I reckon. Thought highly of in the village too they are. The Mothers' Union likes them.

CHURCH: Ha. Success.

DRON: Yeah, they like them. Them think it's the show garden of the village. They have little contests see like, best garden of the village, and best autumn berry display, and stuff like this. Wonderful displays they get with them berries man. And one of their things is *monumental gardening*. I reckon your wife will win that when she's eligible.

CHURCH: Funny, why does it make me despair so much? Fiddling my life away in a garden. The big land man. Ha. What a substitute. And yet, my father had a garden. I remember it well. On the side of the terrace facing the pit. He had this patch, and he would come back at night, from out that earth, with eight kids in the house; have a bath, and go into the garden before pub times. Now this was a tiny garden, and he was a huge man, and he kept it so *neat*.

DRON: That's where you got it from then.

CHURCH: Yes. But with him it didn't seem pointless. I see him, sitting there, thoughtful before he went out drinking, with his whippet and his pigeon shed painted in black and white stripes for Newcastle United. It never seemed pointless to him.

DRON: Pigeon fancier was he? They like pigeons round here.

CHURCH: But up there, in Northumbria, it was a way of life. These pigeons, whirring round and round the evening sky with the pit heaps pointing past them. Way of life. And it never, never struck me as incongruous. This big man, sitting there. In his patch.

DRON: But he'd worked all bloody day hadn't he?

CHURCH: Worked? He'd fought it out.

DRON: A man needs a bit of a rest and peace and quiet, like solitude as they say, when he's grafted. So he has a garden. You're the other way round. That stuff you do isn't work, not man's work. You make the garden your work.

CHURCH: Dron, you are profound. I make the garden my work. I take exercise, I work out my surplus energies. I take long walks all in the pursuit of sweet, bugger all.

DRON: Walks. Ha, I'd rather walk than work. I'd rather sit than walk, rather kip than sit. But you see, I'm allus watching, this reservoy. That's what I've got my chair here for, so's I can watch it while I'm sitting.

CHURCH: That's a commune with nature man.

DRON: I'm watching. 'Cos if it ever bust; it would sweep it all away.

You'd be hanging on to that yellow rope for your lifeline man. It would be the great flood in that village.

CHURCH: Can you hear it?

DRON: What?

CHURCH: The reservoir?

DRON: Sssh.

CHURCH: You can hear it. On top of us.

DRON: I have never met another man, outside of the water business, who heard the water.

CHURCH: But man, I lived on a mountain of coal. That lived, and moved and sighed . . .

DRON: A drink. You like the magnum?

CHURCH: I like the magnum.

DRON: Now let me get this straight, you said to me that although the damson tasted well, and was clearer, yet, the magnum was the wine of quality.

CHURCH: I said that.

DRON: Then I am going to tell you that in the qualities of wine you are a man of great perception.

CHURCH: Well thank you.

DRON: Get that down you. Then I'll tell you something as will clarify my observations.

CHURCH: I seem to have had such a lot. Such a lot in a short time.

DRON: Nah, you got to get a palate you see. That's what they say in hotels, these colonels and bishops and that. 'Oh, I'm just going to get a palate on,' they say. It's like with women ent it. You got to have a good few layers on afore you can enjoy each one proper. It's like if you've just had your wife, you think you've lived, but you've never had a German girl have you?

CHURCH: Unfortunately not.

DRON: Lovely they are. Lovely. Different quality to an English tart. More body. Same as one wine is different from another. If you've just known English women, you mustn't think you're a world wide knocker, none of it. 'Cos German girls is different. Nice they are.

CHURCH: This was in the war?

DRON: Oh yes, yes. You can't expect not to beat the enemy and not have its women now can you? That Mothers' Union down there think they're powerful but Christ if they Russians invaded this country they'd see how powerful they were. You don't know women, occupied by the soldiery. I seen women in their basic state. Being had. That Mothers' Union, that's not women. That's phoney. But anyway, you get a palate on.

CHURCH: This tastes much smoother now.

DRON: Well, it *is* a superior wine.

CHURCH: It has more body hasn't it?

DRON: That's it. Body. I'm glad to have met a man as knows wines proper like.

CHURCH: Oh please, I don't know.

DRON: Find a seat, there, that oil drum. Put that cushion on. The place is a mess just now. I'm not quite settled yet. You caught me at a wrong moment. There, *I'll* sit on the oil drum, you can have the chair.

CHURCH: Oh it doesn't matter. You have the chair. Go on, I insist.

DRON: Hah, well if you're not fussy, I like to have my chair. Sit somewhere.

CHURCH [*standing at the door*]: Farewell, companion. Try to rest. You rounded virgin, moaning for your needs. Farewell, you great wall of contained power. I must be drunk. I'm talking to the reservoir.

DRON: You're not drunk. Just started.

CHURCH: Farewell, you mother giant. Christ, she stands above us like doom. But I know, Dron. I know. My father used to talk to the earth. 'You're restless you bugger,' he would say, or, 'She's in a bad mood today that 'un.' He would sometimes be afraid to go in on the shift. A bad day.

DRON: A wise man, he respected force. It's like the soldiers. Think they don't know the bullets is alive? I've heard a Buff say. 'It's going to be my day, Dron,' and feller you knew he wasn't coming back that night.

CHURCH: I'm glad I met you tonight, Dron.

DRON: And I'm glad I met you.

CHURCH: You've got the earth in you mister. And you've got an independent soul. These are the things I've lost. I've lost the earth. And I've lost my independent soul.

DRON: Women are bitches for ruining a man.

CHURCH: She's a nice girl you know, Dron. But strange. I knew when

I left the pit side that something was going. That I was going to a more artificial set up. A phoney deal. 'Oh,' my father said, 'You're going to better yourself, get to hell out of it,' and we all went, my brothers, my sister, all. But I felt that I was losing. And father felt it. He knew. He used to come and see us. But it was no good. Too posh. Too neat. Too polite. My wife got him in a half a dozen bottles of brown ale to make him comfortable. But it was no use. He didn't even finish them. This was a man who can drink ten in a night. He didn't even finish them. And before the week was up he was gone. Packed his bag and away. Back to the pit heap. God, I was bursting to go with him. 'But it wouldn't be sensible,' my wife said. 'It wouldn't be sensible.' But it would have been *truthful*.

DRON: You're pissed, son.

CHURCH: We are all matchsticks on the face of this earth. Matchsticks. That's what he used to say. Because he had been under it you see? He had been in the bowels.

DRON: Of course he's right. He's a clever feller your old man. What? That water would sweep us all to the Cotswolds if it hit us. These folks think it's been trained, beaten into submission. But it's not like that up here mate. Do you know that there are thousands of tons worth of pressure up there held back by six inches of bloody concrete?

CHURCH: Never.

DRON: It just needs *one weakness* in there. One crack . . . Anyway, take a seat son, make yourself at home.

CHURCH: Farewell, mistress. I'm glad to have met you. I'd forgotten the forces of Nature.

DRON: But they hadn't bloody forgotten you mate had they?

CHURCH: No. No.

DRON: Make yourself at home.

CHURCH: But home, is not as homely as this.

DRON: You like the place?

CHURCH: Like it? It's so cosy.

DRON: I mean, hotels have cellars like this don't they? Barrels. Round, just like this. No furniture, nor nothing, And these toffs, lords and bishops and that would all sit round and taste. Just like this. They called it, 'tasting', bishops minds you. And yet that bloody silly vicar down there, leads the Women's Institute against drink. They all want stuffed, him and all. Bishops, they taste.

CHURCH: Ah.

DRON: This is wine tasting. White wine and red wine. White wine is fish and cheese dish, see; and red wine is meat. Later on, when I get more organized, I'm going to have up here, have, actually in the place, a big slab of cheese there; like for the white, and over there, perhaps a tin or two of corned beef. I've got a bit of bread and a few turnips in now, which to my mind makes a nice meal but I could not offer to guests.

CHURCH: It sounds very nice.

DRON: Now I can see you're not a snob, albeit an educated man.

CHURCH: God, hasn't it shown yet?

DRON: Yes. I can see that you are an educated man. But despite that, a good man and not above a feller. So if there comes a time, in this night, when you fancy a piece of bread and turnip, just say to me, 'Dron,' say, 'I fancy a good piece of bread and turnip,' and so, we'll see about it. To me, it is a good wholesome meal, to me, I mean, you have Nature's finest gifts there, wheat, and a good root. Them's Nature's gifts. So if you fancy yourself a bite, just say.

CHURCH: My wife will have laid on supper. Cocoa and digestives. With the television play. Culture for two.

DRON: B.B.C. is it?

CHURCH: Yes.

DRON: Well, I was thinking of getting myself a little transistor in you know, and listening to B.B.C. on that. No rubbish. Good tunes like, the marching songs say. Good stuff. Lili Marlene and that. Northern Orchestras and stuff. All the quality things. Keeps the intelligence sharp. You got to keep your intelligence keen, or before you know where you are the people in the village are insinuating.

CHURCH: Insinuating?

DRON: Yes. About the drink. Think your intelligence goes. Well. I like a drink but I've got my intelligence.

CHURCH: Oh yes, I find you startlingly, let's say, profound company.

DRON: You do?

CHURCH: I find you a man concerned with things. That's it Dron. You're concerned with life. With the essentials. Like an artist, you're attuned to life, and its enormities.

DRON: Well, I like to think I'm doing a good job.

CHURCH: You're a man in the stream of life Dron. Not like me. In that bungalow I am not in the mainstream of life. It's even built off the main road. *She* wanted a quiet retreat. How much farther can we retreat?

DRON: Drink up boy. Drink up. Don't take on.

CHURCH: My, that last drop tasted like gin.

DRON: Now lissen. I'll tell you what I am going to do. I'm going to do this thing because I can see that you are a man of connoisseuring. Now this is what I'm going to do. . . . You said that this magnum was a good wine, correct?

CHURCH: Correct.

DRON: And you said that it had a certain body?

CHURCH: Correct. Bouquet.

DRON: Bouquet, that's good.

CHURCH: Bouquet.

DRON: Bouquet.

CHURCH: Bouquet.

DRON: Bou-bloody-quet. Now, because you are a man as knows his wines, I am going to give you a cocktail. Yes. A cocktail. Here, red wine and white. Try that.

CHURCH: That's got a certain splendour.

DRON: But *you* know what is the base of that cocktail don't you?

CHURCH: Oh yes. Oh yes. The magnum, the white, is the base of this cocktail.

DRON: Man, you know your wines.

CHURCH: Oh yes. The magnum is the gin of the piece, or as they say, the base; and the other is the flavourer.

DRON: You are a connoisseur, you know that? A natural.

CHURCH: Something of my father has filtered through then? How did it happen? How did I get like this?

DRON: Like that? Pissed?

CHURCH: No. No. Phh. Sterilized. She's a nice girl, you know. I went on a training course with the office down in Gloucester, and I met her there. A nice girl. A southern girl. Sensible and good natured. Just sort of nice. I didn't know anything was happening to me. But Dron, I've lost it. I've lost it.

DRON: Well, I hope you find it feller.

CHURCH: I'm not living. I'm only half alive. It's not her fault, it's not my fault. But it's happened. I've been quietly sterilized.

DRON: I'm sorry to hear it Church. Sorry to hear it.

CHURCH: Oh, I mean, metaphorically speaking.

DRON: Any way of speaking it's a nasty thing to happen.

CHURCH: Before this we were in Cheltenham, in rooms. And I had the feeling, 'You're out of the force of things,' it said. 'The force that through the green leaf sends the fuse,' or something. I thought, if we came here, I'd be back in it. With the growers, with the blossom, and the earth, and the humid climate. But the garden didn't give me it. Did not give me it. Walking here tonight has remade me. I saw that you were of the earth and of the force of things as well. Unbelievable. This magnum is great. Just great man. It's like the finest gin. You're a genius.

DRON: I've had other gentlemen up here you know. I have had the men from the Wine Brewers' Association up here.

CHURCH: Hah, keep them out Dron, keep them out. They'll try to make a specimen of you. Be a natural man. That's it. We must be natural men. Where's the toilet?

DRON: Well, either behind the barrels, or outside if you'd like a drop of fresh air.

CHURCH: I'll go outside.

[*He goes outside while* DRON *fills up. Enter* CHURCH.]

This is the life.

DRON: How's she looking? No cracks?

CHURCH: Don't let the bastards tame you Dron. Like they've tamed me. Don't let them. Don't let them get their hydrometer in your wine Dron.

DRON: You didn't see no cracks out there then?

CHURCH: Hah, that air. Goes down your lungs as sweet as a bird. Like ice.

DRON: You haven't had enough then Church?

CHURCH: Enough? My father would say, 'You haven't had a night of it until you've had too much. A feast,' he would say, 'is as good as enough, if not better.' Gimme a drink Dron.

DRON: There is no cracks up there then Church?

CHURCH: I was in love with a pit yakkers girl once. 'You'll never love me,' she said, ''Cos you're posh.' I heard my father say to her once,

'Oh you'll not marry little Lord Fauntelroy. You're too good for him. You'll marry a big sexy pit yakker.'

DRON: It's the thought of them cracks that does me. *They* don't know down in the village how a man can sit up here, not for a drink, (although mark you I like a drink). But not for the drink alone do I sit it out up here. I care for them. But they stop their menfolk coming up here you know. Oh yes. Many a time fellers used to come up here, but not no more. The women have stopped that. But I'm expecting Perce. Perce will be up. Good grower Perce is. Grow? He'd grow corn on the cob on concrete that man would. That land of his was bad. Oh I know it's near the river, but it's bad land. Bad stuff that land. But Perce, made it pay.

CHURCH: You know that land?

DRON: Know that land? It was my land.

CHURCH: Your land?

DRON: My land, and my father's land. People down the village said, I sold out, 'cos I liked the drink. But not true. Not true. I sold out, 'cos, 'cos, it was bad land, and I felt myself drawn to the waterworks. Perce, he's a good grower. But that land was a wilderness in my time. Couldn't do nothing with it. Perce will be up tonight. You ask him. He'll tell you. It was a bastard of a land.

CHURCH: Dron, I'm hungry.

DRON: You'll like Perce. He likes me.

CHURCH: This gives you a hell of an appetite.

DRON: When I got this place fixed up, with chairs and mebbe a picture and that, I'll get cheese and meat in. Cheese for the white wine, and meat for the red wine.

CHURCH: I could eat bread and turnip Dron.

DRON: Bread and turnip? You sure. I mean. It's just bread and turnip.

CHURCH: I could eat bread and turnip Dron. My father said they used to eat turnips in the trenches.

DRON: Very true and all. Very true. They did that. I was up there with the commandos, and the paratroops ...

CHURCH: And the Buffs?

BOTH: Steady the Buffs.

DRON: And them lads would have eaten horsemuck, but I was there to cook for them. I was there. They never mention that. Women's Institute. I've seen women eat cats. They had it rough the German women. Folks say they didn't have it rough. But I've seen them. German women. Lovely girls, the best in the district, real class, beautiful girls, I've seen them mother and daughters, letting the soldiers drill them for a sandwich.

CHURCH: Terrible.

DRON: A sandwich.

CHURCH: That's terrible.

DRON: Oh yes, they women in the village, thinks they're all respectable and decent, organized, but I've seen women when they were helpless. And listen; it's like you say; these forces of nature, they're never far off. Just a turn of the screw and that Women's Institute could be dispersed and them all on their backs. Why don't they think of that when they'm getting at a man? Heh? Here, sure you want a piece of turnip?

CHURCH: Great.

DRON: I think I'll join you. This wine gives you an appetite.

CHURCH: It does. It does. Cheers! Dron. Cheers! I've never eaten like this since I was a boy. Never, dear God, I didn't know there was a good meal left on this earth. Father, hear me.

DRON: I'm glad you're enjoying it. Hi, what about your cocoa and digestive biscuits?

CHURCH: She can *stuff* them. And the play. This is how she did it. She planned too much. She was too cold and careful. My mother just *loved* my father. Bore his kids, stood by him, for all his faults and his roaring and his drinking. She loved him. We have the house, they had no house, we have the car, they had no car; they had life. They were *one* Dron, I love this meal, I love this night.

DRON: I'm glad you like it.

CHURCH: I don't care if I am getting pissed Dron. I think it's true that people who are pissed see things more clearly than in the cold light of day. I am but a contemptible offshoot of my father. One who has ceased to live. A miner he was. Down in the bowels of the earth he went. How he knew life had wronged him yet he loved every minute of it. And drink. Ha. He drank like a fish. He would come in on a Saturday night. Gone. Gone to the world. Staggering. Abusing. Angry. So angry at it all. Shouting at the pit heaps, talking to the earth.

DRON: Was he a big strong feller?

CHURCH: Yes. Like a wounded buffalo.

DRON: Wounded?

CHURCH: Yes. Rotten with the coal. Coal dust in him. But he fought on like a giant, he fought on.

DRON: He's not dead?

CHURCH: No. Dammit. He grew a silver beard in his old age. Dear old man. Still smoking, drinking, snuffing. He *lived though*. He lived. Eight kids.

DRON: I got an injury in the war.

CHURCH: If he could see me now.

DRON: Burnt I am, down one leg. Burnt from top to bottom.

CHURCH: This is fine alcohol.

DRON: A big jerry can of beans it was, right at the front, for the commandos going in. 'We'll die with a bellyful of beans Dron,' they were saying. When blast, a mortar shell exploded and they all ducked, but I never ducked, I never deserted my field kitchen. Over it came with the blast. All down my legs. Severely burnt. I was honourably discharged you know. That's what them down there don't know.

CHURCH: That's what I've done, refused to know. I've refused to know.

DRON: It's the Mothers' Union. 'He's losing his intelligence,' they say, but they never say, 'he's nearly lost his leg.'

CHURCH: Bugger the Mothers' Union Dron. I'm enjoying this.

DRON: You'll get a name if you're not careful.

CHURCH: I don't care about the Mothers' Union.

DRON: Just wait till your wife is eligible mate. Then you'll care. They're terrible in force.

CHURCH: But, Dron, we're respectable up here.

[DRON *stands up and feels the urge for a piss. He is about to do it behind the wine barrels when he realizes that he's in good company*.]

DRON: Yes. Yes that's what I say. [*He goes outside.*]

[CHURCH *goes to the half barrel tub and peers inside, he puts his finger in and smells it. Re-enter* DRON.]

DRON: There looks a lot of pressure on that reservoy.

CHURCH: Dron. You dirty old beast. What's this?

DRON: It's rhubarb wine on the make see?

CHURCH: Oh, my apologies.

DRON: It's 'cos the rhubarb is in season see? If you put your ear to it you can hear it fizz.

CHURCH: I must apologize. I thought it was the toilet for a minute.

DRON: Hi, I got a proper toilet round the back of the shed you know. Chemicals, and seat and all that. I haven't been in for a long time, 'cos it's such a long walk see? But last time I was there it was in good nick. Oh I've got my standards you know. That's rhubarb wine.

CHURCH: It's big enough to drown in.

DRON: Don't mention drowning to me. Drowning is too near my soul.

CHURCH: My apologies. It is full though isn't it?

DRON: Well, yes. It's full. Full of good wine. Working. Because this is the rhubarb season see? You saw the rhubarb outside, it looks covered in weeds and long in grass but that doesn't harm the wine. All I do is to put the rhubarb *in* here, top up with water, add sugar and leave to work.

CHURCH: Work?

DRON: Work.

CHURCH: Work?

DRON: Work. Change to wine. In this state, this is lethal. It could kill. The Mothers' Union say I am killing myself with alcohol, but I am not killing myself with alcohol and this proves it. I got a grip on myself. I could drink this because it tastes beautiful and fresh like . . . like . . . pop? But I won't. I will wait till it's finished working then I will pour it into that barrel which will be empty.

CHURCH: I see, and when you've emptied this out?

DRON: Ah well then, I will fill it up with the next fruit which is plums, so that way . . . *I am never out.*

CHURCH: Dron. Dron. You drunken bastard. I'm glad I met you. You drunken swine and I don't care. Dron, Dron, old friend. I've come to life. [*He goes to the door.*]

[*Shouting:*] I've come to life. You hear me? We were wrong. Wrong. We were too bloody sensible. We should have lived first and planned later. [*He staggers back in.*]

DRON: How does the reservoy look? No cracks? There's only six inches of concrete there.

CHURCH: That's not much concrete.

DRON: That's what I say. But they don't care.

CHURCH: You say the Scotsman who built it got the sack?

DRON: Yes. Sacked.

CHURCH: What for? Drink?

DRON: Yes. For drinking. He liked a drink.

CHURCH: Can't blame a man for liking a drink. Here, give me one there you mean old sod.

DRON: Take one. Help yourself. You can drink boy. You can drink.

CHURCH: We men of Nature need a drink.

DRON: Ha now that's the thing isn't it? What I say, and this I say with considered aforethought and all seriousness, is that, the blessing of hard work is that it gives a man a thirst. That's the blessing of hard work.

CHURCH: That's profound Dron, that's profound.

DRON: It's like what you said about the man who works hard all day on the land on reservoys or water mains digging. He's a man whose system needs a drink. But, a man as sits in a bloody office all day with numbers and then comes back to a little garden does not need this kind of drinking. You can reach the stage, if you work in an office long enough where your bloody cocoa is too strong.

CHURCH: It's true Dron, that is true.

DRON: There is nothing wrong with drink. Them Mothers' Unioners and the vicar there on about the curses of drink.

CHURCH: They don't know what they're on about.

DRON: *Hi down there. What the hell you on about?* They drink more tea than me don't they? They say that drink is bad for you. But what about tea? It has been proved that tea is bad for you, it's bad for your things. It rots your things.

CHURCH: Things?

DRON: Yes. Their things. It rots their things. Doesn't the Royal Navy give its men rum? Do they or do they not give the sailors rum?

CHURCH: *They do.*

DRON: And we've got the finest Navy in the world boy. Bar none. I know. I fought with the British sailor. But them down there don't want none of that. They don't know who watches this reservoy for them that's a certainty. On about their drink.

CHURCH: But Dron, they don't think your health's affected? Big strong man like you?

DRON: I am a big strong man then? Still? I mean, from where you're standing I'm a big strong man?

CHURCH: You are indeed. Strong. Huge.

DRON: Well, that's it isn't it? The Waterworks wouldn't have me if I wasn't in the prime would they?

CHURCH: They would not.

DRON: A man's a man as likes a drink.

CHURCH: My father could drink.

DRON: The Scotsman could drink.

CHURCH: Poor feller. Getting the sack.

DRON [*goes quiet, confidential*]: Can I tell you something?

CHURCH: You can tell me. Anything.

DRON: Mind you, it's a burden. Once you know this thing, you will never rest again.

CHURCH: But I've rested so long. Tell me.

DRON: You'll never know peace again when I tell you this.

CHURCH: I don't want peace.

DRON: You'll curse the day I told you and sigh for the times when you could sit in your bungalow with an easy heart and watch telly and drink cocoa.

CHURCH: Go on, tell me!

DRON: It's about the Scotsman and the reservoy. He was a big drinker see and he used to come in a lot. Here. And one day, he said to me, 'Dron,' he said (because we were good pals), 'Dron. This is the best wine I've ever tasted but it's made me put that concrete up there too thin.' 'Concrete too thin?' I said. 'Yes. Concrete too thin,' he said. 'When they come to fill it up there'll be a crack up there.' And he showed me exactly where the crack would be. With a piece of chalk. And then they sacked him, and of course I sat up here. And lo and behold, when they filled it up, a crack came, exactly on the chalk marks.

CHURCH: Wow, that's something.

DRON: Then he said, 'After them first cracks, they'll close up,' and sure enough they did. 'But,' he said, and this is the big thing, 'One of these days, maybe soon, maybe late, that reservoy will crack again with such violence as will wash that village to hell and sweep the children from their beds out on to the cold fields.' I tried to tell the engineers as took his place but they all laughed. Oh clever dicks, you know? Oh they thought they knew. But that old Scot was wily. He'd forgotten more than they would ever know. 'One day,' he said, 'Maybe soon, maybe late, that reservoy is going to crack.' That's why I'm here. Watching. [*He is overcome. He nearly cries.*]

CHURCH: You're a fine man Dron. A fine man. Watching. Let me share your burden.

DRON: Eh? You mean that?

CHURCH: Let me share your burden.

DRON: It was my wine as done it you see. I feel responsible.

CHURCH: You're a fine man Dron. A fine man.

DRON: They don't know. Mothers' Union. They think I don't care about nothing? I care about them. I care about them. But she's gone down to join them.

CHURCH: Your wife?

DRON: Yeah. We sort of parted. 'If you're going to sit up there all day,' she said, 'you may as well make it your home.' Well I was glad to so I could watch for cracks and levels, and sleep better knowing that if I failed in my duty, I'd be the first to go. And they call me a waster. They don't know how I feel Church, they don't know how I feel. I'd like to say to them, I'd like to say, 'I think you're a fine body of women,' I'd like to say. But they won't let me. Women! God, when we moved in on Germany I've seen women folk brought down. To nothing but sex organs. For a sandwich the blokes could buy the best girl in the place. The best girl could be bought for a sandwich. You would go into the house, the mother and father and kids watching you. And the girl, or the wife, would take you in the next room and you left the sandwich on the table. For a sandwich you could get any one of them. Girls of twelve you could get for a sandwich. The men made pigs of themselves. They queued up outside my field kitchen for sandwiches; queued up. And I gave them sandwiches. And there wasn't even no meat in. No meat. I kept the meat and traded it for fags. If only I'd put some meat in I'd feel better. So I'm watching this reservoy. What more can I do? I'm trying to pay them back. What more can a man do? But, they think I just came up here to drink.

CHURCH: You're a fine man Dron. That's a dangerous vessel.

DRON: She's active you see? Active. Sometimes a nights I can hear her, active. Lissen. Hear her moving, moaning?

CHURCH: Yes. Yes.

DRON: I think she needs her man. She needs her man, that would settle her.

CHURCH: I feel tingling with life. Like father knew the coal, I know that reservoir.

DRON: Her needs a man. This is a mighty reservoy and is terrible in power. Her needs settling.

CHURCH: Dron. I want to *do* something. Tonight is the night, I want to go home like father. Defying the earth. Father! He would have roared home. Roared like a lion. Roared in and the street would tremble. And the earth would tremble. He'd have gone out there and defied the enemy. He'd have gone out there and sang to it. He'd have gone out and climbed the Mighty Reservoy and sang to the bloody world. Defiant.

DRON: We'll go up there and sing if it'll make you happy.

CHURCH: What. Would you Dron?

DRON: Yeah. So long as you get the muck off your boots.

CHURCH: Shall we Dron? Shall we? Go up there and sing? Shall we?

DRON: Mind you I haven't got a very good voice.

ACT THREE

On top of the Reservoir.

DRON: Get the muck off your boots.

CHURCH: They're not dirty. I been visiting.

DRON: You been with a friend eh?

CHURCH: To a friend's hotel. In the cellar.

DRON: Ha. Wine tasting?

CHURCH: The bouquet was magnificent.

DRON: How much did you say you paid for them boots?

CHURCH: Too much.

DRON: You should have gone to the Growers.

CHURCH: But I'm not a Grower.

DRON: That's nothin'. Anybody can go to the Growers for boots. Even pissed-up parsons can go to the Growers for boots.

CHURCH: Look at the view.

DRON: Look at the aerial mast all lit up.

CHURCH: It is indeed. It is a beautiful sight.

DRON: You and your Cotswold hills. Afore. On about the Cotswold hills.

CHURCH: You're right. The hills aren't important. It's what man does on them.

DRON: Look, an aeroplane. See how it goes.

CHURCH: Great Dron. Man in Nature's terrible power. That's us. You've got a natural sense of beauty Dron.

DRON: Course I have. Look at this reservoy, like a pig's ass.

CHURCH: Like the thigh of a Russian prostitute.

DRON: Hi, your wife's a bit of old cake isn't she?

CHURCH: She's well preserved, but it costs a fortune in preservatives.

DRON: Mine has joined the Mothers' Union. Late member.

CHURCH: To hell with the Mothers' Union. Steady the Buffs and give them a sandwich each. With no meat in.

DRON: Dare I laugh at that Church?

CHURCH: Laugh. Yes. Laugh. Tonight we're going to win man. You will sing to hell with your conscience, and I will sing myself to nature and the force of life. Up we go then.

DRON: Boots clean?

CHURCH: Of course they are.

DRON: Now be serious. I feel something might happen, feel there's something *big* on.

CHURCH: I'll say there's something big on. This is to do with souls man. And the triumph thereof.

DRON: All the same, take the shit off your boots.

CHURCH: O.K. O.K.

DRON: It is an intelligent rule though Church?

CHURCH: It is intelligent.

DRON: They say I'm going you know. They say the drink is removing my intelligence but it's not true, it's not true, I got a grip on my intelligence Church.

CHURCH: Of course you have. You've said some very clever things this night.

DRON: You think so eh? You think so.

CHURCH: Very clever. Now on. On. We must sing up there.

DRON: Can't we sing down here?

CHURCH: No half measures. No half measures.

DRON: There should be a ladder here. The Scotsman would have had a ladder.

CHURCH: He seems to have been a very good man that.

DRON: He was. But he made it too thin. Them cracks will reappear he said then that will be the end.

CHURCH: Come on. Defy it. Let it crack. Defy it to crack.
   [*They climb up to the top.*]

DRON: Come on. Up to the top. Haa.
   Here we are. Look at the view. The village looks nice, all lights in the trees like that.

CHURCH: Note how, on our lane, we have fluorescent drive lights. How pathetic.

DRON: Nice and open though.

CHURCH: We delayed having a family. Get our little nest together. 'Let's be sensible,' she said. Sensible? My father wasn't sensible. He was alive. When a baby does come it won't like it in that house, because I'm damned sure I don't. Let's be sensible. No let's be illogical and happy. Father. Father. Why do you despise me? As if I need ask.

DRON: Well, here we are.

CHURCH: This is what he would have done Dron. He didn't creep home hygienically to bed every night. He stayed out and roared at the moon and abused that deep mountain of coal. He was at one with the elements. Like us Dron, at one with the elements. Here we are. Let's sing to our monster.

DRON: What'll we sing? 'Blaydon Races'?

CHURCH: No. No. That wouldn't do. He would sing that but he'd mean it. We can't be phoney. You just don't sing 'Blaydon Races' in Worcestershire.

DRON: No. That's true

CHURCH: *We*'ll sing your song. What's your song?

DRON: Worcestershire song? I don't think we've got one.

CHURCH: No Worcestershire song? What a mean lot. Keeping themselves to themselves. My father knew them all like he knew his own street. 'Keep Your Feet Still Geordie Hinny', 'The Keel Row', 'Blaydon Races' he knew them all. He knew those Northumbrian songs because they were of the land and the sky and the sea. They were part of his tradition. I have murdered my tradition. It would be phoney to sing them now.

DRON: That's rough.

CHURCH: Come on man. You must have a song that went through your mind when you were tilling the fields long ago. Where is it?

DRON: I used to like 'Farmer's Boy'.

CHURCH: Then let's sing it. Right. 'To be a Farmer's Boy'.

DRON: We used to sing it at the Plough and Harrow when I used to go before the cider got too weak for me.

CHURCH: The cider? Too weak for you?

DRON: I used to like the cider. Till I brewed the plums. First, I'd come up here, just for a sip; then go down to the pub. Then the cider started tasting like water, then it was up here all the time. But it is not making me lose my intelligence Church. You heard the boot rule.

CHURCH: I heard the boot rule. A very intelligent rule. The boot rule is.

DRON: I mean, my brain is not affected. What do they have to say that for? Why don't they know about the crack? It's a heavy load for a man to bear.

CHURCH: Let's sing your song. Right. Are we ready. One, two, three.
[*They sing a few bars of 'To Be a Farmer's Boy'.* DRON *cries.*]
Dron, you're crying.

DRON: Gone are the days.

CHURCH: Now Dron, you're a big fine feller.

DRON: I could make it pay. I could make it pay. I used to have lettuce,
and sprouts, and parsnips, and radish; nothing posh you understand?
But I made a living. No glass mind you, but then, the Vale didn't
have glass in those days. Not like now. It's a field of glass now. But
in them days it was honest toil. I used to sweat. Sure, I liked a cider,
sure, I liked a cider. It gets hot down there in the Vale. 'You're
drinking too much cider,' she would start to say. 'No I am not
drinking too much cider, I can drink a glass of cider with the next
man,' and we would sing 'Farmer's Boy', in the Plough and
Harrow; and she'd say, 'Well, I hope you ent that's all,' and I says,
'I work hard, I eat hard, I drink hard.' And then, you see. Things
got bad like. I mean, there were hard years. There were hard years.
Drought, bad market, frost nipping the blossom, things like that.
I said, 'I've had enough, I can't make the land pay in this year. We'll
sell out, and I'll get a job outside and just keep the land on the hill,
for our own veg.' But she said, 'You've allus been a land man,
you can't let this land beat you.' But I said, 'I'm not beaten, not
beaten, but I'll defy any man to make money out of this land.'

CHURCH: So you sold up?

DRON: Yeah. And moved into the village.

CHURCH: Who'd you sell to?

DRON: *That bloody Perce.* Clever swine ent you Perce? Can you hear
me Perce? Think you're bloody great. Fields of glass and concrete
slabs. And I thought you wuz coming up here tonight? Allus
coming up here ent you?

CHURCH: Poor Dron. Come on Dron. [*He goes over to the hatch and
listens to the reservoir.*] Is she annoyed?

DRON: She's rumbling.

CHURCH: You can't do anything can you you beast? Listen to her
getting all worked up. Crack. Crack. Crack damn you crack.
Let's dance on her. [*He dances on the hatch top singing 'Keep Your Feet
Still Geordie Hinny'.*]

DRON: No. No. It'll break out.

CHURCH: Let her try. Let her try. Come on, Dance.

[*They dance together. Singing a mix of 'Farmer's Boy' and 'Geordie Hinny'.*]

Triumph. Ha ha. She'll not crack now Dron. We've done our worst.

DRON: You've relieved me.

CHURCH: Of course. It just needed a *man* on the job Dron. What? My father cursed the very mountain of coal that he walked on. Now. You are free Dron. And I'm free. We're both free. Tonight, I will walk down to that house, she'll be red eyed and worried. And I'll stalk in, and stink of plum, kick my boots into her nice clean fireless grate and if she's lucky, take her upstairs and give her a sandwich.

DRON: And you'll come up again Churchy? We'll talk about things.

CHURCH: We'll talk, and drink, and write filthy things on this reservoir. Sleep angel, sleep.

DRON: I want to talk about them German girls.

CHURCH: And I want to listen about them German girls.

DRON: Ha ha ha.

CHURCH: 'Give us a sandvich. Give us a sandvich.'

DRON: And you know what I did with the meat?

CHURCH: No what did you do with the meat?

DRON: I got fags with it. I got fags. Fags were hard to come by. Hundreds of fags I got. I was the only man in Berlin with fags at one time. And I didn't enjoy them. I didn't enjoy them fags. I don't smoke no more.

CHURCH: Stop worrying Dron. You've paid it back boy. Men like you can't be held back by conscience man. We've got to be hard. Look, Dron, look. Be strong. Face up to yourself man. Look at me, I'll go back and piss in that pool tonight.

DRON: Hundreds of fags I had while the rest of the Army of Occupation was all smoking cowflap together.

CHURCH: You swine you. No wonder your conscience hurts.

DRON: And that old Perce who didn't come tonight?

CHURCH: Damn ole Perce who didn't come tonight.

DRON: Strings his tomatoes on the trot he does.

CHURCH: We'll enter him for the Grand National.

DRON: Do you know that his land down there was *my* land?

CHURCH: Times were bad then Dron. We know what the weather was like.

DRON: He had it lucky.

CHURCH: Dead jammy.

DRON: And he's missed tonight.

CHURCH: Stringin' his tomatoes at a run.

DRON: Your father would be proud of you tonight Church.

CHURCH: I look good eh? I look good?

DRON: You look great.

CHURCH: And that wife of mine, you know when she can join the Mothers' Union? She can join the Mothers' Union when she's got ten kids to her credit. That's when she can join. One kid don't make a mother, it just makes an outsize virgin.

DRON: That's it boy.

CHURCH: And as for the reservoy. We'll fight it. We'll fight it. Let it moan on.

DRON: Sssh. Lissen.

CHURCH: It's nothing.

DRON: Funny feel.

CHURCH: No. No.

DRON: Sssh. [*They listen.*] Let's go Church. Let's go.

CHURCH: Go? No. No.

DRON: She's bloody active.

CHURCH: Come on. Let's take a look at her.

DRON: Take a look?

CHURCH: Yes. Let's get that grate open. Why, come on. [*They go down and open the hatch carefully.*] Look. Black. And look. The stars are in there.

DRON: Terrible, ent it?

CHURCH: You haven't seen a pit pool. You seen a pit pool?

DRON: No. I haven't seen a pit pool Church.

CHURCH: Deep. And black. Ink. Bottomless. My father used to come home pissed . . . and swim in pit pools.

DRON: There's a man.

CHURCH: He'd swim in that.

DRON: Never! Never in that.

CHURCH: He'd swim in that I'm telling you.

DRON: A mighty man to swim in that.

CHURCH: He'd swim in the teeth of that monster.

DRON: What a man.

CHURCH: Yeah. Look at me. Office boy.

DRON: Yeah. Some man he must have been. One of Nature's men. To swim that.

CHURCH: Dear father, I loved you well, my giant.

DRON: But to swim in that.

CHURCH: Under the stars he would. In the reflected stars.

DRON: A mighty man . . .

CHURCH: He would swim in that.

DRON: Gone are the men who would swim in that.

CHURCH: There are not many men who would swim in that.

DRON: The strain of man who would swim in that is gone.

CHURCH: A man who would swim in that could hold his head high. High.

DRON: A man who could swim in that could call himself a man ever again. But there is no man left who would swim in that. Is there?

CHURCH: I am my father's son.

DRON: No. You wouldn't swim in that. Would you? Oh no you wouldn't swim in that.

CHURCH: Let me see it. Let me see. Yes. He would swim in the teeth of that terrible thing.

DRON: No. No. You'm just an office boy as is drunk.

CHURCH: Drunk? Not drunk. Alive. Awake.

DRON: Her is too much of a match for you man. Her's a claimer.

CHURCH: I have my father in me. I have my father's quick spirit in me yet. Let me take my cardigan off.

DRON: No. I couldn't let you swim in that now could I?

CHURCH: You couldn't stop me Dron. Not now. I must. I must. Man. This is great. Descending into the constellations, like shouting at the earth, this is back to life, back to life. [*He descends.*] Ha. How deep. A dark jewel she is. My God, to be borne up on that. In the dark. There's living. Wait for me Dron, wait for me. Ha, father. See me now. Father. I've found my soul and yours. Wait for me Dron. Wait.
  [*There is a splash. A gurgling. A choking. Then silence.* DRON *closes the hatch. He stands up on it with arms outstretched simulating the drowned figure.*]

DRON [*spitefully*]: You should have took your bloody boots off.

Dron's cabin. Enter Dron.

DRON: Good morning ladies. Good morning all. A solemn time. Sssh, bit of respect. I'm quiet ladies. I'm bearing myself in a manner becoming. Its a terrible shock for a man to find that his work is a killer. Found him floating in my own keeping.

A fine banner there ladies. Hand stitched, by, if I might be so bold, a thousand virtuous hands. There's the plum tree on it and the sign of the Evesham pear. Now there's nice. But now you'll need the water on it. See it was a force ladies. A force of Nature that you didn't contend with. Her was a mighty reservoy ladies as claimed a man as respectable as this. But he had no right going so near ladies, I mean, I'm the only man as has the authority up there with that reservoy ladies. 'Cos I've got my rules.

There's the Vicar, a flash of white and black in the graveyard. Going to give a sermon on Jonah and the Whale.

'Morning vicar,' and Dron will have a pew.

[*Sings.*] 'Oh bid the mighty oceans sleep, for those in peril on the deep.' Here they come now be it? Oh water – swollen remains. Carried by the gentlemen from the office at Cheltenham. Fine men. Carrying their friend to his last. See how the reservoy sits up there ladies? Skulking. But Dron's your master. Its alright now ladies. Dron's your master. There will be no cracking and peace will be in the village.

[*Kneels to pray.*] You can't crack now you've had your man. That water would have swept down and pushed the village aside and kiddies would be swept out into the fields o' night. But quite alright now. Dron, as found the body, is in control. You thought I was losing my intelligence ladies. But I wasn't losing my intelligence, it was just the concentration. Watching that crack. He put the chalk mark up. Yeh, put them up, and said in his Scotch voice, 'They'll appear there.' The strain was great ladies. Sure I took a drink but not no more. I'm back with my wife now, and she works in the hospital kitchens.

Silence now ladies, bit of respect out there, no more clucking there's the ladies; hold on your banner straight and don't let it waver. 'Cos Dron is emerging; 'Photograph please'. A fine man, Dron; an upstanding man Dron, a decent citizen and we have his Olive in the Mothers' Union there's nice. I didn't mean to keep the meat out of them sandwiches, ladies. I watched over youse all, and over your children. I didn't mean to keep the meat from them. I was the only man in Berlin with fags at one time and I didn't enjoy the one of them. That rhubarb fizzes. How nice it is. Like the first cider in the blackcurrant fields, fizzy, quenching. . . . *But one drink would be the last drink.* She'm quiet man. Don't bring her on! Don't bring her on! Less women and children be swept away in their beds and poor bereaved dads go scraping among washed out debris for the remains of their loved ones. A brooch, a teddy bear, a baby's cot. Carried away by a mighty force. Don't worry ladies. Dron is in control. Here we come, out the Church, out in the cold sunshine; is she there? Aye, she's there. Oh mighty wench. You'm had your man. Dron is clean and Dron is respectablized. Out of the wilderness. Good afternoon Perce. A fine grower Perce. I'll give you that and no malice. A fine grower. It wasn't for the want of trying ladies, but God had me cut out for bigger things. A man has to follow his bent. There is some as is cut out for higher things and chosen paths Perce. Aaaah, there's his lady, all in black and bitter mourning for a life cut off. She's been taken to the bosom of the Mothers' Union even though she hasn't got the qualifications yet. And who's the old gentleman with the white hair and beard? The deceased's father? A fine old man. Come to lay his own son to the cold earth. A man who knows the earth. 'Good afternoon sir, and I'm Dron as knows the earth and fetched your son from out his watery tomb. The earth is strong sir. There is forces which you and I know.' Ashes to ashes, dust to dust, water to water. [*He kneels down and looks up at the reservoir.*] You can't undo me. You can't undo a man who has played fair. I'll have a drink. One drink then sleep. One drink. You'm won't crack. You'm been appeased.

[*He rushes to the jam jar and gulps down the last drink and his brain snaps. He groans and then reaches up above his skull for his brain, trying to pull it back into its case. There is an uneasy rumbling from the reservoir. He tries to block it out by covering his ears and shaking his head.*

The Ghost of CHURCH *appears.*]

CHURCH: It's me Dron.

DRON: I knew you'd come in if I had that last drink.

CHURCH: Did you Dron? Did you? Know I'd appear from my watery tomb?

DRON: Yeah. Oh a minute ago it was so nice. I was standing down the village at your funeral, respected and thought highly of. Then I had that last drink. I knew you'd come.

CHURCH: I'm glad you expected me Dron.

DRON: I've had them all here when I've had that last drink. It's my intelligence you see Church.

CHURCH: I see. It goes?

DRON: Yes. It goes. I've had them all here. All people. It used to be rats and black beetles long ago but now it's people, and they're worst. I've had my mother here all bent and worn in land shape with the onion tying and sprout hooving, saying, 'Son, you had the land, your father's land, you've come to this.' I've had my wife here, all bright and clean with her membership card of the Mothers' Union in her coat, and her kids at her hand saying, 'I worked for you but you got the drink in you.' And I've had the women of the Mothers' Union here saying, 'Clackity clack, clackity clack. Stinking waster; leaving wife man, lazy stinking cider drinker, plum juice vendor.' And I've had them German girls and families all standing round quiet, all watching, sons, fathers, brothers, mothers, grannies and the girl just beckoning and whispering, 'Put your sandwich on the table,' and I've put it down and they've all looked at it as if to say. 'No meat. He's kept the meat for fags.'

CHURCH: You're not afraid of me then Dron?

DRON: No. No. I knew you'd come, once my intelligence went.

CHURCH: Poor Dron.

DRON: My rule. What was my rule again? It was a good rule. You said. 'An intelligent rule,' you said.

CHURCH: An intelligent rule it was Dron.

DRON: What was it again? What was it? If only I could remember my rule my intelligence would come flying back like a wood pigeon. Oh my God, my rule, my intelligence.

CHURCH: You're lonely, and going insane.

DRON: No. No. Don't talk about me. Talk about you. Did you find it alright. When you went in there. Was it alright?

CHURCH: You're finished Dron.

DRON: Aw, Church. You'm left your boots on you know. Church, you'm left your boots on. I had a rule about boots. What was it Churchy? What was it? It was an intelligent rule Church wasn't it?

CHURCH: Your rule? You're just a drunken beast. Sitting here, not washing, away from wife, luring men up to make yourself think you're respectable. You aren't respectable. You've even had a man killed now. A right mess you're in.

DRON: But I had a rule. I had a rule Church.

CHURCH: Always scrape the muck off your boots.

DRON: Was that my rule?

CHURCH: That was your rule.

DRON: Always, scrape the . . . muck off your boots.

CHURCH: *Doesn't* sound so good does it?

DRON: You liked it though Church. When you first came up, you liked it, I remember you liked it.

CHURCH: There it is. You'll say anything to humour a fool.

DRON: So that was it? Always scrape the muck off your boots.

CHURCH: The drink has gone into your brain.

DRON: My brain?

CHURCH: First your intelligence goes and then your reason, then you kill your brain.

DRON: Kill my brain? No. It's never going to come to that. I won't kill my brain. I got will power you know. I never went past that stage Church. Let's talk, let's talk. Your father was right wasn't he? You weren't the man to go swimming in that reservoy. Now him, yes, him, I can see that. An old miner but they don't make them like that no more see.

CHURCH: You can't delay it Dron. Your brain is going. It's scattered about. You're killing it.

DRON: I was saying to the ladies as how you broke into my shed and had a drink, when I wasn't here.

CHURCH: Lies aren't going to help you now . . .

DRON: I was down there, down there talking to them, saying as how, you know, a young feller, got in the shed and couldn't take the drink as Dron takes . . .

CHURCH: You got a respectable man up here and killed him in your madness.

DRON: Church. We had a good night boy. But you had no right taking that reservoy on. Her is a Mighty thing.

CHURCH: It was probably a good play tonight.

DRON: And she'll be sitting there still with your cocoa and digestives, hoping for you coming back. Oh there'll be hell on in that village in the morning. What'll they do? What'll they say? There'll be an inquest.

CHURCH: They'll say a young man was lured into the shed and made silly on this poison.

DRON: *Shame* Church. You'm liked it.

CHURCH: They'll root you out Dron. Pull you out of your shed in the morning. And make you face them. But listen Dron, there'll be no morning for you. Have a drink and I'll tell you.

DRON: No. No. I can do without. I got control. I got faculties.

CHURCH: Hoh, the wine is flat now. You're thirsty. Take a drink of rhubarb while it's still fizzing. Now there's a thirst quencher. There's a thirst quencher for you.

DRON: No. No. Oh it's right I'm thirsty. But I got faculties. Mustn't touch the rhubarb.

CHURCH: So thirst quenching.

DRON: It's thirst quenching right enough when it's working. Like the first fizz cider you had as a kid in the hot field getting the black-currants in with your mother sitting on a stool in a straw hat. And your Dad give you your first fizzy cider down there. A nice drink. So thirst quenching. Nice to lie back and drink it. But, I don't see. 'Cos I got will power and faculties.

CHURCH: It's a lot of wine there Dron. Enough to drown in.

DRON: No, not drown, mustn't talk about drown.

CHURCH: Dron, I've come to tell you about in there.

DRON: Yes? About in there. Oh, it must be fearsome in there.

CHURCH: I've come to tell you. About in there. In there. In the Mighty Reservoy. It's right Dron. Her claimed her man.

DRON: I knew her'd claim her man.

CHURCH: Clutched down I was. In that icy, jewel of a thing, cold as ice. She wrestled me down to her ice cold belly Dron, black as coal . . .

DRON: Black as coal . . .

CHURCH: But Dron, I've come to tell you. As I went down, I saw
... torn apart ... a moving, tearing ... *crack*.

DRON: A *crack*.

CHURCH: A huge crack Dron. Dron. You were right. It's a crack.
Growing as slow and as sure as a slug.

DRON: A crack.

CHURCH: Top to bottom. With the icy fingers of the reservoy pulling
it apart, Dron. Ripping it open.

DRON: A crack. Not now. It's after my hours. I've had my last drink.
Not now. Ladies. I watched till twelve.

CHURCH: The mighty reservoy is cracking Dron. Slow, watery,
parting. Like wet cardboard, going. And the water, digging through
it. Listen, can you hear a whisper. It's that water. Edging to the
village Dron, sweeping the children out of their beds and into the
fields under the stars.

DRON: The alarm. The alarm.

CHURCH: Yes. Go to it Dron, get to it.

DRON: I can't move. I've turned to clay.

CHURCH: Move Dron, move. Move to save the ladies and children of
the village. Dron. The hero!

DRON: Can't move. Gimme a drink. [*He tries to fill up the jam jar
but can't. He throws it away. He looks around and plunges his head into
the open-topped tub. The roaring and the drinking are now synonymous.
The more he drinks, the more it roars.*]

CHURCH: It's coming Dron.

DRON: Drink! Drink! [*He puts his head in the barrel and the roar grows
to a crescendo as he is drowning in drink. He reels.*]

CHURCH: Is it just your head Dron? Is it just in your head? Is it
just ... [*ad lib ...*]

DRON: No. The Mighty Reservoy. It's the Mighty Reservoy.
[*The roaring and rushing reach a tremendous crescendo as* DRON
dies of drink. Then it ceases. The ghost of CHURCH *is gone. There is
the sound of a bird. Morning light appears. The Mighty Reservoy is
intact.*]

STEWART CONN

The King

Suppose we kill a king, and then a king,
  and then a king;
princes are waiting everywhere;
suppose by poison or by water, kill a queen;
her daughter sits upon the stair.

(Robert Horan

The King was first presented at the Traverse Theatre, Edinburgh in May 1967, with the following cast:

ATTIE   Phillip Manikum
FARROL   Peter Harlowe
LENA   Annabel Leventon

Directed by Max Stafford-Clark

It was subsequently presented by the same Company during the 21st Edinburgh International Festival.

It is late Friday evening, and almost dark. Outside, singing and shouting. This approaches, then is interrupted as a door opens, off.

FARROL [*off*]: Ssh. After you.

ATTIE [*off*]: No, after you Mr Farrol.

FARROL [*off*]: I insist.

ATTIE [*off*]: Have it your way.

FARROL [*off*]: Here, the groceries are still behind the storm-door. [*Pause.*] Take this while I switch the light on. Steady! In you go. [*Shuffling and clinking of bottles, off.* ATTIE *enters, stumbling in the near darkness. He is weighed down by a brown paper carry-out bag filled with bottles, and a large cardboard box heaped with groceries. He stumbles against something.*] Just a minute, till I find the light. [*Enters and switches on the room light: he too has a carry-out bag, clinking.*] I'll take these through. [*Exits to the kitchen.*]

[ATTIE *slumps into an armchair helplessly. He tries to wipe his free hand across his forehead.*]

ATTIE [*to himself*]: As if we hadn't had enough, without . . . oh, what the hell.

[FARROL *returns breezily, rubbing his hands.* ATTIE *tries to rise, muttering.*]

FARROL: What's up then?

ATTIE: My hand, it's gone numb.

FARROL: What are you for?

ATTIE: Look, Mr Farrol . . .

FARROL: What are you having?

ATTIE: I didn't . . . look, I didn't come round just to lay into your beer.

FARROL: We can drink yours, if that'll make you happy. [*He takes several screwtops from* ATTIE's *bag.*]

ATTIE: But . . .

FARROL: Not gone off, have you? Off the idea? Mugs. In the sideboard. It'll come all right. It'll all be hunkey-dorey, you wait and see.

[ATTIE, *at the sideboard, knocks over a mug.*]

Take it easy, what sort of an impression do you want to make? Put them down there.

[ATTIE *has brought out two beer-mugs.* FARROL *fills them, hands one to* ATTIE.]

Well, sit down. Not there, that's her chair.

ATTIE: Where is she?

FARROL: Cheers!

ATTIE: Cheers! [*He sits.*]

FARROL: Told you she'd gone to bed. We had a row. Having second thoughts?

ATTIE: It's the dummie.

FARROL: What about the dummie?

ATTIE: I'm worried what'll happen to him, that's all.

FARROL: Lock him up for a few months. Best thing that could happen. For his own good, I mean.

ATTIE: I know, but . . .

FARROL: How'd it all happen, anyway? I was in the other bar.

ATTIE: They came in, the dummie and his mate, you know – the big blond one . . .

FARROL: I saw him.

ATTIE: Thought you said you were in the other bar?

FARROL: Get on with it.

ATTIE: Well, they asked for a drink. And Bill refused to serve them. Said they'd both been banned. So they asked for a carry-out. Couple of bottles. Well, that was when it started. Bill came round the bar to them, to put them out. And the dummie went for him. Must've panicked, or something. Next thing the cops were in. And old Bill, he clobbered the dummie. And they were carting him out when he started making signs. And his mate said 'He wants to say something.' And Bill said 'How can he say something when he's deaf and dumb?' And the dummie's mate said 'Give him a piece of paper and pencil, it might be serious, you never know, he might be hurt bad. Go on.' So they gave the dummie a pencil and a piece of paper, and he wrote on it, all very slow and methodical. And he folded it, and handed it to the police. Well I mean, we thought all he wanted was a pee, something of that style. But when the police opened it up, all it said was 'Gestapo Bastards'. So they clobbered him again and carted him off. Well, what do you think'll happen?

FARROL: Serve him right, ask me. Shouldn't think we'd see him around for a while, poor sod.

ATTIE: Say that again.

FARROL: Poor sod. Refill?

ATTIE: Look, Mr Farrol . . .

FARROL: Come along, put a bit of lead in the old pencil, Attie.

ATTIE: I didn't come here just to drink. I mean, it's all very good of you, but . . .

FARROL: But what?

ATTIE: How serious were you? Down the pub there?

FARROL: Perfectly serious. I said I'd have to talk to her about it.

ATTIE: Well . . .

FARROL: I told you, I keep telling you we had a row. She's gone to bed, that's all. I'll go and see if she's awake. And we can see how we stand. How about that? Make yourself at home. It's all yours, Attie, it's all yours.

[*Before* ATTIE *can protest* FARROL *has gone out.* ATTIE *gazes glumly before him.*]

ATTIE: Poor soul, right enough. Kick him to bits they will. Once they get him behind bars. Once they get him in that cell. They'll give him paper and pencil, I can tell you. They'll lay in, so they will. [*He drains his drink and speedily refills it.*] Here's to him anyway. I wouldn't be a dummie for all the . . .

[*He breaks off, and looks round the room. There is a plushness about it, and yet at the same time something austere. Candlesticks on a sideboard, a sofa in one corner, a drinks cabinet, a leather arm-chair. There is also a large old oak chest. Heavy curtains, wood panelling.*

ATTIE *takes this in, then slaps his pockets as though feeling for something. He crosses the room and takes an apple from a silver fruit-dish. About to bite it, he changes his mind and slips it into his pocket. After a moment he crosses to the sideboard, on which stands a wooden cigarette-box. He listens for a moment, takes the cigarette-box, and sits in the chair* FARROL *previously indicated as* LENA's.

ATTIE *lifts the lid of the cigarette-box: it begins to play gaily. Immediately he slaps the lid shut. At this moment* FARROL *enters.* ATTIE *is taken by surprise.*]

FARROL: We're a musical family.

ATTIE: I was just . . . looking . . .

FARROL: Help yourself.

ATTIE: Some . . . some nice . . . ah . . . pieces of furniture.

FARROL: Take one. [*Offers* ATTIE *a cigarette.*] Yes, my wife collects them. She's quite a collector. Do you collect things?

ATTIE [*as* FARROL *lights his cigarette*]: Thanks. The odd thing. Nothing much, what I can pick up.

FARROL: No tastes in particular? I mean, I know so little about you. All I know is what you were telling me in the pub. What you were saying down there. And I don't know if it's true or not. I'm sizing you up.

ATTIE: Don't you worry.

FARROL: Could be a pack of lies, all brag.

ATTIE: Don't say that, Mr Farrol.

FARROL: Just the one line, you talked about. You could have other lines . . .

ATTIE: I'm not the bragging type.

FARROL: Something I don't know about. For all I know.

ATTIE: Stop getting at me. Look, just because you brought me here, that . . .

FARROL: At your request.

ATTIE: Whose!

FARROL: We had an ostrich, once.

ATTIE: An ostrich?

FARROL: That's right.

ATTIE: A real one?

FARROL: Course.

ATTIE: Alive?

FARROL: No, dead.

ATTIE: Thought you said it was real.

FARROL: So it was. But it was dead.

ATTIE: How'd it get here?

FARROL: Flew, I suppose.

ATTIE: Ostriches can't fly.

FARROL: Then why ask?

ATTIE: Well, once it was here, I mean . . . what did you do with it? Stuff it?

FARROL: No. Buried it. [*Pause.*] You not got anything lying around?

ATTIE: Course. Mean to say, who ever heard of a place where there wasn't anything lying around? About the place? Usual things, old clothes, bits and pieces, odd shoe, bric-brac, newspapers, I mean to say . . .

FARROL: Newspapers?

ATTIE: The odd can, sort of thing . . . what?

FARROL: You said newspapers.

ATTIE: So, I said newspapers?

FARROL: Which ones?

ATTIE: How should I know? *News of the World, People, Mirror*, sort of thing. Sort of thing you'd find lying around anywhere. Why make such a meal of it?

FARROL: Refill. [*He refills* ATTIE's *mug, and his own.*] Cheers!

ATTIE: Cheers.

FARROL: So you collect newspaper cuttings, that it?

ATTIE: Who said anything about cuttings? I didn't say cuttings did I, I said newspapers.

FARROL: No, I did. It'd be perfectly natural, don't get me wrong. What sort of cuttings do you keep?

ATTIE: All sorts. Events. That's it, events. World occasions. Of national importance. Snip out the odd one, here and there. As the fancy takes me. You know, Kennedy's Assassination, King's Funeral . . .

FARROL: Which king?

ATTIE: George VI. Didn't know there was another one!

FARROL: What else?

ATTIE: Bombing in Suez, going back a bit that. Hungarian Revolution. Negro Riots in U.S., Miss World, Premier Says No, 6d on Fags, you name it, I got it. And all the sporting headlines, goes without saying. England Win World Cup, Arkle Crippled, Russian Athletes Change Sex, Famous Boxer Murdered . . .

FARROL: So you keep murders?

ATTIE: What? Oh, just well-known ones. Like that one. I mean, he was flyweight champion of the world; greatest since Benny Lynch.

FARROL: Any others?

ATTIE: Why should there be? It isn't as if I specialized in that line. It's just it so happens. I've got cuttings of all sorts of things, Garden Parties, Seat-belts, Niagara Falls . . .

FARROL: What others?

ATTIE: The Wardrobe Case. That's the only other I can think of. Well, you not approve, that it? That what's biting you? Got a thing against wardrobes?

FARROL: No.

ATTIE: What do you want me to do about it?

FARROL: Drink up.

ATTIE: I've had about enough, Mr Farrol. We'd quite a bevy down the pub there.

FARROL: So you had.

ATTIE: But I knew what I was saying, don't get me wrong. I wasn't talking out the back of my head, no sir. I meant every word. When I get into my stride about flowers, I'm right on beam. A different man. I know what I'm about, believe you me. Flowers just come natural to me, I suppose, looking after them, making them grow, bringing them on. Got green fingers, you might put it, a way with flowers. They . . . I suppose they exert a fascination for me. That's what you brought me back for, to look after your garden?

FARROL: My wife's garden.

ATTIE: You wouldn't discuss it in the pub, said it was too busy, too noisy. But I'm the man for the job. Look, if it's bringing on flowers, I'm your man. Soil, nitrates, fertilizers, I know the lot. Back of my hand. Growth, transplanting, terrain, treating, pruning, crossing, specially cross-breeding, that's my speciality. My name's in the records of all the local shows these three shires, years back. Just some sort of power, some magic invested in me, you might say.

FARROL: I've heard about your –

ATTIE: Renown?

FARROL: Scarcely.

ATTIE: What d'you mean?

FARROL: Why are you out of a job? What makes you think my wife would employ you? After . . .?

ATTIE: You don't credit rumour do you? You know local gossip. I left – it can be vicious – because I'd had enough, no other reason. No cloud. You know how a man can be branded. If I was guilty of that, do you think I'd show my face in these parts? I couldn't hold up my head, Mr Farrol.

FARROL: No, you couldn't.

ATTIE: Well.

[ATTIE *drinks.* FARROL *watches him closely.*]

FARROL: It'd be much easier if my wife was here. As I say, the garden has always been her responsibility. The walled garden goes back to Tudor times, you know.

ATTIE: If I wasn't suitable?

FARROL: She'd soon find out. But I wouldn't worry. I think you'll do. You strike me as, well, much more reliable than the last man.

ATTIE: What happened to him?

FARROL: My wife got rid of him.

ATTIE: What happened?

FARROL: She disposed of him, that's all.

ATTIE: How? You can't just, well, dispose of people – just like that.

FARROL: Can't you?

[ATTIE *rises, breaking the mood. He leans forward to pick up a beer-bottle. He eyes the oak chest. He looks at it, then at* FARROL, *then moves away.*]

ATTIE: Huh, I'll tell you where I wouldn't put him. If you like. I'll tell you one place where he isn't!

FARROL: Where's that?

ATTIE: In that chest.

FARROL: How do you know?

ATTIE: Because you'd smell him, that's how I'd know. By now. After two months. Look, you're trying to put the wind up me. Any minute now you'll be trying to make me remember reading in the papers, about some gardener who disappeared two months ago –

FARROL: You're the one that keeps cuttings, Attie.

ATTIE: That doesn't mean I'm as drunk as I'm –

FARROL: Forget it.

ATTIE: All right for you. When you're calling the tune.

FARROL: It's my wife that calls the tune, Attie.

ATTIE: Right then, where is she? Produce her. Bring her out of your hat. How much longer is she likely to be? I said –

FARROL: Search me.

ATTIE: Why hasn't she come down?

FARROL: I told you she was tired.

ATTIE: Thought you had a row.

FARROL: She was tired and we had a row.

ATTIE: I've only your word for it that she's upstairs in bed.

FARROL: You'll have to take my word for it. I know what you're thinking.

ATTIE: I'm thinking it's time I went. You're nuts.

FARROL: That'd make it all the more likely.

ATTIE: Oh sure, your wife's in there. In that chest. I can just see her, can't you? Crammed in at the bottom. With the gardener on top of her.

FARROL: Aren't you going to open it then?

ATTIE: Why?

FARROL: To see what's in it. To satisfy your –

ATTIE: I know what's in it. Bugger all. Look, your wife's upstairs.

FARROL: Trying to convince yourself, eh? Have you heard her? Moving around? Don't you think she'd have put in an appearance before now? You reckon she'd leave the groceries behind the storm-door till half past ten on a Friday? You're joking!

ATTIE: It's got nothing to do with me.

FARROL: If only you knew!

[*A pause, as they eye one another. Suddenly* FARROL *shouts:*]
Lena!

[*But there is no reply. After a pause* FARROL *laughs:* ATTIE *rises.*]
Don't say I didn't warn you, that's all.

[ATTIE *lays down his beer-mug and crosses to the chest.* FARROL *sits watching him, playing with an empty brown paper bag.*

ATTIE *stares at the chest, then bends and unfastens it.*

He looks at FARROL, *then back at the chest.*

FARROL *rises unobtrusively.*

ATTIE *spreads his arms on the lid of the chest. As he is about to raise it* FARROL *brings the paper bag down over* ATTIE's *head.*

A muffled oath from ATTIE: FARROL *laughs.*

ATTIE, *the bag still pressed over his head, makes blindly for* FARROL, *and blunders into the chest.*

ATTIE *teeters, and then stops. At this point* LENA *enters.*

ATTIE *stands still, and suddenly rips the bag from his head. He is face to face with* LENA.]

FARROL [*formally*]: Attie, Lena. Lena, Attie. Consider yourselves old friends. Attie was looking for you, dearest, weren't you Attie? A real flower of the fields, Attie. Is all forgiven, sweetheart? Tell me all is forgiven. I was telling Attie, darling, that we'd had a little trouble, a minor altercation, earlier this evening. He was very impressed. Lena hasn't been too well, you see, Attie. But she's loving and generous and forgiving. What would you like to drink, my love? Guinness or Guinness?

LENA: Sit down and don't make a fool of yourself.

FARROL: My love! [*To* ATTIE] You don't believe me? That she's generous? How about this? [*He takes two boxes from the sideboard.*] Have a deck at these. Virgin white. Expensive as hell. None of your Moss Bros, that little lot. Price tag still on them – she forgot to take it off, the loving devil. How d'you fancy a pair of shirts like these Attie, nine guineas a time, eh?

LENA: Stop making an ass of yourself. Put them back, where they belong.

FARROL: You'll embarrass Attie.

LENA: I may as well have a Guinness. Precious little chance of getting off to sleep while –

FARROL: Drink coming up. [*He pours, refills the others.*]

ATTIE: I'd best be off, Mr Farrol.

FARROL: What? When Lena has just given in? A Guinness is as good as a capitulation, coming from Lena. Your glass.

ATTIE: I'm . . . I mean, I'm sorry to have disturbed you.

FARROL: Attie's a worried man, Lena. Tell her all about the dummie. No? Don't say I don't do my best for you. Cheers anyway. Happy times!

[*They drink.*]

Trouble with Lena, Attie, is she sleepwalks. Goes to bed too early, has to unwind. Quite subconscious. Never knows when she's at it, that's her trouble. Could be at it now, all I know. Difficult to tell. Even to an experienced observer. Probably no idea we're here at all. Then snap, and she's out of it. Back to normal. Shallow level now, tell by her irises. That ought to interest you, eh? Soon she'll be my own generous, loving Lena again. Soon she'll –

LENA: Drop dead!

FARROL [*shrugs*]: What the heck.

LENA [*to* ATTIE]: Give me a cigarette!

[ATTIE *feels in his pockets. He remembers the cigarette-box. He looks at* FARROL *who offers no assistance.* ATTIE *crosses to the cigarette-box, lifts it and takes it to* LENA. *He opens it, and the music plays as she takes a cigarette.* ATTIE *replaces the box, and lights* LENA'*s cigarette. He stands holding the burning match, as she exhales. Then, softly:*] Don't burn your fingers.

FARROL: What did I tell you, Attie?

LENA: Strange, to see my husband's face when he discovers he's been right after all.

ATTIE: Yes, I've a high regard for him.

LENA: I can be extremely sensitive to things, in my sleep. I can sense certain things. Such as the presence of . . . I almost said a stranger. But you aren't exactly a stranger, are you?

FARROL: Course not.

LENA: What are those boxes doing on the floor? Put them where they belong. And we can get down to business. You've come about the rose-garden?

FARROL [*removing the shirt-boxes*]: Are we not rushing it a bit?

LENA: Not if that's why he's come. Is it?

ATTIE: That's right.

LENA: We're beginning to understand one another already.

ATTIE: Yes.

LENA: Have you any credentials?

ATTIE: References?

FARROL [*returning*]: You know he hasn't got –

LENA: I don't mean written references. Written recommendations never made a gardener. I'm talking in practical terms. What have you grown in the past? What success have you had at local shows? Up and down the country? I have to know this. Because my rose-garden isn't just any rose-garden. It's very special. I can't let any Tom, Dick or Harry handle my affairs.

ATTIE: I love roses. I can recite all their names.

LENA: That isn't the question.

ATTIE: You can't care for roses unless you have love for them. But as for paper qualifications, well I can't help there. It isn't something you can, well, commit to paper . . . just like that.

LENA: It isn't something you can rationalize?

ATTIE: I love flowers. If that isn't good enough for you, nothing is. But it all depends on circumstances. I don't mean just terms. But the over-all picture. All I did was ask Mr Farrol there about prospects. I didn't commit myself at any stage. Just to sound him.

LENA: But if I say I'm willing to take you?

ATTIE: I'd have to think it over.

FARROL: Not backing out?

ATTIE: No . . . but, about terms . . .

LENA: There's no need for you to worry about terms. I dictate the terms. That seems to be the whole thing settled.

ATTIE: Not so fast.

FARROL: You can't be as desperate as I thought. As you led me to believe. If you can turn down –

ATTIE: Who's turning down?

LENA: Then you accept?

ATTIE: I can't afford not to.

LENA: Good. You'll have to stay on the premises, of course.

ATTIE: Well yes, that's okay. . . . I'd have to, you know, collect some things, that's all.

LENA: That will be seen to, in the morning.

ATTIE: But –

LENA: That's part of the contract. Clause 1, you might say.

FARROL: You can bed down in this room overnight.

ATTIE: What sort of a hold is it you want over me?

LENA: You came of your own free will.

ATTIE: And I can leave of my own free will. Can't I? I mean, make no mistake about that. There's nothing you can do, either of you, to stop me. Contract's a contract, fair enough. Fully realize that. Gentleman and his bond. But you haven't any hold, no real hold, over me. What I do. Where I go. I mean, how could you have! I'm a free agent, mark my words. What I mean is, if I wanted – I said *if* – I could up and go right now. Nothing to stop me. This instant. You appreciate that? All I'd have to do would be to pick up my carry-out – what's left of it – yes, and my cap . . . and, *if* I wanted to, understand . . . just a supposition, talking in terms of a working hypothesis . . . [*he has in fact lifted his cap and the bag, and is sidling softly round the room*] . . . otherwise I'd lose my self-respect. You wouldn't want that. Man has to have his pride. All I have to do, just showing I'm capable of it, would be to say thanks for the little party, Mr Farrol, and good night, and ... well ... take my leave ... just like this!

[ATTIE *suddenly makes for the door. It is locked. Neither* LENA *nor* FARROL *has moved.* ATTIE *comes back centre, and throws his cap down.*]

FARROL: Here, I'll put down the sofa for you. Cushion'll do for a pillow. Fine and comfortable. Better than a hayloft, must say that for it, eh Attie? Mustn't turn down the comforts of life. Couple of blankets underneath, that's them. Fine and dandy.

[*The sofa has been folded down to make a bed.* ATTIE *rubs his eyes.*]

ATTIE: Okay, so I'm ready for a kip. What's it matter where you kip down, I always say. I accept your ... your terms, whatever they are. On one condition: you leave the rest of the Guinness.

FARROL: Don't say it hasn't worked out, Attie. For the best. Don't say I haven't done what I can for you, all along the line.

LENA: Goodnight, Attie.

[LENA *exits.* FARROL *makes to follow, but* ATTIE *halts him.*]

ATTIE: There's ... there's just the one thing, Mr Farrol. ... I mean, what if I ... during the night, I mean ... after all that beer ...?

FARROL [*gestures*]: Through there. But you needn't get any fancy ideas. The windows aren't big enough to let a rat out. Sweet dreams!

[FARROL *exits.* ATTIE *is stock-still for a moment. Then he shrugs and turns away. The door is locked. He wipes the back of his hand across his forehead. He takes the apple from his pocket, is about to bite into it, but instead replaces it on the fruit dish.*

He pours another mugful of beer, but as he is on the point of drinking he changes his mind and puts the mug down hurriedly.]

ATTIE: Sweet dreams, my fanny! [*He exits to the toilet.*]

[*Blackout*]

Some hours have passed. As the lights come up ATTIE *is sprawled on the make-shift bed surrounded by empty bottles and apple-cores. He yawns.*

Rising, he stretches himself and crosses to the sideboard. He touches the cigarette-box gingerly. As he opens the lid the tune starts. He closes the lid sharply, and listens.

An idea strikes him. Taking the box, he disappears under the blankets. Movement. When he surfaces there is a cigarette in his mouth, and the box is closed again. Pleased with himself, he replaces the box and lights the cigarette.

After a few puffs his gaze settles on the chest. He moves towards it, slowly. He bends and touches the lid, looks round at the cigarette-box, and straightens up again. He stubs his cigarette and returns to the chest. Slowly he raises the heavy lid, and gives a low whistle.

From the chest he takes a crown with gems and band of ermine. He carries the crown carefully to the centre of the room and lays it down. He walks round it, studying it. He lifts it, but lays it down again. Taking out a comb, he tidies his hair and puts the comb back in his pocket. He wipes his hands.

Lifting the crown, he sits in LENA's *chair. He holds the crown at arm's length over his head.*

ATTIE [*making the sound of a fanfare*]: Too too-too-roo-too ta-too . . . !
    [*Slowly he lowers the crown towards his head. A rap at the door.* ATTIE *freezes. Another rap. And swiftly he puts the crown back in the chest and closes the lid. He sits casually on the chest.* LENA *enters, wearing a rich red dressing-gown over a white night-dress.* ATTIE *rises.*]

LENA: I came to see whether you were comfortable.

ATTIE: Bit of a draught, that's all.

LENA: I thought perhaps you mightn't be able to sleep. It's thundery.

ATTIE: It's luxurious. Why, it's as good as . . . as a palace.

LENA: A palace?

ATTIE: Compared with some of the places I've known. Had to get accustomed to. Kipped in, like.

LENA: I think it's actually started raining.

ATTIE: Wouldn't know. Dry enough in here.

LENA: Out in the garden, I meant.

ATTIE: Why should that interest me? Whether it's raining – ?

LENA: Wasn't that why you came?

ATTIE: It's damp.

LENA: Thought you said it was dry?

ATTIE: All these bottles.

LENA: A minute ago you said it was like a palace.

ATTIE: Palaces can be damp. Can't they? Often as not. Don't start telling me about palaces. I know palaces. Palaces are my home ground. Going to wrack and ruin, majority of them, no one to look after them properly. Same with their gardens. Palace gardens, trampled on, churned up, half a dollar a time and no litter. Ancient homes. As if that made any difference. To the destruction.

LENA: You haven't seen your garden yet?

ATTIE: My garden?

LENA: That was the agreement.

ATTIE: How could I have seen it?

LENA: From outside?

ATTIE: All I've seen were the walls. Too high to get over, you know that. You must know that. You'd need tin ribs anyway, need a ruddy suit of armour, for those walls. Cut your liver out trying to scale them. With bits of glass, broken bottles stuck in. . . . Where's Mr Farrol?

LENA: Upstairs, sleeping. . . . He was tired.

ATTIE: Not starting all that over again, are we?

LENA: I couldn't sleep. So I thought I'd look for company.

ATTIE: Has he got tin ribs?

LENA: I thought I'd ask your advice. Straight away. About the roses. Most of them are old plants. Time some of the beds were renewed. Given new occupants. What would you suggest?

ATTIE: Depends on the soil. So many things.

LENA: Then there's the pruning. Your speciality. And the twin ramblers on the trellis to be made secure. And possibly a hardy breed, for the north-facing wall. What do you suggest, Attie? Iceberg? Peace? Elizabeth of Glamis?

ATTIE: Look, I'm not experienced enough in roses. Haven't got the know-how. Not to your level. I'd stay and do my best, but the garden'd suffer. You need someone who's . . . well, akin. I'm not in that league, Mrs Farrol . . .

LENA: Lena.

ATTIE: That's right. Lena. I'd do all I could, but it wouldn't be good enough. There'd be no guarantee. I haven't got what it takes, not rose-wise. You'd be better off with a professional – a man that knows his onions, where roses are concerned.

LENA: Go on.

ATTIE: That's it. That's my say. I don't want to give the impression of false pretences.

LENA: You're not backing out on our agreement. Not now. Not if I have my way of it.

ATTIE: I'm damn well –

LENA: Don't worry, Attie. I'll make it well worth your while.

ATTIE: You've got it all wrong. I'm not cut out for this sort of thing.

LENA: You underestimate yourself.

ATTIE: Mind if I have a . . . have a smoke?

[LENA *offers the box to him. He takes a cigarette, as the tune plays. She shuts the box. This time she lights his cigarette.*]

LENA: You're trembling, Attie.

ATTIE: I'm shivering.

LENA: I'm the one that ought to be shivering. It's chilly outside. All I'm wearing is a thin night-dress, under this dressing-gown. With nothing beneath, Attie. Nothing at all. Between it and my skin. See how thin it is. Next to my skin. Following the line of my body, from here . . . right down . . . to here. . . . You're not the one who should be shivering, Attie. You're so close I can almost feel you, sense your body trembling, close to mine. Close to my body . . .

ATTIE [*helplessly*]: My cigarette's gone out!

[*She takes it from between his fingers and lays it aside. Slowly, the lights change to a red glow.*]

LENA: Do you really not know what to do, Attie? Really and truly? Have you not had any experience? Come, come, I'm sure you must've had some experience, somewhere. In your life-time. Just think. Try to remember. You think about it, Attie. Doesn't some instinct tell you? So that you can take the opportunity when it's offered to you? Just like that, Attie? On a plate?

ATTIE: Look Lena . . .

LENA: Look, Attie!

ATTIE: Mr Farrol –

LENA: Has nothing to do with it. This is between you and me, Attie. You and me. Do you understand? Think how wonderful it would be? Imagine! Close your eyes and imagine how wonderful it would be. Think of the satisfaction. To us both. Especially to you. Can't you imagine it? The first seed, the slow flowering, the sweet slow flowering, the petals unfolding slowly and tenderly in the balm of the air, the chill giving way to warmth, being displaced, the seed thrusting its way in and up ... and up ... and up, to the air. All the world compressed and tightening, then slackening, slaking off, the whole flower rising and blooming, the petals spreading and perfuming the garden, the sweetness, the honey, the perfect luxury of it, the full flower there, there in front of you, before you, in your grasp for the taking, for the picking, the plucking, the pruning, your hand to do the plucking. ... All yours, Attie ... yours ...

ATTIE: Lena ...

LENA: The petals thrust back, giving off their perfume, soft as silk, the silken petals, the honey dropping and flowing and running, the whole garden dripping and flowing with honey, and you deep at the centre, the centre of it all. ... The roses, Attie. ... The roses, the rose-garden all yours, to take for your very own, the petals opening, your fingers flexing and slipping inside, sliding between the opening petals, the stamens erect, then drooping, the scent of pollen perfuming the air, the blue midnight air heavy and dripping with the scent of honey, of pollen drifting, the scent of honey, of spices, blue in the night air, blue and green, and shot with gold ... with velvet ... and gold ...

ATTIE: ... and gold

LENA: ... and gold

ATTIE: ... and gold

LENA: ... and

ATTIE: ... gold

LENA: ... and

ATTIE: ... gold

LENA: ... and

BOTH: ... gold
  and gold.

  [*A pause.* ATTIE'*s breathing. Then:*]

ATTIE: Lena ... Lena ...

LENA: You're not trembling now. You're not shivering or trembling.

ATTIE: I could go a smoke!

LENA: No. It's forbidden.

ATTIE: But –

LENA: It's taboo. You can't have it, now.

ATTIE: Look, I'd better be –

LENA: It's all right.

ATTIE: What if he – ?

LENA: He won't. Besides, do you think it would matter? If he did? You disappoint me. As if that could make any difference to our contract.

ATTIE: It mightn't make any difference to us, but –

LENA: Attie . . .

ATTIE: Look, I've every right –

LENA: No real right. Any longer. Not even your body is your own, now. Relax, Attie, while you can. And let warm seas flow over you. Over your mind.

ATTIE: You're . . . you're going on as if you owned me. As if I belonged to you.

LENA: Isn't that a fair assumption, after what has happened?

ATTIE: I don't think so at all. It's as if, as if you were a queen or someone. That's it, a queen. Owning me. As though I was a subject. One of your subjects. You think I don't know? That's where you're wrong. I know what I'm up against. What's going on. I've a pretty shrewd notion. Because I know, you see. I know. I've found out. You didn't know that, did you? That's not according to plan.

LENA: What do you know, Attie?

ATTIE: Now it's you that's asking the questions. The boot's on the other foot.

LENA: What do you know?

ATTIE: About the crown. I know about the crown.

[*A roll of thunder, overhead.*]

LENA: How could you know about that?

ATTIE: That shook you. It's in that chest.

LENA: I thought it was locked.

ATTIE: Well, it wasn't locked. And I opened it. And found what was inside . . .

[LENA *smiles.* ATTIE *tails off.*]

You're having me on again. You didn't think it was locked. How could you possibly think it was locked? You're toying with me, that's all. I might be a mug in some ways, but –

LENA: Toying with you?

ATTIE: You needn't pretend. Any longer. I can see through you. You're transparent.

LENA: Attie . . .

ATTIE: I was a mug even to want to believe you. After all that, with him.

LENA: So you know about the crown?

ATTIE: Yes, I know about your crown. Don't expect a bloke to sit up all night chewing his toe-nails, do you? Well, what d'you expect?

LENA: My crown?

ATTIE: Your crown. Or is it his? Bloody Farrol's? Is that it? His big secret? Can just see him in it. Up and down the front street on a Saturday afternoon, I can just hear him say, 'I'm not loitering, Constable, I'm waiting for my equerry.' Or if he doesn't quite make it, you know, back from the Arms at night. I can just see him lying there flaked out in the gutter. And two old ladies walking past. And one turning to the other and saying 'I say, my dear, I do believe someone has thrown out a perfectly good king.' That'd please him. Kingly Farrol. Farrol the First! Lying there, outside the Arms, spewing himself up.

LENA: He doesn't wear it, at the moment.

ATTIE: You're telling me. It's in that chest.

LENA: I wonder if it would fit you?

ATTIE: Of course.

LENA: You sound very certain.

ATTIE: I tried it on. Perfect fit. Tight as an old sock.

LENA: We thought it might fit. That's why you're here.

ATTIE: Look, my skull doesn't button up the back. You thought it might fit? You didn't even know –

LENA: So long as you've tried it, and it fits. You'll have to go through with it now. You couldn't very well back out now.

ATTIE: It's very kind of you, I mean to say, but I couldn't . . . well, it wouldn't be any use to me. Except to pawn it, hawk it or something. I couldn't go to the match wearing it on a Saturday afternoon. I'd get mobbed, I'd get murdered. No, it's safer where it is.

LENA: Don't worry. You won't leave this room in it.

ATTIE: That's a relief. Is there any more Guinness?

LENA: Have you forgotten? That's taboo.

ATTIE: What you want, Lena, what you want's some kind of a dummie. You want me to be king, that it? To sit here, day in and day out, night after night, satisfying you? Well you're not on.

LENA: Not satisfied?

ATTIE: Look, Lena, I couldn't cope. Honest. It just isn't in me. It might not really fit. When it's worn in. After all. I maybe made a mistake. An error. Yes, probably the beer that did it. Like as not I got it wrong. Got carried away. I'm ... what I'm trying to say, I'm not the type. Why don't you get someone else?

LENA: It's too late for that, Attie.

ATTIE: Too late?

[Overhead, a roll of thunder.]

LENA [at the window]: It's still raining. Torrents. Outside. In the garden. I thought you might have prevented it.

ATTIE: Me?

LENA: You.

ATTIE: I'll ... I'll be back in a minute.

[ATTIE exits to the toilet. Pause. The other door opens, and FARROL enters. He is in striped pyjamas, and a dark dressing-gown.]

FARROL: Thunder always wakens me. Where is he?

[LENA gestures.]

FARROL: Still raining outside. Torrents.

[ATTIE re-enters, sees FARROL, and halts.]

FARROL [to ATTIE]: Thought you might have prevented it.

ATTIE: What?

FARROL: The storm, what do you think?

ATTIE: Come off it.

FARROL: From what you told me earlier, in the pub –

ATTIE: You didn't take that seriously, did you? I mean, you didn't ruddy well take that – ?

FARROL: It's what you said, isn't it?

ATTIE: I can't remember.

FARROL: How you could work spells on the weather. Charms. Work a charm on the crops. On the trees. On growing things.

ATTIE: I said?

FARROL: How you could make the crops grow, and the trees bear fruit, the grain mature, and the bee store her honey. How you could make the rains come, and water the land.

ATTIE: I said that? I must've been drunk.

FARROL: I heard you say –

ATTIE: I was speaking to the others.

FARROL: But I heard you.

ATTIE: Overheard me. I wasn't speaking to –

FARROL: You were speaking to those that'd believe you. Give credit to what you had to say. Buy you drinks, set you up pints, on the strength of what you were promising to do. Of your promises. You would ripen the fruit, bring forth the blossom, make the head heavy . . .

LENA: You would care for the roses, send sun and shower, would give perfume and colour.

FARROL: You would make the sun your brandy-cask. You would gather the rain-clouds, water the land.

LENA: And they believed you.

[*A pause.*]

FARROL: Does the crown fit?

LENA: Yes.

ATTIE: No.

FARROL: We'll soon find out. We'll get you to try it on.

LENA: He tried it on himself.

ATTIE: And it didn't fit.

LENA: So you did try it on.

ATTIE: No.

FARROL: We'll see for ourselves. Whether it fits or not. Turn round.

[ATTIE *does so.*]

And again . . . and again . . . face the front. Stand still. Pick up that cover. . . . Fold those blankets. Careful, careful . . . watch the bottles. Mess you've made.

[ATTIE *obeys orders.*]

LENA: Careful.

FARROL: Watch your feet.

LENA: Act like a man.

FARROL: Ready?

LENA: Ready?

ATTIE [*breathlessly*]: Re—ady.

FARROL: You haven't even started yet. Not in trim, your trouble. Come on, come on, have to find something to prise that chest open with. Could do with an axe, none handy, have to make do best we can. Or an iron spar. None handy? Need something. In there, try in there, must be something lying around, pick-handle or something. Heavy oak, you know. Hurry up, get a move on, we haven't all night.

[ATTIE *has exited to the toilet, and comes back breathlessly with an iron rod. He offers this to* FARROL, *who laughs.*]

What's that for, you bloody fool? It's not locked.

[FARROL *subdues* ATTIE, *who slumps to his knees.* LENA *and* FARROL *open the chest.* LENA *takes out the crown.* FARROL *positions* ATTIE. *Ceremonially* LENA *places the crown on* ATTIE'S *head.* FARROL *drapes* LENA'S *dressing-gown on* ATTIE, *like a red cloak.*]

Right!

[*From the chest* LENA *brings a brass bell. This is placed in* ATTIE'S *right hand. The rod is placed in his left hand. His arms are crossed on his breast. They walk round him, admiringly.* ATTIE *is mute. Overhead, a roll of thunder. They glance up, then at each other.* ATTIE *does not notice. Then he seems to come to.*]

ATTIE [*indicating the bell*]: What's this?

FARROL: A bell.

ATTIE: What's it for?

FARROL: To keep the rains away.

[*Pause.* ATTIE *laughs nervously.*]

ATTIE: Reminds me of a story. That. About a man – stop me if you've heard it – about a man who'd spent a number of years, yes, a good few years, in Africa. Darkest Africa. And –

FARROL: I'll tell you something. Are you listening?

[ATTIE *nods.*]

You know where Uganda is?

[ATTIE *nods.*]

Among certain tribes in Uganda ... are you listening to me? Really concentrating on what I'm saying?

ATTIE: I'm listening.

FARROL: Among certain tribes in Uganda the king was responsible for feeding his people. But every so often there are the monsoons. And the danger of rain destroying the crops. If there was too much rain, the seed would rot, the grain be destroyed, the people starve. They had to rely on the king making the rains go away.

ATTIE: How?

FARROL: I'm answering your question. The king had a bell. A little bell. And he rang it, to make the rains stop. He ordered the rain to stop, and rang his bell. And the crops were saved.

ATTIE: And if the rains didn't stop?

FARROL: They took the king, and they killed him.

ATTIE: How did they kill him?

FARROL: There were various ways.

ATTIE: Why did they have to kill him?

LENA: To save the land.

FARROL: From pollution. To save themselves.

LENA: To give themselves new life.

[*Pause.*]

ATTIE: Why are you telling me this?

FARROL: Why don't you sit down? After all, even kings have the right to relax.

ATTIE: I'm not a ruddy king – how often do I have to tell you?

FARROL: You're far too modest.

[ATTIE *is made to sit. He is still in position, arms folded, as on a throne.*]

ATTIE: Well?

FARROL: Better start ringing your bell.

LENA: You don't want the roses to be swept away? And drowned?

ATTIE: But a bell won't stop –

LENA: The rain?

FARROL: And if the rains don't go off, the king has to be killed.

ATTIE: You can't kill a king.

FARROL: Kings are always being killed.

LENA: Over and over again.

FARROL: After they've served their purpose.

ATTIE: Look, if I were to ring the bell, the rains might go off. But that wouldn't mean I'd stopped them. I can't stop the rain.

FARROL: You're the king.

ATTIE: If I'm the king, then surely I'm entitled to draw up the rules? What's the point of a king, if he doesn't enforce his own rules?

FARROL: All the king can do is obey. Till his strength fails.

ATTIE: Nothing wrong with my strength. My strength isn't failing. Ask her.

FARROL: Your strength as king. Not in other things.

LENA: Your strength to stop the rain.

ATTIE: So, you give me a stupid, pissing little bell, and tell me to stop the rain?

FARROL: It is up to you –

ATTIE: I know what's up to me. It's up to me –

LENA: To be king. With crown and sceptre, with silver bell and cloak of velours. To act like a king, As a king should. With pomp and with majesty. All dominion and power. The three shires and beyond. Over baron and serf, to hold your sway. Heaven and earth in the palm of your hand.

ATTIE: For God's sake . . .

FARROL: In God's name!

ATTIE: Then I'll show you. If I'm the king I'll bloody well be king. And act like one. I'll wield dominion and power, you wait and see. And you know what'd really do you good, teach you a lesson? If I did stop the rain. That'd shake you, really shock you, eh? After the high-handed way you've treated me. If it worked. If, now that I'd become king, there really was some secret power invested in me. That would humble you. And my aim is to humble you. I see that as part of my kingly duty.

FARROL: Go on.

ATTIE: That would astonish you, open your eyes. If I was to ring my bell, and the rains were to cease. That would prove my power, my hold. Prove I was stronger than you. And in my rightful place. Stronger than your stupid little, pissy little game. With its petty rules. But you bargained without one thing. My strength. Without me. She gave me the power. Invested in me. You weren't here. When it was decreed. I'm regal. Your king. You'll come at my every beck and call. My merest whim. You'll kneel before me. At my wish and command. I'll dominate you utterly. Kneel! Kneel, before your king! You thought I was your plaything? I, your domino? That I was nothing but a braggart? That it was nothing but bravado? I'll see you learn. The hard way. Down on your knees, before me!

[*When* LENA *and* FARROL *are kneeling, he continues.*]

I'll humour you. I'll ring your little bell. But only for so long as suits me. After that things will change. Soon I'll have you kissing my arse. Do you hear? With this bell, I can stop the skies. I have power invested in me. I am master of the seasons. My world is awash with flowers, it trails with roses. I drink from the brandy-cask of the sun. Am master of storm and tempest, of moon and stars. I am king. Do you hear? King! Now I shall behave like a king.

[*Overhead, a thunder-roll.* ATTIE *looks up, ringing the bell.*]

I command you, order you, do you hear ... I who have been appointed king of the heavens, anointed ruler of the skies, it is I who order you ... in my name ... I decree and command ... in the name of the king ... let the storm cease, the rains cease, the heavens seal themselves ...

[*Another thunder-clap, close.* FARROL *rises, slowly. Still* ATTIE *rings the bell.*]

Do not the vast heavens hear? Let them then obey! The heavens seal themselves ... at my kingly behest ... in the king's name!

[*Thunder and lightning. With one hand* ATTIE *keeps ringing the bell. The other covers his eyes.*]

Obey! Obey! Why don't ... they heed me? I ... am ... the ... king ... ordained and anointed ... where is my strength? My power. ... I cannot see. ... I am ... alone ... my strength ... my strength ... is sapped ...

[*He lolls, exhausted, making a last despairing effort to ring the bell. As he grows weaker* FARROL *approaches him and removes the crown.*]

My ... power ... is ... gone ...

[FARROL, *the silk sash from the dressing-gown in his hands, closes on* ATTIE *from behind.* ATTIE *extends his arms as if in final appeal. With the sash,* FARROL *strangles him.* ATTIE's *body slumps to the floor. Silence, but for* FARROL's *breathing. A pause, as* FARROL *looks down at* ATTIE, *then at* LENA *who is still kneeling.*]

FARROL: I must see to the garden.

[*Slowly* FARROL *exits.* LENA *looks up, rises and crosses to* ATTIE. *Stooping, she loosens the sash from his neck, and arranges the dressing-gown over his body like a cloak. She takes his head gently in her lap.*]

LENA: Attie ... Attie ...

[*A pause, then* FARROL *enters, carrying a bunch of roses in bloom. He crosses to* LENA, *who does not look up.*]

FARROL: That's all. There don't seem to be any more left.

LENA: Put them down there.

FARROL: It looks as though they've all been destroyed by the rain. [*He lays the roses beside her. Crossing to the window, he draws the curtains aside so that the early light strikes her.*] Looks as though the storm has passed. It's clearing, outside.

LENA: Why does it always have to spoil everything?

[*FARROL shrugs. He exits, silently. LENA is placing the roses on ATTIE's body. Now, cradling his head in her arms, she breaks down.*] Why does everything … always … have to be spoiled? [*She rocks to and fro, weeping.*]

[*Slowly to Blackout*]

IAN HAMILTON FINLAY

Walking Through Seaweed

CHARACTERS

FIRST GIRL
SECOND GIRL

The scene is a city street of the 1960s, at dusk. Two teenage girls have sauntered up to look in a shop-window. Three doors away is a cafe with a juke-box, its raucous or wistful pop songs carrying faintly into the street.

Music: any wistful pop song.

FIRST GIRL: See them toffee-apples in the window?

SECOND GIRL: Yep.

FIRST GIRL: Real old-fashioned they look. – Fancy toffee-apples . . .

SECOND GIRL: You ever ate toffee-apples?

FIRST GIRL: Yep. Sure we ate them. Lots of times. When I was wee we was great on toffee-apples. But I wouldn't eat one now. It'd be undignified.

SECOND GIRL: Maybe I could go in the shop and get one of them toffee-apples . . .

FIRST GIRL: And eat it now – out here in the street? Not when you're out with *me* you don't eat a toffee-apple . . .

SECOND GIRL: Oh well, all right. . . . But I think it would be nice to have eaten one of them toffee-apples.

FIRST GIRL: It's O.K. for kids to eat toffee-apples. But we ain't kids now. We're sixteen.

SECOND GIRL: Yep. Grown-up women.

[*Pause. The pop song grows momentarily louder.*]

How do you like that one that's on the juke-box in the cafe now?

FIRST GIRL: I never heard that one before.

SECOND GIRL: It was on the telly.

FIRST GIRL: Was it? When?

SECOND GIRL: Last Sunday.

FIRST GIRL: We ain't got a telly yet.

SECOND GIRL: No.

FIRST GIRL: Everyone around us – they've all got tellys . . .

SECOND GIRL: Yep.

FIRST GIRL: Isn't that Cliff, or someone, singing?

SECOND GIRL: It sounds like it's Cliff . . . or someone. . . . Yep.

FIRST GIRL: It's sort of sad.

SECOND GIRL: Yep. – I like that. [*Pause.*] You want to go in the cafe and listen to the juke-box?

FIRST GIRL: In a minute. When we've looked in the window here. [*Pause.*] It's sort of, maybe, *too* sad – that one.

187

SECOND GIRL: I like the sad ones. I don't like them cheery ones much.

FIRST GIRL: Maybe it *ain't* Cliff singing.

SECOND GIRL: It *sounds* like him – or someone. . .

　　[*Pause. The music begins to fade.*]

Them toffee-apples look real good. You can see the apple-skin right through the toffee too . . .

FIRST GIRL: Yep. There ain't much toffee . . .

SECOND GIRL: There's plenty toffee. It's just you can see right through it, to the apple-skin.

FIRST GIRL: It'll be mostly water and sugar.

SECOND GIRL: And d'you see them liquorice-straps?

FIRST GIRL: Which?

SECOND GIRL: There – by the sweetie-cigarettes. You see them?

FIRST GIRL: Yep. We ate them too.

SECOND GIRL: So did we.

FIRST GIRL: All of us ate them liquorice-straps.

SECOND GIRL: You know what I always think of when I see them old-fashioned rolled-up liquorice-straps?

FIRST GIRL: No.

SECOND GIRL: Seaweed.

FIRST GIRL: What?

SECOND GIRL: Seaweed. [*Pause.*] You ever walked through seaweed – that seaweed that grows by the sea – you know? That seaweed that's all slippery . . . And mostly brown – like them straps of liquorice?

FIRST GIRL: No.

SECOND GIRL: You never walked through it?

FIRST GIRL: No.

SECOND GIRL: You never took your shoes and stockings off – and sort of – paddled through it?

FIRST GIRL: No. I'd be scared to.

SECOND GIRL: Why'd you be scared to?

FIRST GIRL: There might be *things* in it.

SECOND GIRL: What kind of things would there be in seaweed?

FIRST GIRL: Oh, I dunno. Crabs maybe. – Maybe there'd be crabs in it would come and bite you – and – [*Pause*] I'd be *scared* to walk through seaweed.

SECOND GIRL: You just don't know *what's* in seaweed.

FIRST GIRL: That's what I'm telling you. I'd be scared to walk in seaweed. – Maybe there'd even be a lobster in seaweed. – Did you ever go in a rest-ur-ant and *eat* a lobster?

SECOND GIRL: Not yet. But I'm going to – soon.

FIRST GIRL: Maybe – maybe if you go around the place walking in seaweed – maybe you'll never get to eat a lobster. Maybe a lobster will have eaten *you*.

SECOND GIRL: Oh, but it's lovely to walk in seaweed. . . . You take off your shoes and your socks – and you carry them . . . and you go walking all through it – right up to your ankles in it – like you was on a tight-rope . . .

FIRST GIRL: Like you was on what?

SECOND GIRL: Like on a tight-rope – You know, a tight-rope . . .

FIRST GIRL: Oh, a tight-rope, like in the circus?

SECOND GIRL: Yep.

FIRST GIRL: I seen a circus – a real big one – on the telly once . . .

SECOND GIRL: Well, if you saw the circus you'd see a tight-rope.

FIRST GIRL: Yep. There was lions – and things – and some of them elephants too.

SECOND GIRL: Yep? And a lady on a tight-rope?

FIRST GIRL: Yep.

SECOND GIRL: Well, that's a tight-rope. – And walking through seaweed – it's like on a tight-rope – all slippery – and you got to walk carefully. . . . Some of it looks like them straps of liquorice. And there's some, when you walk on it, goes off pop! [*Pause.*] That kind's like a lot of little . . . like. . . . Well, I dunno, but it can go off pop.

FIRST GIRL: I seen that sort. You can make it pop.

SECOND GIRL: Yep. – You can pop it if you stand on it hard enough.

FIRST GIRL: I popped it myself sometimes. – You know, with my shoes on.

SECOND GIRL: Well, some of the seaweed – it's that funny pop-stuff, and others is kind of longer, like them straps of liquorice there. That's the kind that's always the slipperiest. – You got to walk on it very carefully. . . . You got to walk carefully or maybe you'd slip . . . and then you'd get your dress all wet. . . . So you hold your arms out.

FIRST GIRL: How?

SECOND GIRL: Well, like the lady did on the tight-rope. Holding your arms out – that helps you balance – but you got to take just small steps . . . or you'd maybe fall.

FIRST GIRL: I never went in for walking through seaweed. – Well, I *have* walked through it. But just with my shoes on.

SECOND GIRL: That ain't *really* walking through seaweed.

FIRST GIRL: I'll tell you something, it can spoil your shoes.

SECOND GIRL: I always take my shoes *off*.

FIRST GIRL: So far as I'm concerned, you can keep that seaweed.

SECOND GIRL: Maybe you *have* to walk through seaweed – if you want to get *past* the seaweed and down to the *sea*.

FIRST GIRL: There's a lot of it grows on the top of rocks.

SECOND GIRL: There's a lot of it grows all over the seaside. – And if you want to get to where the sea is, well, you've got to walk through it. . . . But you've got to walk careful . . .

FIRST GIRL: Yep. It can ruin a pair of shoes.

SECOND GIRL: Not if you take them off and carry them.

FIRST GIRL: That's O.K. for *you* – you ain't *scared* of seaweed.

SECOND GIRL: What's to be scared of in seaweed?

FIRST GIRL: Well, maybe – crabs – or –

SECOND GIRL: Or what?

FIRST GIRL: I dunno. You can't *see*, though . . .

SECOND GIRL: Yep. You can't see *what's* in seaweed. I like that. It's sort of exciting . . .

FIRST GIRL: You got funny ideas of what's exciting . . .

SECOND GIRL: You scared of crabs?

FIRST GIRL: Uh-huh. I ain't as scared of crabs as I am of spiders. But I'm scared of crabs. Crabs can *bite*.

SECOND GIRL: I never yet got bit by a crab.

FIRST GIRL: You just wait. – Walking through seaweed.

SECOND GIRL: I walk through it – up to my ankles – in my bare feet – just like a dancer!

FIRST GIRL: You *said* like a telly-tight-rope-lady.

SECOND GIRL: O.K. like a telly-tight-rope-lady. Or like a dancer. . . . It makes me *feel* like a dancer . . .

FIRST GIRL: I like dancing.

SECOND GIRL: So do I.

FIRST GIRL: I like rock-an'-roll and jiving.

SECOND GIRL: I like that too – it's lovely.

FIRST GIRL: Everyone goes jiving.

SECOND GIRL: Yep. [*Pause.*] You got a boy friend?

FIRST GIRL: Yep. I got lots of them.

SECOND GIRL: You got lots of boy friends?

FIRST GIRL: Yep.

SECOND GIRL: What d'you do with them?

FIRST GIRL: Not much. . . . Go jiving.

SECOND GIRL: That all?

FIRST GIRL: Go to the pictures.

SECOND GIRL: That all?

FIRST GIRL: What else? – Go jiving, go to the pictures. Play the juke-box in a cafe. What else?

SECOND GIRL: I got a boy friend.

FIRST GIRL: Have you?

SECOND GIRL: Yep. I got a boy friend. And he's sort of special. I mean – I mean I've just the one special boy friend – and do you know what he and I do?

FIRST GIRL: No.

SECOND GIRL: Well, guess – go on. Remember about – about the seaweed, and – . Remember he's my one special boy friend. . . . Now you try and guess what he and I do . . .

FIRST GIRL: Go to the pictures?

SECOND GIRL: No.

FIRST GIRL: Go jiving?

SECOND GIRL: No.

FIRST GIRL: If you had enough money, you could go jiving – or something – every night.

SECOND GIRL: Oh, he and I got plenty money. He and I are *loaded*. – But we don't go jiving.

FIRST GIRL: No? Can't he jive then?

SECOND GIRL: Yep. But he doesn't want to. – He ain't like an ordinary boy. He's special.

FIRST GIRL: All the boys nowadays go jiving.

SECOND GIRL: You're supposed to be guessing what he and I do . . .

FIRST GIRL: No pictures. . . . No jiving. . . . I suppose you go in a cafe and play the juke-box . . .

SECOND GIRL: No. We never play a juke-box.

FIRST GIRL: Sounds like your boy must be a square.

SECOND GIRL: No, he ain't a square.

FIRST GIRL: Well, what d'you do? You'll have to tell me.

SECOND GIRL: Me and my boy friend – I told you he's special – *we go walking through seaweed*.

FIRST GIRL: You don't!

SECOND GIRL: But we do. – We go – in his car – down to where the sea is, and then – then we take off our shoes . . . and we walk through the seaweed . . . it's ever so lovely!

FIRST GIRL: You must be crackers – you and your boy friend.

SECOND GIRL: We are not crackers. He's a very nice boy. [*Pause.*] And while we're walking along through the seaweed – he's ever such a nice boy – he takes hold of my hand . . .

FIRST GIRL: What does he do?

SECOND GIRL: When we're walking?

FIRST GIRL: No, what does he *do*? What does he work at?

SECOND GIRL: He's – he's in advertising.

FIRST GIRL: What's his name?

SECOND GIRL: His first name's Paul.

FIRST GIRL: You ain't just making all of this up, are you?

SECOND GIRL: How'd I be making it up? I told you his name, didn't I – Paul. His name is Paul and he's ever so handsome. . . . He has nice dark hair and he's . . . kind of smooth . . .

FIRST GIRL: It doesn't sound to me like a nice, smooth, handsome boy that's in advertising – a kind of a boy like this Paul – would want to go walking through a lot of seaweed . . .

SECOND GIRL: I beg your pardon, but he *does*. Let me tell you – he wouldn't *mind* getting bit by a crab. [*Pause.*] The fact is, he's *fond* of crabs.

FIRST GIRL: Is he?

SECOND GIRL: And we never do get bit.

FIRST GIRL: What kind of a seaweed is that seaweed?

SECOND GIRL: Well, I'll tell you. . . . We walk through every kind of seaweed – the liquorice stuff like all them straps there – and also **the** other poppy kind. . . . And as we walk, we hold hands.

FIRST GIRL: It sounds square to me.

SECOND GIRL: Well, it isn't. – We could take you along with us one day. . . . You could come along with me and Paul, and we could all three of us go walking in the seaweed . . .

FIRST GIRL: I think your Paul must be bats.

SECOND GIRL: He is *not* bats. He's a very sensible boy. He only sometimes gets fed-up of being in – the office. . . . He gets tired of – the office – and on Saturdays – he wants a change. . . . He gets sick-fed-up-to-the-teeth with that old office. . . . So we go and walk through seaweed . . .

FIRST GIRL: Where d'you work yourself?

SECOND GIRL: In a factory.

FIRST GIRL: How come you happened to meet this Paul fellow who's so handsome and works in advertising?

SECOND GIRL: You sound like you don't believe me.

FIRST GIRL: I'm only asking – how come you met him?

SECOND GIRL: We met . . . at a dance. [*Pause.*] You know – like me and you did. [*Pause.*] I suppose you weren't seeing your boy friends that night?

FIRST GIRL: No.

SECOND GIRL: Sometimes . . . you feel like being more on your own . . . Yep . . .

FIRST GIRL: I never met any handsome smooth fellows – out of advertising – at a dance . . .

SECOND GIRL: Well, maybe you will . . .

FIRST GIRL: I never even *saw* any fellows who looked like that . . .

SECOND GIRL: Well, it's just your luck. – And then Paul and I have the same tastes . . .

FIRST GIRL: Yep. You both like walking through that seaweed . . .

SECOND GIRL: Yep. That's our favourite thing. [*Pause.*] Don't you ever get fed-up with going to the pictures? Don't you ever get sick-fed-up-to-the-teeth with just ordinary boys? And work? And all that . . .?

FIRST GIRL: I dunno. I don't think about it.

SECOND GIRL: Where d'you work?

FIRST GIRL: In a factory.

SECOND GIRL: Same as me.

FIRST GIRL: Yep. Same as you. But I never met – at a dance – any handsome fellow out of advertising. I *read* of them in magazines. I read of *lots* of them in that magazine my Mum gets. ... Tall, dark and smooth. ... And come to think of it, *their* name was Paul.

SECOND GIRL: Paul is a very common name in advertising.

FIRST GIRL: Yep. But I never met one *real* such fellow ...

SECOND GIRL: Maybe you will, though ... someday.

FIRST GIRL: Maybe. Yep. [*Pause.*] I only hope if I do he don't have a taste for walking through seaweed. ... Seaweed – and eating toffee-apples –

SECOND GIRL: You have to walk through seaweed sometimes – if you want to get down to where the sea is ...

FIRST GIRL: Who wants to get to the sea?

SECOND GIRL: I do sometimes. I like it. [*Pause.*] It ain't like a factory – the sea. It's big – and it's deep, and – . Well, I dunno. But I like the sea.

FIRST GIRL: You're a queer one, you are.

SECOND GIRL: What's the name of *your* boy friend?

FIRST GIRL: I already told you – I ain't got just *one* boy friend. I got lots of boy friends. I got hundreds.

SECOND GIRL: Who?

FIRST GIRL: I can't remember their names off-hand ...

SECOND GIRL: Are they Beats?

FIRST GIRL: No they ain't.

SECOND GIRL: Do you think I'm a Beat – a Beat girl?

FIRST GIRL: Yep. The things you say – you must be a Beat. Though – well, you ain't *dressed* like a Beat. But walking in seaweed – *that's* sort of a Beat thing ...

SECOND GIRL: My Paul walks through seaweed. And he ain't a Beat – he's an advertising man.

FIRST GIRL: What do they do in them places?

SECOND GIRL: Advertising places?

FIRST GIRL: Yep. Advertising places. What do they do there?

SECOND GIRL: Well, I dunno. ... I suppose. ... Well, they sort of – advertise things ...

FIRST GIRL: What does *he* do?

SECOND GIRL: Paul?

FIRST GIRL: Yep. What does Paul do in that advertising place?

SECOND GIRL: He. – Well, he never talks much about it. You don't think of – of work when you're walking in the seaweed, see? You feel *romantic*.

FIRST GIRL : All the same you must know what he *does*.

SECOND GIRL: Well, as a matter of fact I do know. What he does is – is – is go to conferences.

FIRST GIRL: Conferences?

SECOND GIRL: Yep.

FIRST GIRL: I read about them conferences in my Mum's magazine . . .

SECOND GIRL: Uh–huh.

FIRST GIRL: It seems like advertising's *all* conferences. There's this boy – the one called Paul, you know – the one who's sort of smooth, and dark, and handsome – and what he does is, go to conferences.

SECOND GIRL: Uh–huh. Well, that's like Paul. Paul goes to conferences.

FIRST GIRL: Then, after the conferences – when they've knocked off advertising – then this boy Paul – this handsome smoothy – he goes and meets his girl and they go to a rest-ur-ant. They sit and eat lobsters and and maybe he's *too* smooth.

SECOND GIRL: My Paul isn't too smooth.

FIRST GIRL: Maybe. But what about the other one?

SECOND GIRL: I ain't *got* another one.

FIRST GIRL: Oh ain't you? Come off it . . .

SECOND GIRL: But I *told* you – we're special.

FIRST GIRL: What about the one with ginger hair and a snub nose. The engineer.

SECOND GIRL: I don't *know* any engineers.

FIRST GIRL: I bet *he* wouldn't walk through seaweed though. I bet the ginger one with the snub nose spends *his* Saturdays at a football match.

SECOND GIRL: I don't love *him*. I love Paul.

FIRST GIRL: You don't care about the engineer, eh?

SECOND GIRL: No. If you want to know, I can't stand him. – All he *ever* wants to do is – go and jive.

FIRST GIRL: That's what I said. He does the same things like everyone else does.

SECOND GIRL: But Paul – he's different.

FIRST GIRL: Yep. He's different. You're telling me he is! Any boy who spends his Saturdays just walking through seaweed is different. He's a head-case. [*Pause.*] Ain't you even *scared* of what might be in it? Ain't you scared of all them crabs and things?

SECOND GIRL: No. I'm more scared of every day.

FIRST GIRL: What?

SECOND GIRL: Every day. The factory, and all that. – Just working and – [*Pause.*] You know, when we've walked all through the seaweed – that kind like liquorice and the other poppy kind – when we've walked all the way through the seaweed, hand in hand –

FIRST GIRL: I thought *you* said you walked with your arms held up.

SECOND GIRL: That's right. Like a tight-rope-lady.

FIRST GIRL: Then how come you can hold hands?

SECOND GIRL: Oh, when Paul and I are walking through the sea-weed – we only hold up our *outside* hands.

FIRST GIRL: Then how d'you carry your shoes and socks?

SECOND GIRL: What?

FIRST GIRL: If the two of you's holding hands and you're holding up your hands like the telly-tight-rope-lady – you only got *two* hands – how d'you carry your shoes and socks? Eh?

SECOND GIRL: Well – Well, what d'you think? We left them up where the car is. See?

FIRST GIRL: Oh? [*Pause.*] One of these days you and Paul – you're going to be *sorry* for walking through seaweed.

SECOND GIRL: Why?

FIRST GIRL: You're going to get bit. That's why.

SECOND GIRL: We never get bit. But we just *might* though. That's what's nice about walking through seaweed – that you might get bit . . . just a *little*. . . . [*Pause.*] Them crabs don't scare *me*. I ain't scared of crabs. They're kind of on *our* side.

FIRST GIRL: What? Whose side?

SECOND GIRL: Me and Paul's side.

FIRST GIRL: No one's on your side. Except you.

SECOND GIRL: Yes they are. The crabs are. All wee things like crabs and – and wee things like that – they *like* me and Paul. [*Pause.*] Do you tell all of them boy friends things?

FIRST GIRL: No. They're just boy friends.

SECOND GIRL: I always tell my Paul *lots* of things.

FIRST GIRL: Do you?

SECOND GIRL: Yep. He's special. I tell him everything.

FIRST GIRL: I can picture it.

SECOND GIRL: What?

FIRST GIRL: You and him – walking in seaweed. – The pair of you standing, walking – right up over the ankles too – in all that seaweed. – All of them crabs ready to bite you – and you and him just standing there telling things . . .

SECOND GIRL: Well, I always feel like telling things there in the seaweed. [*Pause.*] And then – like I was saying to you – when we've walked right through it – all through the seaweed – and us holding hands too – holding our hands and telling our secret things –

FIRST GIRL: What sort of secret things?

SECOND GIRL: Like you tell yourself in bed at night . . .

FIRST GIRL: When I'm in bed at night I go to sleep. If we had the telly I'd sit up later though. Everyone round us has the telly. Only *we* ain't. You feel right out of it.

SECOND GIRL: You can come round some night and see our telly.

FIRST GIRL: That ain't the same as if it was your *own* telly.

SECOND GIRL: No. . . . Well, I was saying – when we've walked all through the seaweed . . .

FIRST GIRL: Yep?

SECOND GIRL: Then me and Paul – he's a real smooth fellow – we come to where the sea is . . .

FIRST GIRL: Yep?

SECOND GIRL: Ain't you listening? We come to the sea.

FIRST GIRL: I'm listening. [*Pause.*] I like those records too. . . . All we got at home's an old wireless. . . . My other sister – she's got a radiogram.

SECOND GIRL: We come to the sea and – it's ever so beautiful.

FIRST GIRL: Some of them's beautiful. I like the cheery ones.

SECOND GIRL: I ain't talking about those records on the old juke-box – I'm telling you about Paul and me: we come to *the sea.*

FIRST GIRL: Well, the sea ain't *much* – in my opinion. I don't care *that* much about the sea that I'd risk my life – and spoil my shoes maybe – just walking through a lot of seaweed, all full of crabs and things, to get to it. [*Pause.*] You could get bit like that. It just ain't nice.

SECOND GIRL: What ain't nice?

FIRST GIRL: Ain't I telling you? – Seaweed ain't nice. And the sea ain't nice. And having no telly ain't. Eating toffee-apples ain't nice either. I wouldn't put a *toe* in that seaweed . . .

SECOND GIRL: But it's – beautiful – the sea.

FIRST GIRL: Yep. I seen it.

SECOND GIRL: Did you ever dream of it?

FIRST GIRL: I don't have dreams. – Only once I dreamed we'd a telly . . .

SECOND GIRL: Yep.

FIRST GIRL: A great big telly with a screen as big as the screen in a picture-house. Not one of them wee old-fashioned picture-houses screens. . . . A big screen, about a hundred yards across . . .

SECOND GIRL: Yep?

FIRST GIRL: With a plastic-plated cabinet.

SECOND GIRL: I ain't never dreamed of a telly set . . .

FIRST GIRL: Another time I had a dream of a radiogram – and once I dreamed I was married to a disc-jockey.

SECOND GIRL: Well, there you are. You *do* have dreams.

FIRST GIRL: Yep. Well. . . . Maybe . . .

SECOND GIRL: I dreamed – I dreamed of the sea once. . . . It was all – kind of dark – and – it was all big and dark – and – . Well, it was – beautiful!

FIRST GIRL: It was a beautiful radiogram in my dream. It was kind of Hi-Fi Stereoscopic. Posh! You didn't even have to press the button. You just had to *think* and it went and switched itself on.

SECOND GIRL: Yep? You know what the sea was like in my dream?

FIRST GIRL: It was Hi-Fi Stereoscopic – with *five* extra loudspeakers.

SECOND GIRL: It was just kind of like *home* – it was just kind of like what a *real home* is . . .

FIRST GIRL: What?

SECOND GIRL: I said – the sea in my dream – it was all big and dark and – just like home!

FIRST GIRL: You talk like a funny picture I saw.

SECOND GIRL: I could have stayed there by it – forever!

FIRST GIRL: It made me want to giggle. *Everyone* giggled.

SECOND GIRL: But my Mum came and waked me up.

FIRST GIRL: What?

SECOND GIRL: I had to wake up – out of my dream.

FIRST GIRL: I wonder why I dreamed of a great big radiogram?

SECOND GIRL: I suppose you'd like to *have* a great big radiogram.

FIRST GIRL: Yep.

SECOND GIRL: Maybe you could come with us down to the sea. Or – well, if Paul had to work some Saturday – if he got asked to do overtime – at advertising – we could go there . . . just the two of us.

FIRST GIRL: And walk through that seaweed – !?

SECOND GIRL: I could hold your hand – like Paul holds my hand – .

FIRST GIRL: You ain't like a magazine fellow that would make me feel all right about that seaweed. . . .

SECOND GIRL: I'd hold it tight. – Ever so tight. [*Pause.*] You and I – we could hold hands – we could go walking – like dancers – like on a tight-rope – all down through all that seaweed – and we'd tell each other things – all our secret things. – Yep, you and me – we could walk through the seaweed – all the way – right to the sea! [*Pause.*] You got to walk through seaweed or – or you don't get anywhere. And seaweed – it's full of crabs and things. . . . But you got to walk through it – hand in hand – with some other person – because it's lovely too – you got to walk – like a dancer – like two dancers – all through the seaweed – right to the sea . . . !

FIRST GIRL: All my life I kept out of seaweed. I stayed away from seaweed. It ain't well – nice stuff. You can go and walk in all that seaweed – you can go if you want to – but not with *me*!

SECOND GIRL: I like the look of them toffee-apples . . .

FIRST GIRL: They're just for kids. [*Pause.*] Let's go in the cafe now. [*Pause.*] I like that one that's on the juke-box. Though it's kind of sad. . . . Come on, let's go . . .

SECOND GIRL: Yep. Let's go in the cafe and play the juke-box. – Maybe some of all of them boy friends of yours will be in the cafe – perhaps.

[*The music grows louder. It is a record – something like – Bobby Darin's* 'Beyond The Sea'.]

Somewhere . . .

Beyond the sea . . .

[*The two girls saunter off as the music grows still louder – then slowly fades.*]

IAN HAMILTON FINLAY

The Estate Hunters

Only the samovar hummed drearily,
and everything was the same as before.

(From a Russian novel.)

CHARACTERS

MR FARQUHARSON

JOHN

TWO FISHERS

SCENE ONE

A kitchen in a tenement. A summer evening. Through the window are the jumbled roofs of other tenements, shipyard cranes and factory chimneys. MR FARQUHARSON, *age sixty, sits at the table, while his small son* JOHN *makes a pot of tea.*

MR FARQUHARSON: Is that tea ready, my boy?

JOHN: Yes, father. Almost.

MR FARQUHARSON: And is it strong?

JOHN: Yes.

MR FARQUHARSON: Black?

JOHN: Yes.

MR FARQUHARSON: How many spoons did you put in the teapot?

JOHN: Four. One for me, one for you, one for the pot – and one extra.

MR FARQUHARSON: Put another spoon in for me, my boy. And let me have that newspaper, will you – .

JOHN: Here you are. [*Takes the newspaper from below the cushion on the armchair, and passes it.*]

MR FARQUHARSON: Thank you, my boy. And now my fountain pen . . .

JOHN: Where is the pen?

MR FARQUHARSON [*jokes*]: How should I know? Just look around for it. It can't have vanished. It must be *somewhere* . . .

JOHN [*opens a drawer. Finds the pen*]: It was in the drawer beside the spare fishing-tackle.

MR FARQUHARSON: Thank you. Splendid. Then there's only one last thing . . .

JOHN: What?

MR FARQUHARSON: My spectacles.

JOHN: Your – . But you've got them *on*!

MR FARQUHARSON: Well, so I have. And I never noticed. [*Pause.*] All right my boy, you can pour the tea now. No. Wait.

[JOHN *looks at his father.*]

You're quite sure you didn't forget to let it stew for a couple of minutes?

JOHN: No.

MR FARQUHARSON: And it's nice and black for me, is it?

JOHN: Yes. It's like tar.

MR FARQUHARSON: Good. Splendid. Then you can go ahead and pour it out.

JOHN: I'm *trying* to . . .

MR FARQUHARSON [*looking*]: What – ?

JOHN: I'm trying to pour it. It won't pour . . .

MR FARQUHARSON: That sounds to me like *very* good tea, my boy.

JOHN [*pokes with his finger in the teapot*]: I made a mistake with the number of spoons, I think. I think I must have put *four* spoons in the teapot *twice*.

MR FARQUHARSON [*thoughtfully*]: Plus one extra . . . makes nine spoons . . .

JOHN: I think so. About that . . .

MR FARQUHARSON [*pretends to be cross*]: 'About that' – what do you mean, my boy? And you expect to be a fisher – . You want to grow up and be a big boy, and catch a lot of trout – and you can't even count the spoons – . [*He shakes his head.*]

JOHN: It's all right now. It was only the spout of the teapot was choked with tea-leaves.

MR FARQUHARSON: Well, I don't wonder.

JOHN: But what we *ought* to have is a proper mustard tin.

MR FARQUHARSON: A mustard tin – . What for, my boy?

JOHN: To put the tea in the pot with. A mustard tin instead of a teaspoon. Haven't you noticed – all the fishers put the tea, and the sugar, in their billycans from a mustard tin.

MR FARQUHARSON: But not when they're at home, in their own houses, I shouldn't expect.

JOHN: They make good tea . . .

MR FARQUHARSON: Well, we might try it. See you remind me to bring a tin of mustard up with me from the shop tomorrow. I have some in stock.

JOHN: But you aren't *going* to the shop tomorrow.

MR FARQUHARSON: Well, that's so. I'd forgotten. But neither I am.

JOHN [*anxious*]: You didn't forget we're going into the country for the whole day tomorrow, fishing?

MR FARQUHARSON: No, I certainly didn't forget. [*Pause.*] We'll just have to make do without the mustard.

JOHN [*puzzled*]: The . . . mustard?

MR FARQUHARSON: Well, there you are. And you think *I* have a bad memory. . . . Didn't you just ask me to bring you a tin of mustard home from the shop?

JOHN: Oh, father – . Really. Don't you see, it isn't the mustard we want – it's *the tin*.

MR FARQUHARSON: Oh, is it – . Well, that reminds me . . .

JOHN: What?

MR FARQUHARSON: I knew there was something I was meaning to ask you. It's been in my head ever since I came in here. And now I remember. It's my tin cup. Did you remember to pack my tin cup for tomorrow? When you're out in the country you get thirsty, and then there's nothing in this world even half as good as a drink of water from some little burn.

JOHN: Well, the tin cup's packed. And here's your tea. [*He pours it out and sets it on the table.*]

MR FARQUHARSON: Thank you, my boy. Thank you. All we need now is my fountain-pen . . .

JOHN [*sighs*]: I passed it to you already. It's there – see? – under your saucer. [*Pause.*] Are there many 'For Sale' advertisements in the paper tonight?

MR FARQUHARSON [*looks in the newspaper*]: Well, let's see . . . yes. Yes, there are. . . . There are one . . . two . . . three . . . four whole columns.

JOHN: Then what's the first place that's for sale. Read it out.

MR FARQUHARSON: Don't rush me, my boy.

JOHN: I'm not rushing you.

MR FARQUHARSON: Yes, you are. Don't argue with your father. The younger generation is always rushing. [*Pause.*] Was that clock wound last night? What's the time?

JOHN [*looks at the alarm-clock on the mantelpiece*]: Ten past eight.

MR FARQUHARSON [*taken aback*]: Oh, is it – . Already. Still, we have practically the whole of the evening to go through these advertisements. Bring a chair in here by me.

JOHN: All right. [*He puts a chair in at the table, kneels on it chin-in-hand, and waits.*]

[*After a pause*] Aren't you going to read out the first advertisement?

MR FARQUHARSON: In just a minute, my boy. Don't rush me. . . .
You can't just rush into a thing of this sort. It takes time. It may
even take *years*.

JOHN: I don't think we'll ever find a place that suits us . . .

MR FARQUHARSON: Of course we will. Are you ready now? Are
you listening?

JOHN: Yes . . .

MR FARQUHARSON: Then I want you to listen very carefully, and
tell me if this first place is a place we would want to buy.

JOHN: Yes, yes. I know that.

MR FARQUHARSON: Well, here's what it says. [*Reads.*] 'For sale.
Stately country mansion. Thirty bedrooms. Dining rooms.
Lounges. Maids' accommodation. Etc., etc. Plus 2,000 acres.
Pheasant, grouse shooting. Salmon fishing. Trout.' [*A long pause.*]
Well?

JOHN [*uncertain*]: We *don't* want to buy it . . .?

MR FARQUHARSON: My boy, I am asking *you*. I don't have to tell
you that there are only the two of us. So it's up to you, too, to
say what you think.

JOHN: How big is 2,000 acres?

MR FARQUHARSON: How big – . Well, let's see . . . you know that
back-green down there below the window?

JOHN: Yes.

MR FARQUHARSON: Well, try to think of the back-green, *including*
the dustbins, and then multiply it – well, 4,000 times.

JOHN: Whew – !

MR FARQUHARSON: What do you say?

JOHN: I think we don't want to buy it. I think it would be too big
for us.

MR FARQUHARSON: Well, there you are, you see. That's just what I
think too. As a matter of fact, we couldn't buy it. A place like that
would be – pretty expensive. But of course that's no reason for us
not to give it our careful *thought*. [*Pause.*] And so you agree it's
not a place for us to buy?

JOHN: No. Yes, I mean. What's the next place?

MR FARQUHARSON: Don't rush me . . .

JOHN: I'm not rushing you . . .

MR FARQUHARSON [*continues*]: And even if we *could* afford to buy it,

I may say I wouldn't want to. I have never had any inclination to fish for salmon. What about you?

JOHN: No, I haven't either, I think.

MR FARQUHARSON: And besides, there's another point that's just occurred to me. Neither of our rods would hold a salmon. So – where's that fountain pen got to? – I'll just score it out. [*Does.*] There – . My boy?

JOHN: Yes . . .

MR FARQUHARSON: Speaking of rods . . .

JOHN: They're both rubbed with oil and all ready for tomorrow.

MR FARQUHARSON: Well, that's splendid. I'm glad to hear it. But – speaking of rods – what I want to say is, are you absolutely positive you didn't forget to pack my tin cup?

JOHN: No, I didn't forget. Everything's packed.

MR FARQUHARSON: We're all prepared to set off first thing?

JOHN: Yes.

MR FARQUHARSON: I know one thing you *did* forget to pack, though.

JOHN: No, I didn't . . .

MR FARQUHARSON: Yes, you did.

JOHN: What?

MR FARQUHARSON: Those new wet-flies.

JOHN: Well, I didn't. They're packed too. Everything's packed. The new wet-flies, and your tin cup, and the dry-flies, and the minnow, and – and the old wet-flies, and a hook in case we want to use the worm.

MR FARQUHARSON [*horrified*]: What – ?

JOHN [*hesitant*]: I put in a hook in case we want to use the worm . . .

MR FARQUHARSON: Where did you get it? – You didn't *buy* it?

JOHN: No . . .

MR FARQUHARSON: Well, what then?

JOHN: I found it . . .

MR FARQUHARSON: Where? Not in *this* house – .

JOHN: No. Stuck in the branch of a tree. When we last went fishing. It was stuck in a branch over the water, and that was how I knew it couldn't be – like *you* said it was – a little burn that had never been fished.

MR FARQUHARSON: My boy, I did not say that burn was a little burn

207

that had never been fished. I only said – when we first got there – that it *might* have been a little burn that had never been fished.

JOHN: But it had been fished, though, because I found the lost hook stuck in the branch.

MR FARQUHARSON: Well, I could see that for myself. Just as soon as we'd started fishing, I could see we weren't the first ones who had fished for those trout. Not by a long way . . .

JOHN: They wouldn't look at our flies at all . . .

MR FARQUHARSON: Well, that's so. I don't deny it. But – do you want us to descend to using *a worm*, my boy? What sort of fishers do you think we are?

[*An awkward silence. There is no answer.*]

Eh?

JOHN [*wistfully*]: It would be nice if we could catch a trout . . .

MR FARQUHARSON: My boy, to listen to you saying that, anyone would think we had *never* caught a trout . . .

JOHN: But it would be nice if we could catch *another* trout . . .

MR FARQUHARSON: Well, and why shouldn't we?

JOHN: I don't know . . .

MR FARQUHARSON: Well, there you are. [*Pause. Then for the thousandth time*] My boy, it's my opinion that there are a lot of little burns scattered up and down this country that have never, ever, been fished.

JOHN: Yes . . .

MR FARQUHARSON: Yes. So they are sure to be *full* of the most innocent little trout.

JOHN: Yes . . . I suppose so . . .

MR FARQUHARSON: You suppose so? But my boy, I am telling you. Those burns will be simply *seething* with trout that have never, ever, so much as *seen* a wet-fly.

JOHN: But what if they know it's the *wrong* fly?

MR FARQUHARSON: Those little trout – . Don't talk such rubbish. How could they know it's the wrong fly? When they're so innocent – when they have never been fished for – just *any* fly would be the right fly for *them*.

JOHN: You really think we'd catch one?

MR FARQUHARSON: One . . .? One . . .? You're a pessimist. We'll catch dozens.

JOHN: When?

MR FARQUHARSON [*drawn up*]: Well, er, tomorrow . . .

JOHN: But suppose we can't find that sort of burn? Suppose it's just like last time? Last time we couldn't find even *a pool* where there wasn't someone fishing before we got there. We were late in getting away. All you kept saying was, 'Don't rush me.' And we just walked and walked and walked, and you made us carry all that heavy tackle, and by the time we got started and set the rod up, it was time to come away.

MR FARQUHARSON: Well, that's so. I have to admit it. But – well, the place we went to last time wasn't lonely enough. That was all . . .

JOHN: Yes. But we had to go just where the bus went.

MR FARQUHARSON: Well, just you wait till we get ourselves a car. As soon as we can afford it, we'll buy ourselves a little car, and – .

JOHN [*interrupts*]: But tomorrow we won't have a car.

MR FARQUHARSON: No. Tomorrow we won't. . . . But still . . .

JOHN: What?

MR FARQUHARSON: Well, but still. . . . But still we may catch a trout . . .

JOHN: Oh, I don't think we'll ever find a burn that has never been fished. *Or* a place that suits us . . .

[*Music. The light starts to dim.*]

MR FARQUHARSON: What. . . . Don't talk such rubbish. Of course we'll find a burn. *And* a place. Our needs are very modest. All we want is a little cottage. – A little country cottage, with oil-lamps – and of course with a burn that's not too far. A little burn that has probably never been fished. So the trout will all rise like mad, and – and they'll splash the water right up on our window, and . . . and we'll not be able to sleep – we'll not get a wink of sleep – the whole night. But it won't matter if we don't sleep because there'll be no shop to go hurrying down to. There'll be no shop – and no tenements. Just the hills and the trees all around us – and the little burn . . .

SCENE TWO

The same. The following morning. Bright sunlight. JOHN *looks out of the* window. MR FARQUHARSON *stands by the table which is absurdly strewn with rods and creels.*

MR FARQUHARSON: Now let's see. . . . Have we got everything? The two rods. . . . [*Lifts them.*] Yes. And both creels. . . . Yes. And you're quite positive you packed my tin cup? It would be a disaster if we were to go off without it. Just suppose we got thirsty. . . . Suppose we were wanting a drink of the burn water and then we found we had left it behind? Eh? [*Pause.*] What's the time on that clock, my boy?

JOHN [*turns*]: It's almost ten.

MR FARQUHARSON: What – . And we've been up since six. That clock must be wrong. It's unbelievable how the time flies. What are you doing, standing there at that window – . You ought to be helping me to pack.

JOHN: There's been an accident.

MR FARQUHARSON: What – . What sort of an accident? Is it serious?

JOHN: It's a coal-horse. It's fallen down in the street.

MR FARQUHARSON: And can't they help it up again?

JOHN: No. I don't think so.

MR FARQUHARSON: Why not?

JOHN: It's an old horse, I think. At least it looks like an old horse. And there's a big crowd standing around it. They must be going to shoot it soon, I expect.

MR FARQUHARSON: Well, that's a shame.

JOHN: Yes, isn't it – . Oh. Here's a policeman . . .

MR FARQUHARSON: What?

JOHN: A policeman. He's just come. He's got out his notebook and he's speaking to the coalman. No. No, that can't be the coalman. . . . That's the coalman there, that's kneeling – .

MR FARQUHARSON: What?

JOHN: That's the coalman that's kneeling, putting straw under the horse's head. And stroking its nose. He's making it comfortable till they come and shoot it. And – .

[*The doorbell suddenly jangles.*]

MR FARQUHARSON: Goodness. There's the postman. That clock must be right after all. . . . Go on, my boy – go into the lobby and see what he's brought us. But don't bother me with any bills today. We haven't the time to be bothered with bills.

[JOHN *goes out into the lobby and comes back holding a letter.*]

JOHN: There's a letter for you. And it's typed.

MR FARQUHARSON: Is it sealed or unsealed?

JOHN: Sealed.

MR FARQUHARSON: Then find me my spectacles. Be quick. No. Just you open it. But hurry. What does it say?

JOHN [*opens the letter and reads it*]: Oh –

MR FARQUHARSON: Don't tell me it *is* a bill, after all . . .

JOHN: No. It's from the estate-people.

MR FARQUHARSON: The – . What estate-people? What are you talking about?

JOHN: Don't you remember? The people you wrote to in reply to the advertisement in the paper last week.

MR FARQUHARSON: Oh. Them. Yes. . . . Well, what do they say?

JOHN: They say they're willing to sell you the estate.

MR FARQUHARSON [*very embarrassed*]: Oh, are they – . [*He coughs.*] Hmn. Well. . . . Well, we'll see about it later. We simply haven't got the time to think about it now if we're going fishing. Just put the letter away in the drawer – yes – and come and help me check over this stuff.

[JOHN *sighs loudly.*]

What?

JOHN: We've checked it already. We've checked it *twice*. We're going to be late again, just like last time. I knew it. We won't find even *a pool* by the time we get there. [*Sighs.*] What's the use . . .

MR FARQUHARSON: All right, my boy. We won't check it. We'll go at once. We'll catch a tram.

JOHN: There's no good you saying that *now*.

MR FARQUHARSON: What – ?

JOHN: All the trams are held up by the accident.

MR FARQUHARSON: Then – here, catch hold of this rod, my boy – we'll take a bus into the bus-station.

JOHN: All the buses are held up as well, now.

MR FARQUHARSON: The buses too – . That's awkward. But – .

Well, we'll just start and walk towards the bus-station. We may get a lift.

[*They begin to pick up the equipment as the curtain slowly comes down.*]

SCENE THREE

In the country. Evening of the same day. In the foreground, a burn with a pool; in the background, pine trees and an old stone bridge. The rays of the setting sun slant redly through the pines.

At first, as the curtain rises, it might almost be 'a burn that has never been fished'. But then a fisher, that is, an angler in a working-man's suit and a shirt with no collar, comes down the bank and starts to fish in the pool. After several casts with the wet-fly he hasn't caught anything, and he goes away.

Another fisher comes up to the pool. He also casts, and, at the third or fourth cast, his fly gets caught up in a tree by the water. He tries to disentangle it but finally breaks the cast. Goes away . . .

MR FARQUHARSON *and* JOHN *then appear on the bridge. For a moment they stand silhouetted against the sun's rays. They are absurdly laden with equipment, and are tired, dirty and hot. They have walked for miles and miles.*

MR FARQUHARSON *sits, exhausted, on the rear parapet while* JOHN *comes forward to look into the pool.*

MR FARQUHARSON [*mops his brow with his handkerchief*]: Keep back my boy! Keep back!

JOHN: I *am* keeping back.

MR FARQUHARSON: No, you're not. You're looking. [*Pause.*] If I have told you once, I have told you a hundred times, you mustn't show yourself to the trout.

JOHN [*looks over the parapet*]: Maybe there aren't any trout. . . . Oh! Yes, there are! Look! Oh! Here's one.

MR FARQUHARSON [*shouts*]: Don't shout, my boy! Don't shout! You must go up cautiously. They can *hear* as well as *see* . . .

JOHN [*points*]: And there's another! Here's another! Here's another! Oh, come and look at it! Come and look! [*He is beside himself with excitement.*]

    [MR FARQUHARSON *gets up – it is an effort – and comes forward to the parapet.*]

MR FARQUHARSON [*solemnly, after a pause*]: Well, my boy, this looks to me as if it might be a little burn that has never been fished.

JOHN: Then let's *start* fishing.

MR FARQUHARSON: Don't rush me, my boy. Don't rush me . . .

JOHN: I'm not rushing you. I'm not. I'm only saying we ought to start and fish.

MR FARQUHARSON: Well, but now we've found a burn, I really think the best plan would be for us to come back and fish in it some other day. Don't you?

JOHN: No. I don't want to fish some other day. I want to fish *now*. I can't wait. I'll *die* . . .

MR FARQUHARSON: Well, but what about the bus? It's the last one, you know. Suppose we miss it? Eh?

JOHN: We won't miss it. . . . Hurry. You put the rod up and I'll open the creel and get out the flies.

MR FARQUHARSON: All right, my boy. But I want you to do something for me first.

JOHN: What?

MR FARQUHARSON [*solemnly*]: Just a little thing. Unpack my tin cup and go down there and fetch me up a drink of the burn-water.

JOHN: Then you get the flies and set the rod up. Promise?

MR FARQUHARSON: Yes. But go cautiously when you're down there. . . . Don't scare the trout.

    [JOHN *comes down to the pool. He fills the cup and passes it over the parapet, to his father.* MR FARQUHARSON *drinks elaborately. Stands the cup on the parapet. Sets up the rod. Meanwhile,* JOHN *discovers first an empty beer bottle, then the fly that was lost in the tree.*]

[*As he sets the cup down*] Ah. That was delicious, my boy. Just delicious . . .

JOHN [*as he finds the fly*]: Oh – .

MR FARQUHARSON: What is it?

JOHN: I've found a fly here.

MR FARQUHARSON [*misunderstanding*]: You have – . Well, that's a stroke of luck for us. Now you must try to match it with one of ours, my boy.

JOHN: I don't mean that sort of fly.

MR FARQUHARSON: What?

JOHN: It isn't a real fly, that was flying about. It's a fisher's fly. It was caught in this tree.

MR FARQUHARSON: Caught in the tree – . How do you suppose it got there?

JOHN: I suppose it means this burn *has* been fished.

MR FARQUHARSON: I'm afraid it looks like that, my boy. Still. Still, perhaps it has *almost* never been fished. Eh?

JOHN: Yes. Almost never. . . . Perhaps.

MR FARQUHARSON: But I think we ought to leave it and come back another day, a bit earlier. Don't you?

JOHN: No. I want to fish now. I'm *going* to fish now, even if you aren't. Are you ready?

MR FARQUHARSON: Yes, my boy. I suppose I'm ready . . .

JOHN: Then you stay up there and cast from the bridge, and I'll stay down here and keep watch on the flies in the pool. Right?

MR FARQUHARSON: Very well, my boy. But remember, no shouting. And no dancing about either. You've to behave yourself down there, do you hear?

JOHN: Yes, yes, yes. I know that. But hurry. . . . Hurry . . .

MR FARQUHARSON: Don't rush me, my boy, don't rush me. . . . And don't forget to be listening for that bus.

JOHN: Yes . . .

MR FARQUHARSON: Well, are you ready?

JOHN: Yes. . . . Yes . . .

MR FARQUHARSON [*raises the rod*]: Then here we go . . . [*He casts. That is, he makes half-a-dozen ludicrous practice-casts, the line cracking each time like a circus-whip. Finally he lets the flies simply fall over the parapet.*]

JOHN [*jumps about in wild excitement*]: Hurray! Hurray! Hurray!

MR FARQUHARSON [*calls down*]: Contain yourself, my boy. Contain yourself . . .

JOHN: Yes, yes. . . . Yes.

MR FARQUHARSON: Can you see any trout down there now?

JOHN: Thousands.

MR FARQUHARSON: What?

JOHN: Hundreds. . . . Hundreds of trout.

MR FARQUHARSON: Stand still. And don't exaggerate.

JOHN: I'm not. I'm not. There's dozens of trout. Just down there. [*Points.*]

MR FARQUHARSON: Are there – . And do they look innocent?

JOHN: No. . . . Not *very* innocent.

MR FARQUHARSON: And where are the flies? Can you see them yet?

JOHN: Yes, Yes, here they're coming now. Drifting down the stream. But – . Oh dear – . Oh – . Oh dear . . .

MR FARQUHARSON: What? What is it, my boy.

JOHN: It's the flies . . .

MR FARQUHARSON: Well, but what about them?

JOHN: They've hooked on to each other. They're in a great big fankle.*

MR FARQUHARSON: Are they? Dash it – . Is it a really bad fankle?

JOHN: Yes. No. Sort of . . .

MR FARQUHARSON: Then I'd better just reel them in.

JOHN: No, don't. Don't. Wait just a tick . . .

MR FARQUHARSON: Very well. If you say so. But where are they now? Can you see where they are?

JOHN: Yes. They're almost up to where the trout are swimming.

MR FARQUHARSON: Any rises?

JOHN: No. Not yet. Oh – .

MR FARQUHARSON: What? Was that a rise then?

JOHN: No. Now the trout are swimming *away* from the flies. [*Pause. Then, an outburst.*] Oh, how I hate them! How I hate them! They're just like horrible corner boys – only instead of pointed shoes they have those horrible, ugly pointed fins. And they don't even *run* away from the flies – they just look sly and sidle off . . .

MR FARQUHARSON: Never mind. I'll reel up and try again, eh?

JOHN: No, wait. Wait just a second. Wait till the flies have gone right down to the bottom of the pool. *Please.*

MR FARQUHARSON: But what about that bus, my boy?

JOHN: I'm listening for it . . .

MR FARQUHARSON [*excitedly*]: A rise!

JOHN: What?

* *fankle:* a knot.

MR FARQUHARSON: There was a rise! I felt a rise!

JOHN: It's not a rise. It's just the rapids. The flies have gone right down the pool, and now they're in the fast water, and it's plucking at the line. It only *feels* as if it was a rise . . .

MR FARQUHARSON [*absorbed*]: Another rise! A whole lot of rises! It must be the Evening Rise! Stand back!! – Stand well back!! I am going to STRIKE!!!

[*He strikes. The line flies up, and up, and into the tree that stands by the water. A pigeon coos and streaks out.*]

MR FARQUHARSON [*flatly, disappointed*]: My boy, do you think you can climb that tree for our flies?

JOHN [*uncertain*]: Yes, I expect so . . .

[*He goes to the foot of the tree. Looks up to the top of it. A horn blares distantly.*]

MR FARQUHARSON: The bus – ! There's the bus – ! The bus is coming now, my boy. Be quick! Be quick!!

[*There is a moment of panic as the curtain falls.*]

SCENE FOUR

The kitchen. Late the same night. A crescent moon shines in the window.
MR FARQUHARSON *again sits at the table while* JOHN *makes the tea.*

MR FARQUHARSON [*with forced heartiness*]: Is that tea ready, my boy?

JOHN [*tired and dispirited*]: Yes, father.

MR FARQUHARSON: Thank you. Splendid. Then you can pour it out. [*Pause.*] Just wait till tomorrow night – .

JOHN: Tomorrow night – . What for?

MR FARQUHARSON: I'm going to bring you home that mustard tin you wanted.

JOHN: Oh, that – . It doesn't matter . . .

MR FARQUHARSON: What? But of course it matters.

[JOHN *sets his tea on the table.*]

Thank you. [*He notices* JOHN's *face.*] Why, my boy, you've got a touch of the sun.

JOHN: What? [*Goes slowly to the window.*]

MR FARQUHARSON: You've got the sun on your face today. [*Pause. Sips his tea. Tries to humour* JOHN.] Delicious. This tea couldn't be better if it *had* been made with a mustard tin. – Now that newspaper – where's it got to?

JOHN: I don't know . . .

MR FARQUHARSON: There it is there. On the cushion on the chair, my boy . . .

    [JOHN *hesitates, then passes it. Goes back to stand at the window.*]

MR FARQUHARSON: Thank you. . . . You're a good boy. And now you can come and help me.

JOHN: Help you – . What to do?

MR FARQUHARSON: What – . What a funny question. To look for a place for us, of course, my boy. There are a lot of places in tonight's paper. One . . . two . . . three . . . four . . . five whole columns. What do you think of that?

JOHN: I wish. . . [*Breaks off.*]

MR FARQUHARSON: Well, what do you wish? Go on.

JOHN: I wish we *had* caught a trout today . . .

MR FARQUHARSON: And so do I. So do I. Still. . . . Still, we almost caught one, didn't we?

JOHN: When?

MR FARQUHARSON: Don't you remember? At the very end. Just before the bus came. When I struck. – And we almost caught a pigeon.

JOHN: That was just the rapids . . .

MR FARQUHARSON: Still. Still, we'll be sure to catch a trout *next* time. Eh?

JOHN: No, we won't . . .

MR FARQUHARSON [*surprised*]: What? What do you say?

JOHN: No, we won't catch a trout next time . . .

MR FARQUHARSON: You're tired, my boy, that's all. You're a wee, sleepy boy. Now come and help me look through these advertisements.

    [JOHN *shakes his head slowly.*]

MR FARQUHARSON [*looks up from the newspaper*]: What? Aren't you coming to help me?

JOHN: I don't want to do the advertisements.

MR FARQUHARSON: But *I* want you to, my boy. Just suppose that tonight was the very night there was a place that exactly suited us? Suppose there was a little cottage with – .

JOHN [*interrupts in a flat voice*]: There won't be.

MR FARQUHARSON: Eh – . Don't say that. [*Pause.*] What are you doing there?

JOHN: Nothing . . .

MR FARQUHARSON: Then come away from that window and sit down here, by me.

[JOHN *shakes his head.*]

What are you looking at? What's out there?

JOHN: Nothing . . .

MR FARQUHARSON: Nothing – . Then what are you thinking about?

JOHN: Nothing. . . . Yes. Yes, I'm thinking about the horse.

MR FARQUHARSON: The horse – ?

JOHN: The horse that had fallen in the street today.

MR FARQUHARSON: Oh. In the morning. I remember. The poor, old coal-horse. It had fallen down in the street. But it can't *still* be there?

JOHN: No. There's only the straw . . .

MR FARQUHARSON [*puzzled*]: Straw?

JOHN [*as if to himself*]: They were laying straw under its head. They were stroking its nose. They were going to shoot it . . .

MR FARQUHARSON: Please, my boy. You'll have me crying in a minute. [*Pause.*] If you won't come and sit beside me, at least you'll listen while I read out the first place. You just listen very carefully, and then say exactly what you think.

JOHN [*softly*]: I think it wouldn't suit us . . .

MR FARQUHARSON: What – . But how do you know it wouldn't? Have you read it? Eh?

JOHN: No. But I just *know* . . .

MR FARQUHARSON: But you can't know beforehand. And I think it might be the very place for us.

JOHN [*turns*]: Yes . . . ?

MR FARQUHARSON: Yes. It doesn't actually say so, but I expect there'll be a little cottage they would let us have fairly cheaply. And there's sure to be a burn. Don't you think there'll be a burn?

JOHN: Yes . . .

MR FARQUHARSON: Yes, I feel sure there'll be a burn. Why, it'll probably be a burn that has never been fished. Never, my boy – do you understand that? Never. Never. . . . Not once. Not ever since God said: 'Let there be light' – and there was light on all its little pools.

JOHN: Yes. On the little, brown pools. On the ferns, too. On the rocks . . .

MR FARQUHARSON: Yes. . . . But not *too* much light, because, if you have too much light, it isn't good for fishing. Did you know that?

JOHN [*goes slowly up to his father*]: Yes. . . . Too much light isn't good for fishing.

MR FARQUHARSON [*delighted*]: And so you *are* going to help me. . . . Well, that's splendid. . . . This tea is delicious, my boy. Delicious. And tomorrow, we'll get a mustard tin. . . . You really ought to have had a drink of that beautiful burn water. . . . But what am I talking about? Oh, yes. We were going to look through the advertisements. . . . So you do think there'll be a burn?

JOHN [*with tears in his eyes*]: That has never been fished? Yes, I do. Yes, honestly Daddy, I'm sure there will be . . .

[*Pause. They both face the window. The light in the kitchen starts to dim. Music.*]

There'll be a little country cottage – with oil-lamps – that we can afford to buy quite easily. And of course there'll be a burn, too. And it'll never have been fished. Not once. And so the trout – they'll be *so* innocent. . . . All night they'll be rising like mad, and – . Oh, Daddy, Daddy, it will be so wonderful! We'll never – neither of us – sleep a wink all night – not a wink all night – for the rises – of the trout!!

[*The stage is dark. The window throws its golden light on their faces. They are smiling and crying. Slow curtain.*]

B. S. JOHNSON

You're Human Like the Rest of Them

CHARACTERS

HAAKON, *a teacher, about thirty*
PHYSIOTHERAPIST, *about forty-five*
TEACHER ONE, *about fifty*
TEACHER TWO, *about forty*
MISS HAMMOND, *gym mistress, big, about thirty*
SEVERAL OLD AND MIDDLE-AGED MEN, *hospital out-patients*
CAPON, ECKERSLEY, *and several other schoolboys*

Although written and printed here as a stage play, *You're Human Like the Rest of Them* was first presented as a film with the assistance of the Production Fund of the British Film Institute. The première was at the National Film Theatre on 5 May 1967, and the cast was as follows:

HAAKON	William Hoyland
PHYSIOTHERAPIST	Anne Hardcastle
TEACHER ONE	Barry Cole
TEACHER TWO	Gordon Gridley
MISS HAMMOND	Carole McCullagh
MIDDLE-AGED PATIENT	Gianni Zambardi

Photographed by David Muir assisted by Brian Grainger
Recorded by Ann Wolff assisted by Hank Onrust
Art Director: John Furse   Music: David Lord
Directed by the author
Edited by the author and Bruce Beresford

The film was awarded Grands Prix at both the Tours and Melbourne International Short Film Festivals in 1968, and was *invité d'honneur* at the Cracow International Short Film Festival in the same year.

Acknowledgements: This play was commissioned by the Royal Shakespeare Company and first published in *Transatlantic Review 19.*

Darkness. Then a lantern slide punched up on a screen. It represents a stooping human male figure, in outline from the right side, with the spine and spinal nervous system marked in different colours from the outline. A PHYSIOTHERAPIST *stands beside the screen holding a short pointer, with which she indicates appropriately during her little lecture, which she has obviously given many times before.*

PHYSIOTHERAPIST:

>Here you see the spine – Your attention please/
>The spine, stretching from the base of the skull/
>To this tail or tail-like extremity/
>The spine is made up of separate parts/
>Vertebrae, we call the parts vertebrae/
>They're made of bone, the vertebrae, bone, bone/
>They move in relation to each other/
>When you bend your back, they move together/
>>[*It should now be possible to see that the nurse is lecturing to a small group of men aged from thirty upwards, dressed in badly-fitting dressing gowns and clutching fibre cases. They sit on stacking cantilever chairs, less than comfortably.*]

PHYSIOTHERAPIST:

>They're kept apart, so they don't rub or grate/
>By a cartilage

PATIENT ONE: What's that then?

HAAKON: Gristle/

PHYSIOTHERAPIST:

>Listen and you'll know. Cartilage is like/
>Cotton, strands of cotton, on the outside/
>Hard, but on the inside it's not, it's soft/
>It's gelatinous, gluey, it's all soft/
>Now, most people seem to think that the back/
>That the spine can bear any weight at all/
>It can't. They bend over to pick up – Ouch!/
>The spine just wasn't designed to do that/

PATIENT ONE:

>How's that then?

HAAKON: What do you mean, designed?

223

PATIENT TWO: Yes?/
PHYSIOTHERAPIST:
  You're all here because you asked for too much/
  You all asked your backs to bear too much weight/
PATIENT THREE:
  Well, I'm eighty
HAAKON: It's a good age
PATIENT THREE: It's not/
  It's a bloody awful age
PHYSIOTHERAPIST: That's enough/
  When you put a lot of strain on your back/
  Then you may move a cartilage or disc/
  You've all heard of a slipped disc, haven't you?/
  You see, the spine was never designed to/
  Bend over like this . . .
HAAKON   Faulty construction!/
PHYSIOTHERAPIST:
  The muscles are too weak
PATIENT TWO: Eh?
PHYSIOTHERAPIST: They only/
  Connect short pieces of bone together/
  The correct way to pick something up is/
  To bend at the knees and make use of these/
   [indicates on lantern slide appropriately:]
  Long and very strong muscles in your legs/
HAAKON:
  What I want to know is, how is it that/
  Since we can obviously do these things/
  But our backs can't do them properly?
PATIENT TWO: Yes?/
PHYSIOTHERAPIST:
  The fact remains that the spine is just not/
  Designed to
HAAKON: Who designed it, then?
PATIENT THREE: Why not?/
PATIENT TWO:
  Yes, why make it like that?
PHYSIOTHERAPIST: I don't know why/

PATIENT ONE:
     Yes, why?
HAAKON: Doctors can't answer 'why' questions/
     Any more than the vicars can
PATIENT THREE: No
PATIENT ONE: Why?/
PATIENT TWO:
     But who designed it like this then?
PATIENT THREE: God!
HAAKON: Yes!/
PATIENT THREE:
     It's God's fault!
PATIENT FOUR: Another cock-up!
HAAKON: But whose/
     Fault is it if you don't believe in God?/
PATIENT THREE:
     Yours
PATIENT ONE:
          Your fault
HAAKON: My fault?
PATIENT THREE: Yes, your fault, mate, yours!/

[*Blackout*]

Spot picks out an interior wall, with a flight of plaster ducks – small, medium, and large – on it. Another spot picks up entry of HAAKON. *He comes in wearily, but then sees ducks, drops to the floor in a shooting posture, and imitates shotgun firing: three shots and a clunk as one duck falls off wall make up first four syllables of first line.*

HAAKON:
     Bompf! Bompf! Bompf!
                         [*Clunk!*]
TEACHER ONE:
     Tiresome histrionics/
     Haakon, do you have to in the staffroom?/
          [*Lights up: a school staffroom, with at least three teachers: armchairs, tables, noticeboards: everything consistent – e.g.*

*piled crockery, cups of tea, children's voices in playground off –
with the end of lunch break.]*

TEACHER TWO:

Three shots from a double-barrelled shotgun?/

HAAKON:

Pedant.

TEACHER ONE:

And I thought your back was injured?/

MISS HAMMOND:

Yes, how are you?

HAAKON: Better. Or perhaps worse/

Depends how you look at it. I'm nearer/

Yes, nearer at any rate, I'm nearer/

RADIO ANNOUNCER:

'From the Midlands we present the Archers,/

An everday story of count ...'

*[HAAKON goes over to radio, switches off abruptly at exactly
this point.]*

HAAKON: Yes, quite./

Just listen to this: at the hospital/

They gave us a little lecture about/

The spine

TEACHER ONE: We'd like to talk about that too/

The spine – or rather about spinelessness/

Is what we hear about you true, Haakon/

That you were in some bank on Saturday/

When a gunman attempted to rob it?/

HAAKON: He didn't attempt it – he succeeded/

TEACHER ONE: And you stood there and did nothing at all?/

HAAKON: What was I sposed to do – get myself killed?/

Only a few months ago there was this/

Hero who picked up this adding machine/

And threw it at a bandit and you know?/

The next thing the nearest little girl clerk/

Had half her face blown off by a shotgun/

TEACHER TWO: Well, in my day we called that cowardice/

HAAKON: Well, today we call it stupidity/

And look, whose money was it anyway?/

You just don't think about things hard enough/
Do you know that the banks made a survey/
And decided that safety precautions/
Installing alarms and traps and so on/
Would cost too much and robberies were cheaper?/
The amount they lost through theft was far less?/
Did you know that?

TEACHER TWO: That's not the point!

HAAKON: It is!/
It's exactly the bloody point, you see/
You just don't think about things hard enough/
No, let me tell you about this morning/
There were all these old men with back trouble/
And the hospital wasn't any use/
They just blamed it on to God as usual/
But that's

MISS HAMMOND: Of course they didn't. That's silly/

HAAKON: Just you shut your little mouth, Miss Hammond/
I'm trying to say something important/

MISS HAMMOND: Just silly

HAAKON: I know your sort, Miss Hammond/
Your sort draw the line at actual entry/
[*Exit* MISS HAMMOND.]

TEACHER TWO:
Haakon! Are you not feeling well?

HAAKON: As well/
As anyone – that's what I want to say/
We're all rotting away, slowly rotting/
And for some it's not even slow, either/
We just rot, corrode, decay, putrefy/
And there's nothing we can do about it!/

TEACHER ONE:
That's childish rot, Haakon, just damned childish!/

HAAKON: Because you first realized it as a child/
Doesn't make it childish equals useless/
We rot and there's nothing that can stop it/
Can't you feel the shaking horror of that?/
You just can't ignore these things, you just can't!/

[*The bell signifying the end of lunch break sounds.* HAAKON *turns away, says, much more quietly:*]

HAAKON: You just can't ignore these things, you just can't/

[HAAKON *goes to his locker, takes out some books, goes out: no sooner has the door shut than he opens it again and stands in the doorway.*]

HAAKON: Oh, a girl in 4B called Helen Hunt/
Told me she found a purse in the playground/
So if anyone's lost a leather purse/
Will they please go to Helen Hunt for it/

[HAAKON *makes a theatrical gesture in keeping with this old music-hall joke: and exits.*]

[*Blackout*]

Enough props – desk, chair, blackboard – to indicate a classroom. Enter HAAKON. *Noise of kids gradually subsides.*

HAAKON: What lesson are we sposed to be doing?/
Anyway, there's something more important/
I'm not myself today

CAPON: Who are you then?/

ECKERSLEY:
But why can't we have Civics as usual?/

HAAKON:
You'd rather have the usual, Eckersley?/
The usual useless information?

ECKERSLEY: Yes/

HAAKON:
Right then. How many halfpennies in a mile?/
Secret is to know the diameter/
One inch. More. More useless information/
Do you know how to recognize your cows?/
Now your Ayrshire is a brown and white cow/
Don't confuse with the black and white Friesian/
And here's one you haven't heard of before/

The Red Poll which as its name might suggest/
Is a deep chestnut brown not red at all/
And from the Channel

CAPON: Sixty-three thousand/
Three hundred and sixty

HAAKON: What? What?

WHOLE CLASS [*shouts*]: Halfpennies!

HAAKON:

Capon, I shall work you one in the spud!/
Now, Guernseys are sort of soft brown and white/
And Jerseys are much the same colours but/
They have funny faces. Which reminds me/
Did you hear about the old bull who said/
'I'd like a nice tight jersey for Christmas'?/
[*Shocked, delighted, reproving noises from class.*]

CHILD ONE:

What's up with him today?

CAPON: He's not himself/

HAAKON:

Who am I then? Don't answer that. Quiet!/
You ought to be able to take that now/
We make you too many allowances/
Too many for your presumed innocence/
Too many for your snotty-nosedness/
We wrongly emphasize slight differences/
To the cost of common humanity/
For – and let's be very sure about this – /
You are human just like the rest of them/
You are human just like the rest of them/
And your one certainty is that you'll die – /
Our dying is the only certainty/
[*Someone laughs.*]

HAAKON:

Shut up you little bastards, just shut up!/
I'm trying to teach you something real, real!/
Something that I've learnt for myself this time/
Something that has to do with all of you/
You're all going to die but before then/

You're going to decay, rot, for years, rot/
Slowly your bodies are going to rot/
Slowly, mind, just slowly, for years, slowly/
And painfully, your bodies just give up/
They just stop working, function by function/
I saw old men this morning with their skin/
Cross-wrinkled like the neck of a tortoise/
Skin lined and loose like a flaccid penis/
Then, after pain, comes death, you are cut off/
Like a city street-end by the railway/
    [*Long pause.*]

HAAKON:

Only one cheer for dear old God

CAPON: Hooray!/

CHILD ONE:

He's off his squiff

CHILD TWO: Mad, mad

CAPON: Straight round the twist/

HAAKON:

Already you cover up like adults/
Know you can live only by illusion/
You must choose to believe that I am mad/
    [*Long pause.*]

HAAKON:

A parable, children, a true one, true/
    [*During following speech dim all except for spot on* HAAKON's
    face.]

HAAKON:

There were these lizards, at the zoo, lizards/
In a sort of glass-fronted cage, prison/
And they fed these lizards with big locusts/
The lizards were about twelve inches long/
And the locusts were about two inches/
The locusts couldn't get away, of course/
They had no defence against being killed/
The only thing a locust could do was/
To make itself an awkward thing to eat/
By sticking out its arms and legs and wings/

To make itself an awkward thing to kill/
So shall I: I have to die, but by God/
I'm not going to pretend I like it/
I shall make myself so bloody awkward!/

[*By means of music and lighting a comic apotheosis of* HAAKON,
*a complete reversal of mood, takes place: he is given medals by
functionaries, presented with a loyal address, praised in dumb-
show, he is exalted and gradually stands more and more
upright, noble as a result of his suffering. At peak, blackout.*]

GEORGE MACBETH and J. S. BINGHAM

The Doomsday Show

A CABARET

The Doomsday Show was first performed at The Establishment Club, London on 20 July 1964, with the following cast:

LEADER	George MacBeth
THE MAN	Harvey Hall (later William Buck)
THE GIRL	Frances Hooker
	& Caroline Hunt

'The Doomsday Lullaby' was sung on tape
by Penelope Lee.
The poem 'I Am That I Am' was spoken on tape
by Brion Gysin.

NOTE

Although *The Doomsday Show* was jointly conceived and written by George MacBeth and J. S. Bingham, it contains a high proportion of pre-existing material: acknowledgements are due (among others) to Peter Porter for part of his poem 'Your Attention, Please', to Adolf Hitler for part of his Last Will and Testament, to Brion Gysin for his permutated poem 'I Am That I Am', and to Peter Marinker for 'The Doomsday Chant'.

THE DOOMSDAY SHOW

Props: one metronome, three burned books, a powerful 'searchlight' torch, two rolls of film, two pairs of wallpaper scissors, one set of 'Fin du Globe' cards, one swivel typing-chair, one small table, two umbrellas, one tape recording of the poem 'I Am That I Am'.

Lighting: two tight downward vertical spots at the two sides of the stage, one tight upward vertical spot below the space immediately in front of the typing-chair.

Microphones: two movable stand microphones near the two front vertical spot positions; one tape-recorder in the lighting control-room.

Cast: two men and a girl. One of the men is dressed in a black sweater and black trousers, the other (henceforward referred to as the LEADER) is dressed in a white shirt, black and straight-bottomed leather tie and black trousers. The girl is dressed in a black sweater and black ski-pants tucked into black calf-length black boots. All three wear arm-bands on which are sewn letter Ms, but the leader's is white on black, the others' black on white. All three wear dark glasses.

(*N.B.* In the interests of variety, a larger number of performers may take part, particularly five, using four vertical spots.)

Set: A 'collage' construction like a Victorian hinged screen made out of newspaper cuttings and photographs inter-cut and cut across to produce a jigsaw of sex and violence, including, for instance, a Gatling gun piercing a *Playboy* nude, fashion plates divided by First World War trenches, etc. Behind this screen, the props are arranged. Centre stage the swivel typing-chair is standing with its back to the audience. In front of it the metronome, torch, books, etc. are arranged on a small table.

THE DOOMSDAY SHOW

The show begins with house lights dimmed, followed by this announcement, previously recorded, broadcast over the loudspeaker system.

LOUDSPEAKER: We present THE DOOMSDAY SHOW, featuring the Metrognomes.

[*At this point the 'Doomsday Lullaby' is played over the loudspeaker system. The song is sung by a solo woman's voice. The tone of the music is that of a sentimental late-night song.*]

[*During the song the* LEADER *has come on stage and sat down on the swivel typing-chair. He is picked up in the vertical spot as the song ends. The effect is a sort of Dr Strangelove figure, lit in a sinister light from below, surviving the holocaust. His linking speeches, though not his speeches within turns, are pre-recorded and played on tape over the loudspeaker system.*]

LEADER: After Doomsday, the surface of the world was devoid of any form of life. But *beneath* the surface of the world, a few last remnants of life remained. A handful of survivors lingered on in the Paris Underground – their names: THE METROGNOMES.

[*While the* LEADER *is speaking the remaining performers have entered and moved in darkness to their positions at the sides of the stage directly below the downward vertical spots. As the tape reaches the word 'Metrognomes' the* LEADER *switches on the metronome on the table in front of him to a slow tick. At this cue the two vertical downward spots come on simultaneously and reveal the Metrognomes standing with arms folded and legs apart. They are held in the spots for two seconds and then plunged again into darkness. The tape continues.*]

The Metrognomes survived only through the creation of a highly disciplined society of their own, under the control of their leader, the umpire metrognome. This society expressed itself through a number of game-rituals, game-rituals which had two purposes. First, they served to while away the time. Secondly, they were therapeutic: they helped them to keep sane by alienating fears relating to their predicament.

The Metrognomes remembered very clearly their terror when they first heard the broadcast warning of the Doomsday cataclysm. To soften this terrible memory, they tried to make a joke of it. They played a game like musical chairs, which they called 'Sheltering from the Bomb'.

[*Both spots come on simultaneously. The* LEADER *stops the metronome. The performers are seen standing to attention with umbrellas held like rifles against their right shoulders. As the* LEADER (*not his voice on tape*) *reads the ten-minute warning they listen attentively as if ready to break ranks and run for shelter at some expected signal. Sometimes one will half-unshoulder his umbrella, thinking the announcement is about to end. The effect should be of a group playing musical chairs and waiting for the music to stop.*]

Your attention please. The Polar DEW has just warned that a nuclear rocket strike of at least one thousand megatons has been launched by the enemy directly at our major cities. This announcement will take two and three quarter minutes to make, you therefore have a further seven and a quarter minutes to comply with the shelter requirements published in the Civil Defence Code – section Atomic Attack. A specially shortened Mass will be broadcast at the end of this announcement – Protestant and Jewish services will begin simultaneously – select your wavelength immediately according to instructions in the Defence Code.

[*As the* LEADER *stops, the performers un-shoulder their umbrellas and rapidly start to put them up. As they complete the operation, they turn together and look apprehensively at the* LEADER. *He smiles and slowly shakes his head. The performers re-roll their umbrellas and again stand to attention. The* LEADER *continues.*]

Do not take well-loved pets (including birds) into your shelter – they will consume fresh air. Leave the old and bed-ridden, you can do nothing for them. Remember to press the sealing switch when everyone is in the shelter. Set the radiation aerial, turn on the geiger barometer. Turn off your television now.

[*As the* LEADER *pauses, the performers half lower their umbrellas, but he continues without stopping.*]

Turn off your radio immediately the services end. This announcement is ending. Our President has already given orders for massive retaliation – it will be decisive.

[*As the* LEADER *stops, the performers race to put up their umbrellas. The last to do so – the man – is 'out'. The* LEADER *points at him and his spot goes off. The* LEADER *continues.*]

Some of us may die. Remember, statistically it is not likely to be you. All flags are flying fully dressed on Government buildings – the sun is shining. Death is the least we have to fear. We are all in the hands of God, whatever happens by His Will. Now go quickly to your shelters.

[*This time when the* LEADER *stops reading the remaining performer, the* GIRL, *half raises her umbrella and then freezes. Her spot is turned off. The* LEADER *starts the metronome, a little faster than before. The tape continues.*]

The Metrognomes understood the bewilderment of a society in

disintegration, the pain and terror of trying to preserve stability in the midst of threats from within. And their thoughts turned with more fascination than before to the problems of an earlier society, an earlier society which had also ended in an underground tunnel. For them, the last days of Hitler were a macabre but gripping charade.

[*The* LEADER *stops the metronome. The loudspeaker system broadcasts a prepared recording of a brief extract from one of Hitler's speeches, succeeded by the familiar montage of Sieg Heils. The* LEADER *speaks – not on tape – in a rapid, urgent tone recalling wartime* Universal *newsreels.*]

But now, Russian troops are already fighting in the outskirts of Berlin. Below the ruins of the Reichschancellery, in the bowels of the Führerbunker, Hitler attempts to control his crumbling empire with the help of Martin Bormann, Eva Braun and a handful of loyal generals. Outside the bunker, elsewhere in Germany, Goering and Himmler plot to take over power. These are the words they *actually used.*

[*From now on the* LEADER *speaks his cue lines in the same urgent tone of voice throughout the turn.*]

Martin Bormann, Führerbunker, telegrams Admiral Doenitz.

[*The right spot is turned on. In it the* MAN *is seen drawing out a roll of film. He begins to speak, reading from his film in a German accent, but varying his delivery to suit the needs of the text. He reads as if involved in what he is saying and doing his best to act it out convincingly.*]

MAN: Doenitz! Our impression grows daily stronger that the divisions in the Berlin theatre have been standing idle for several days. All the reports we receive are controlled, suppressed, or distorted by Keitel. The Fuehrer orders you to proceed at once, and mercilessly, against all traitors.

[*The right spot is turned off.*]

LEADER: S.S. Colonel.

[*The left spot is turned on. In it the woman is seen drawing out a roll of film. She begins to speak, also reading in a German accent, and in the same way as the man.*]

GIRL: Do you know what this is? Prussic acid. It cost 11,000 marks, this little thing. One drop of it on your tongue and you

flop to the ground, as though you'd been struck by lightning.
[*The left spot is turned off. For the remainder of this turn the lighting and reading arrangements alternate as already described.*]

LEADER: Bormann to Doenitz.

MAN: Instead of urging the troops forward to our rescue with orders and appeals, the men in authority are silent. Treachery seems to have replaced loyalty! We remain here. The Chancellery is already in ruins.

LEADER: Heinrich Himmler, at Hohenlychen.

GIRL: Everyone is mad in Berlin.

LEADER: Adolf Hitler to Keitel.

MAN: I expect the relief of Berlin. What is Heinrich's army doing? What is happening to the Ninth Army? When will Wenck and the Ninth Army join?

LEADER: Himmler to Aide.

GIRL: I almost think, Schellenberg, that you are right. I must act in one way or another.

LEADER: General.

MAN: Just you wait. Don't despair! Everything will be well! The presence of the Fuehrer and his confidence have completely inspired me. This place is as good as a fountain of youth for me!

LEADER: Himmler to Count Bernadotte.

GIRL: The Fuehrer's great life is drawing to its close.

LEADER: Hitler to General.

MAN: Himmler! A traitor must never succeed me as Fuehrer! You must go out and ensure that he does not.

LEADER: Schellenberg.

GIRL: My position with Himmler is now very difficult. In certain circumstances I must expect to be liquidated. I hit on the idea of sending for an astrologer from Hamburg, personally known to Himmler, whom I took with me in order that an astrological session might absorb some of the bitterness of his disappointment.

LEADER: Hitler.

MAN: Everyone has deceived me! No one has told me the truth! The armed forces have lied to me!

LEADER: Hermann Goering telegrams.

GIRL: My Fuehrer! In view of your decision to remain at your post in the fortress of Berlin, do you agree that I take over, at once, the total leadership of the Reich, with full freedom of action at home and abroad, as your deputy, in accordance with your decree of 29 June 1941? If no reply is received by ten o'clock tonight, I shall take it for granted that you have lost your freedom of action.

LEADER: Hitler.

MAN: An ultimatum! A crass ultimatum! Nothing now remains, nothing is spared me, no loyalty is kept, no honour observed; there is no bitterness, no betrayal that has not been heaped upon me.

LEADER: General.

GIRL: In these circumstances it is very difficult to discuss practical matters.

LEADER: Hitler.

MAN: I will not fall into the hands of an enemy who requires a new spectacle, exhibited by the Jews, to divert his hysterical masses.

LEADER: Schellenberg.

GIRL: I managed, with the help of the astrologer, to put forward the proposals for a more limited solution so convincingly that Himmler withdrew for an hour to think it over.

LEADER: Bormann.

MAN: Doenitz! Since all divisions have failed to arrive, and our position seems hopeless, the Fuehrer dictated last night the attached political Testament.

LEADER: Himmler.

GIRL: A bad business.

LEADER: Adolf Hitler writes.

MAN: It is untrue that I, or anybody else in Germany, wanted war in 1939. It was wanted and provoked exclusively by those international politicians who either came of Jewish stock or worked for Jewish interests.

Goering and Himmler, by their secret negotiations with the enemy, without my knowledge or approval, and by their illegal attempts to seize power in the state, quite apart from their treachery to my person, have brought irreparable shame on their country and the whole people.

Now, before the end of my life, I have decided to take as my wife the woman who, after many years of true friendship, came to this town, already almost besieged, of her own free will, in order to share my fate. She will go to her death with me at her own wish, as my wife. I must insist that my body and the body of Eva Braun be destroyed before all others.

LEADER: Eva Braun to Servant.

GIRL: You may safely call me Frau Hitler.

LEADER: A soldier.

MAN: The Fuehrer is dead.

[*The right spot is turned off. The* LEADER *starts the metronome a little faster than before. The tape continues.*]

LEADER: The Metrognomes were a small and hopeless band. They knew no other survivors of the holocaust – only the insects in the tunnels. Pestered as they were by the noise of insects' wings, they were driven into fantasies about the future. They invented imaginary successors to the human race – the Giant Ants. And they mocked at religion by pretending to *be* Giant Ants, intoning a requiem for the death of the last man.

[*The* LEADER *stops the metronome. Both spots now come on simultaneously and the two performers speak their lines one after another in an intoning, liturgical sing-song, as if speaking Church Latin; they stand to attention, with their hands together as if in prayer. The* LEADER *also holds his hands together as if in prayer.*]

MAN: Long long ago when the world was a wild place planted with bushes and peopled by apes, our Mission Brigade was at work in the jungle.

GIRL: Hard by the Congo once, when a foraging detail was active scouting for green-fly, it came on a grey *man*, the last living man, in the branch of a gum-tree stalking a monkey.

MAN: Silent, he crouched there, then jumped. With a long swing down from his branch, he had angled his spear too quickly, before they could hold him, and hurled it hard at the soldier leading the detail.

GIRL: How could he know Queen's orders were only to help him? The soldier winced when the tipped spear pricked him. Unsheathing his sting was a reflex.

MAN: Later the Queen was informed. There were *no more men*.

GIRL: Where had the men gone?

MAN: Over the earth, dear.

GIRL: Ground by the teeth of the termites.

MAN: Blown by the wind.

LEADER: Like the dodo's.

[*The* LEADER *says his line in exactly the same sing-song style as the others dwelling in a final cadence on the long 'o's' of 'dodo's', which he pronounces as 'do-o-do's'. The spots are turned off. The* LEADER *starts the metronome a little faster than before. The tape continues.*]

LEADER: The Metrognomes knew that they could never have children. But they still felt the sexual urge as strongly as before. For them, sex and frustration were inevitably connected. They saw the human body as a pair of giant scissors – and they pretended to *be* giant scissors, opening and shutting in a barren parody of the act of love.

[*The* LEADER *stops the metronome. At this point there is the dry rasping of a single pair of scissors, opening and shutting in the darkness. It should sound like the joyless copulation of a metal insect. The* LEADER *cocks his head at this noise, as if listening. His next words are spoken as a mocking question, almost an interrogation, as if speaking to an unseen presence.*]

Scissor-Man?

[*Again there is the sound of scissors. The* LEADER *now speaks firmly, as if confirming something to a child.*]

Scissor. Man.

[*The* LEADER *continues. He now speaks as if pretending to be a scissor-man, speaking directly to the audience and writhing in snake-like frustration as he talks.*]

I am dangerous in a crisis with sharp legs and a screw in my genitals. I slice bacon-rind for a living.

[*The right spot is turned on. We see the* MAN *holding a large pair of scissors with both hands directly in front of him. As he opens the scissors they form an X like the spreadeagled shape of a man. He opens and shuts the scissors in a steady, heart-beat rhythm throughout the* LEADER'S *next speech.*]

At nights I lie dried under the draining-board, dreaming of Nut-crackers and the Carrot-Grater. If I should catch him rubbing those tin nipples of hers in the bread-bin (God rust his pivot!) so much for secrecy. I'd have his washer off.

[*The* MAN *now rapidly opens and shuts his scissors for three seconds.*]

And then what?

[*The left spot is turned on. The* GIRL *is seen holding her scissors in the same grip as the* MAN. *They both open and shut in synchronization, to a slightly faster heart-beat tempo, throughout the* LEADER'*s next speech.*]

It scarcely pays to be 'Made in Hamburg'. Even our little salt-spoon can sound snooty with an E.P.N.S. under his armpit. Even the pie-server who needs re-dipping. In sixteen stainless years dividing chipolata-links I am still denied a place in the sink-unit. And you can imagine what pairing-off is possible with a wriggle

[*On the word* wriggle, *the performers rapidly open and shut their scissors and then revert to their fast heart-beat rhythm.*]

of cork-screws in an open knife-box. So I keep my legs crossed. I never cut up rough. I lie with care in a world where a squint leg could be fatal. I sleep like a weapon with a yen for a pierced ear.

[*Both performers rapidly open and shut their scissors for three seconds. The spots are turned off and the loud scissor sound continues for three seconds in the darkness. The* LEADER *bends over and starts the metronome, very slightly faster than before. The tape continues.*]

The Metrognomes had soon forgotten the urbane and cultured civilization of the past. But they expressed their nostalgia for it through a game-ritual which became increasingly fragmentary and romantic as their memories dimmed. They lived in a James Bond world of the mind, a world in which the only art was the pornography of violence, in which even a book was a strange novelty whose purpose they could hardly understand.

[*The spots are turned on. The* LEADER *stops the metronome. The performers are seen holding up burned books and examining them. They turn them over, sniff them, shake them, pretend to bite them. The* LEADER *picks up the third of the burned books and opens it, appearing to read the title-page. He sounds amused, disbelieving.*]

Author's note? Consultants of this dictionary-novel may find it convenient to work according to some programme dictated by a sequence of letters. This might be a sentence such as, WHO'S FOR TENNIS? [*He pauses.*] Naturally, one may want each letter entry to occur only once in which case, in the example given, the programme will be WHO'S FR TENI?

[*The performers clap their books shut and alternately snap out the letters* W-H-O-S-F-R, *as if answering their names in a military roll-call.*]

MAN: W

GIRL: H

MAN: O

GIRL: S

MAN: F

GIRL: R

MAN and GIRL: Who's – for – tennis!

[*The spots are turned off. The* LEADER *continues to read.*]

LEADER: A full reading of the dictionary is not necessary to appreciate the main elements of the story, nor will complete acquaintance with the entries solve the mystery.

[*The* LEADER *pauses and appears to turn over some more pages. For the remainder of the turn he speaks as if consulting a dictionary and then giving a clue like the B.B.C. mystery voice in* Twenty Questions.]

W for Wombat.

[*At this cue both spots come on. The* GIRL *is seen appearing to consult her burned book, as one might turn up an entry in a dictionary. She holds the stand microphone as if making love to it and whispers very close to the mouth-piece. As she begins to read, the* MAN *starts to mime the actions described in the text. He mimes as if hearing the words for the first time, and so concentrating hard to see what will come next.*]

GIRL: Inez Lawson-Emery had nothing on. Not even the radio, Cusumba reflected, as he pressed his bloodshot eye against the ivory key escutcheon of her bedroom door. In the nun-shaped aperture of cream and gold fur exposed to the eye the most striking novelty was the maroon corduroy wombat on her dressing-table. Its beady eye stared fixedly into his own beside the superb coppery buttocks enthroned on their Danish leather stool. Now, he thought, and was through the door with his hand on the shutter as the long tanned body rose to its full height on the pony-skin.

[*The spots go off.*]

LEADER: H for Herring-boning.

[*The spots come on. The* MAN *is seen appearing to consult his burned*

book. He too holds his stand microphone as if making love to it,
and speaks very close to the mouth-piece. The GIRL *starts to mime,*
as he reads, according to the same notes as the MAN.]

MAN: The Count squeezed the tiny rubber cylinder in his fingers.
The plastic measurer lay glistening slightly in the candle-flame on
the edge of his bed. He smelt the exciting raw odour of petrol.
Once, twice, he nipped the pierced end of the little container: and
smiled grimly to himself as the bulging drops oozed and dripped
into their slowly filling bath. Outside the window, Miles Ellington
had moved the catch on his Derringer.

[*For the remainder of this turn the lighting and reading arrangements*
alternate as already described until all the letters of the programme
WHO'S FR *are exhausted.*]

LEADER: O for Oxydol.

GIRL: The white suds bubbled in the lavender basin. Inez caught her
creamed face in the glass. My God, she thought, what wouldn't
I give to be a man for once. Her cool nails moved on the taut skin
of her bust, slipped to the side, released the firm catch. In the pale
orange light from the wall fitment Ninian watched the proud
nipples lift and pout as their pink shell dropped in the foaming
bowl. It was several minutes before she grasped the full im-
plications.

LEADER: S for Sikorski.

MAN: The great fans of the Russian helicopter beat the air. Through
the snow-encrusted perspex Immelman could see the tiny black
figure far below on the glacier. What was the stupid bastard doing
there? He slipped the brown octagon of a zube between his teeth
and crunched thoughtfully as his wasp-coloured machine hovered
over the snowfields. There was work to do here for the de-coding
unit at a quick guess.

LEADER: F for Film.

GIRL: The film spread easily over her damp skin. Cool, glossy and
crackling, it encased her bosom like a layer of varnish. They would
never think to look for it there. For a moment she felt a stab of
nostalgia for the old methods, the negatives in the bran barrel, the
contact prints listed in a cigar catalogue. But the weakness passed.
She was soon striding over the creaking boards of the tea-chalet
towards the chair-lift.

LEADER: R for Rubber.

MAN: The glass bubble spun on its metal wire. As she fought for breath in her gas-mask, Inez could see the world whirling like a storm of snow in a paper-weight. Her lashing ski-boot flung open the gilt-edged complete Huysmans and she watched the elaborate pages of *À Rebours* unfurl on the wet rubber as Ellington bent over her prostrate body. In a wave of dizziness she could feel the escalating roundabout of passion engulf her.

[*The spots go off.*]

LEADER: The Ski Murders remain the enigma they always were.

[*The* LEADER *starts the metronome, a little faster than before. The tape continues. As it begins, the upward spot on the* LEADER *goes off, so that the stage is in complete darkness.*]

For the Metrognomes the world had lost its plot. They no longer believed in redemption or love or art. They could only struggle against the chaos of social breakdown; but there was another and more terrible enemy inside their own skulls – the ever-present threat of *mental* breakdown. Sometimes they seemed to hear their own thoughts echoing in the darkness like the voice of a man struggling to keep himself from going mad. And they tried to mime what it meant.

[*The* LEADER *stops the metronome. He picks up the 'search-light' torch and sends a quick succession of short stabbing jets of light straight ahead of him into the faces of the audience. At the same time the prepared recording of the permutated poem* I Am That I Am *is broadcast over the loudspeaker system.*]

LOUDSPEAKER: I AM THAT I AM AM I THAT I AM? THAT I AM AM I I AM THAT AM I AM I THAT I AM I THAT AM AM I THAT AM I AM I AM I I THAT AM THAT AM AM I I etc.

[*The effect of the* I Am That I Am *recording is that of a man having a nervous breakdown in the Grand Canyon. It involves echoing permutations of the basic phrase* I AM THAT I AM, *speeding up and slowing down of magnetic tape, and superimposition of distant takes on takes close to the microphone. As the recording progresses, at irregular intervals of 6 to 10 seconds the spots go on – alternately – to show the performers registering puzzled, then agonized, and finally desperate responses in the form of statuesque tableaux. The stabbing*] *torch-jets continue throughout the turn and for about three seconds after the recording climaxes. The leader starts the metronome, a little faster than before. His upward spot comes on. The tape continues.]*

LEADER: More and more the Metrognomes worked out their problems by playing games. Chaos and the threat of disaster seemed everywhere, and they came to believe that life had always been on the brink of disaster, that men had always been secret agents in a desperate battle against extinction, communicating by S.O.S. messages that never arrived or only arrived too late. They constructed a highly stylized card game ritual which expressed this sense of *total* cataclysm. A *Doomsday Game*, in fact. Or, in their language, *Fin du Globe*.

[The spots come on, showing the performers standing with feet apart and arms folded. The LEADER picks up the Rules card from the top of the Fin du Globe pack and reads it out slowly and carefully. Meanwhile, the metronome is still ticking.]

Rules. The game is best played with a dealer and two players who are known as North, South, East and West. Before each game the pack is shuffled and cards handed to each of the players.

[The LEADER lays down the Rules card and snaps his fingers. The performers turn towards him. He picks up the Fin du Globe pack. He pretends to shuffle the cards and hand them out. As he finishes he snaps his fingers and the spots are turned off. The metronome is still ticking. For a moment there is silence, then the LEADER calls out North, throwing out his arm as he does so to point to the right spot. As one of his compass points is called and his spot is turned on, the appropriate performer reads out the first card in his hand. He should combine the urgency of someone reading a telegram with the urgency of the characters who write the messages on the cards. The first hand should consist of five cards, in a pre-arranged order. The following are two specimen first hand cards with specimen cues and directions.]

North.

[The right spot is turned on. The MAN reads out his first card.]

MAN: Curaçao. Dick Wrigglesworth to Solly Jaggers. The artificial whale is already inside the harbour. Momssen has cabled that every man will do his duty. Five, four, three, two, one, zero. That was it. Congratulate me, Solly, the whole of Bolivia is in Javan hands.

LEADER: South.

[*The right spot is turned off. The left spot is turned on. The* GIRL *reads out her first card.*]

GIRL: Rotterdam. Miss Anstruther to Courtelle. The marijuana was in the joy-stick. You had better make your getaway in the Puss Moth. I suggest a straight course over Chesham and Princes Risborough. Remember what Jacob said. There is no meaning or purpose; only the codes.

[*The 'sixth' card and its consequences are as follows. After the fifth card the* LEADER *calls out the pre-arranged compass point. For example:*]

LEADER: West.

[*The left spot is turned on. The* GIRL *pretends to read her next card.*]

GIRL: Fin de l'Ouest.

[*The* LEADER *stops the metronome. The left spot is turned off. The* LEADER *starts the metronome, a little faster than before. As in the previous hand he calls out one of the three remaining points of the compass, throwing out his arm to point to the appropriate spot. Each performer reads as before when called. This hand consists of seven shorter cards. The following are two specimen second hand cards with cues and lighting directions.*]

LEADER: South.

[*The left spot is turned on. The* GIRL *reads out her first card.*]

GIRL: Amritsar. They tell me that Crazy Horse has escaped from Berlinnie. With that hair-do he can hardly hire a jaguar. Still it is no smiling matter.

LEADER: East.

[*The left spot is turned off. The right spot is turned on. The* MAN *reads his next card.*]

MAN: Porsanger Fjord. Our ambassador has handed an ultimatum to the Gambian Foreign Minister. There is no hope of a settlement with the Greeks. If the English back their minelayers in the Skagerrak we are done for.

[*The 'eighth' card and its consequences are as follows. After the seventh card the leader calls out the pre-arranged compass point. For example:*]

LEADER: North.

[*The right spot is turned on. The* MAN *pretends to read out the next card in his hand.*]

MAN: Fin du Nord.

[*The* LEADER *turns off the metronome. The right spot is turned off. The* LEADER *starts the metronome, a little faster than before. It is now ticking very fast indeed. There is a sense of the seconds slipping rapidly away towards Armageddon. As in the two previous hands, the* LEADER *calls out one of the two remaining compass points, throwing out his arm as he does so to point to the appropriate spot. Each performer reads as before when called. This hand should consist of nine very short cards. The following are two specimen third hand cards with cues and lighting directions.*]

LEADER: East.

[*The right spot is turned on. The* MAN *reads out his first card.*]

MAN: I have just heard the news. The giant pandas have stripped the bamboo forests as far as Kanchenjunga.

LEADER: South.

[*The right spot is turned off. The left spot is turned on. The* GIRL *reads out her next card.*]

GIRL: The Portuguese destroyers have relieved Marangatam. Sir Giles was caught – quite literally – with his trousers down.

[*The 'tenth' card and its consequences are as follows. After the ninth card the* LEADER *calls out the pre-arranged compass point. This is not, however, a choice of South or East but the new direction South-East. As he calls this out he throws out both arms, pointing at each of the remaining performers.*]

LEADER: South-East.

[*The left hand and the right hand spots come on simultaneously. The girl and the man speak in unison.*]

GIRL and MAN: Fin du Globe.

[*Both spots and the* LEADER's *upward spot are turned off. The loudspeaker system broadcasts a prepared recording of a gong struck very close to the microphone and resonating for several seconds with considerable distortion. This sounds like some form of enormous, but stylized, explosion. The* LEADER *rises from his chair and leaves the stage. Full stage lights come on. The* MAN *leads the Doomsday Chant, which both performers speak in rhythmic unison, as if repeating an American College Chant.*]

The MAN and the GIRL:

> Put on your Doomsday sweater,
> The more lead the better,
> And we'll watch the mega-deaths without a fear.
> Feel my heart-beats quickening

[*On the word 'heart-beats' each performer strikes his heart with his right hand.*]

> As those mushroom clouds keep thickening
> And we'll raise this rousing cheer.

[*On the word 'mushroom' the performers raise their right clenched fists to the sky.*]

> D–O–O–M–S–D–A–Y

[*On the spelled out D–O–O–M–S–D–A–Y, each performer goes down on his right knee and stamps out each letter with his left foot while moving his right arm and clenched right fist in an accompanying hammer-movement.*]

> DOOMSDAY!

[*On the final Doomsday! both performers spring into the air, stretching out their arms and legs to form a spreadeagled X. All lights go out.*]

MORE ABOUT PENGUINS

Penguinews, which appears every month, contains details of all the new books issued by Penguins as they are published. From time to time it is supplemented by *Penguins in Print*, which is a complete list of all books published by Penguins which are in print. (There are well over three thousand of these.)

A specimen copy of *Penguinews* will be sent to you free on request, and you can become a subscriber for the price of the postage – 4s. for a year's issues (including the complete lists). Just write to Dept EP, Penguin Books Ltd, Harmondsworth, Middlesex, enclosing a cheque or postal order, and your name will be added to the mailing list.

Some other books published by Penguins are described on the following pages.

Note: *Penguinews* and *Penguins in Print*
are not available in the U.S.A. or Canada

David Storey's famous novel

THIS SPORTING LIFE

The world of professional Rugby football is a
tough world, and Arthur Machin allows little
sentimentality in telling the story of this sporting
life. It is a physical life, fouled by the grime,
sweat, intrigue and naked ambition of a northern
industrial city. From pathetic Mrs Hammond,
who suffers Machin's crude affection, to Weaver
and Slomer, the game's backers, David Storey's
characters are drawn from the raw side of life.

Also in Penguins

RADCLIFFE

Not for sale in the U.S.A.

Peter Terson is also in the Penguin Modern Playwrights

ZIGGER ZAGGER *and* MOONEY AND HIS CARAVANS

When the National Youth Theatre performed Peter Terson's *Zigger Zagger*, its hectic pace and shattering impact drove the audience into the obsessed lives of the football fans on the terraces. In the *Sunday Times* J. W. Lambert wrote: 'Peter Terson's astonishing entertainment gains body from its continual tension between surface exhilaration and underlying hopelessness. . . . Very funny and distinctly alarming, *Zigger Zagger* is true theatre.'

By contrast, *Mooney and His Caravans* is a social drama with a small cast. By turns funny and disturbing, it records the successive stages in the humiliation of a weak husband, and the paradoxical strengthening of the love which his unfaithful wife feels for him.

THE APPRENTICES

The Apprentices brings the energy of *Zigger Zagger* to the factory yard and the situation of working-class youth. The *New Statesman* critic wrote: 'Terson looks behind the pimples and the callow growling, and where the middle class would see only a "yob", Terson finds spirit, energy and an emotional honesty which, were it recognized and encouraged, might bring colour to the cheeks of a grey, sickly world.'